MODERN BRITISH PLAYWRITING:
THE 1950s

VOICES, DOCUMENTS, NEW INTERPRETATIONS

David Pattie is Professor of Drama at the University of Chester, UK. He is the author of *The Complete Critical Guide to Samuel Beckett* (Routledge, 2001) and *Rock Music in Performance* (Palgrave, 2007), and he co-edited a collection of essays on Kraftwerk (*Kraftwerk: Music Non-Stop*, Continuum, 2010). He has published extensively on a wide range of topics, including Samuel Beckett, contemporary writing for the stage, Scottish theatre and culture, political theatre, popular music and popular culture.

MODERN BRITISH PLAYWRITING: THE 1950s

VOICES, DOCUMENTS, NEW INTERPRETATIONS

David Pattie

Series Editors: Richard Boon and Philip Roberts

Methuen Drama

Methuen Drama

1 3 5 7 9 10 8 6 4 2

First published in Great Britain in 2012 by Methuen Drama

Methuen Drama, an imprint of Bloomsbury Publishing Plc

Methuen Drama
Bloomsbury Publishing Plc
50 Bedford Square
London WC1B 3DP
www.methuendrama.com

Paperback ISBN 978 1 408 12927 2
Hardback ISBN 978 1 408 18197 3

Available in the USA from Bloomsbury Academic & Professional, 175 Fifth Avenue /3rd
Floor, New York, NY 10010.

A CIP catalogue record for this book is available from the British Library

Typeset by Mark Heslington Ltd, Scarborough, North Yorkshire
Printed and bound in the UK by MPG Books Ltd, Bodmin, Cornwall

CONTENTS

GENERAL PREFACE

This book is one of a series of six volumes which seek to characterise the nature of modern British playwriting from the 1950s to the end of the first decade of this new century. The work of these six decades is comparable in its range, experimentation and achievement only to the drama of the Elizabethan and Jacobean dramatists. The series chronicles its flowering and development.

Each volume addresses the work of four representative dramatists (five in the *2000–2009* volume) by focusing on key works and by placing that work in a detailed contextual account of the theatrical, social, political and cultural climate of the era.

The series revisits each decade from the perspective of the twenty-first century. We recognise that there is an inevitable danger of imposing a spurious neatness on its subject. So while each book focuses squarely on the particular decade and its representative authors, we have been careful to ensure that some account is given of relevant material from earlier years and, where relevant, of subsequent developments. And while the intentions and organisation of each volume are essentially the same, we have also allowed for flexibility, the better to allow both for the particular demands of the subject and the particular approach of our author/editors.

It is also the case, of course, that differences of historical perspective across the series influence the nature of the books. For student readers, the difference at its most extreme is between a present they daily inhabit and feel they know intimately and a decade (the 1950s) in which their parents or even grandparents might have been born; between a time of seemingly unlimited consumer choice and one which began with post-war food rationing still in place. Further, a playwright who began work in the late 1960s (David Hare, say) has a far bigger body of work and associated scholarship than one whose emergence has come within the last decade or so (debbie tucker green, for example). A glance at the bibliographies for the earliest and latest volumes quickly reveals huge differences in the range of secondary material available to our authors and to our readers. This inevitably means that the later volumes allow a greater space to their contributing essayists for original research and scholarship, but we have also actively encouraged revisionist perspectives – new looks – on the 'older guard' in earlier books.

So while each book can and does stand alone, the series as a whole offers as coherent and comprehensive a view of the whole era as possible.

Throughout, we have had in mind two chief objectives. We have made accessible information and ideas that will enable today's students of theatre to acquaint themselves with the nature of the world inhabited by the playwrights of the last sixty years; and we offer new, original and often surprising perspectives on both established and developing dramatists.

Richard Boon and Philip Roberts
Series Editors
April 2012

Richard Boon is Emeritus Professor of Drama at the University of Hull.

Philip Roberts is Emeritus Professor of Drama and Theatre Studies at the University of Leeds.

ACKNOWLEDGEMENTS

I'd like to thank Sarah Bay-Cheng and John Bull for participating in the project; Philip Roberts, for his patient and assiduous editing; and Jacqui and Cameron, for general support and hilarity.

Finally, I would like to extend my sympathy to the family of Professor Luc Gilleman. Luc had been seriously ill for some time, and died before this book made its way into print; he produced an excellent chapter, in the most difficult circumstances. This book is dedicated to him.

INTRODUCTION TO THE 1950s

'They are scum,' was Mr Maugham's famous verdict on the class of state aided university students to which Kingsley Amis' *Lucky Jim* belongs; and since Mr Maugham seldom says anything controversial or uncertain of wide acceptance, his opinion will be that of many. Those who share it better stay well away from John Osborne's *Look Back in Anger* (Royal Court), which is all scum and a mile wide.[1]

If, at any point in the future, prizes are given for the most quoted British theatre review of the twentieth century, it is easy to surmise that this review will be close to the top of the list. *Look Back in Anger*, first staged by the Royal Court Theatre on 8 May 1956, has become a key part of the narrative of twentieth-century British drama. Certainly, in retrospect, its premiere is only one of a number of significant theatrical events in the middle of the decade (others being the creation of the English Stage Company in 1954; the premiere of Samuel Beckett's *Waiting for Godot*, directed by the young Peter Hall, in 1955; Peter Brook's earliest productions; the Berliner Ensemble's visit to London in 1956; and so on); but even once this is granted, the play's place in history is probably unassailable. Even after various revisionary readings (by, among others, Rebellato and Shellard)[2] *Look Back in Anger* is still regarded as a firebreak, dividing the 1950s sharply in two (see Billington, Gilleman and Sierz).[3] To one side are the plays of Terence Rattigan, the verse dramas of T. S. Eliot and Christopher Fry, the commercialised West End, the well-made play, drawing-room dramas and flamboyant musicals; on the other, the Royal Court generation – the radical, impatient, questioning and clear-eyed anatomists of post-war Britain. It is a potent story, because it has a pleasing simplicity; far easier to identify one key moment where everything seemed to change, than carefully to pick apart the various strands of an inevitably complex reality. More than this, the idea that Osborne's play is of epochal significance takes root very early; by the time that John Russell Taylor publishes *Anger and After* (an influential overview of playwriting in the 1950s) in 1962, the key elements of what Aleks Sierz calls the *Look Back in Anger* myth[4] are already in place.

It is worthwhile dwelling on this for a moment; one reason that cultural narratives form this quickly is convenience – all of the elements of the story already exist within the culture of the time, and a text becomes significant because it seems to summarise and encapsulate those elements. For evidence of this, the best place to go is to Tynan's justly famous review, quoted above; and the first thing to note is that Tynan begins by quoting another, equally celebrated review. The novelist and playwright W. Somerset Maugham uses his article on Kingsley Amis's novel *Lucky Jim* (1954) as a platform to attack, not the novel itself (which he finds remarkable), but the kind of person the novel describes – the new, young and profoundly unsavoury products of a debased university system:

> They do not go to the university to acquire culture, but to get a job, and when they have got one, scamp it. They have no manners, and are woefully unable to deal with any social predicament. Their idea of a celebration is to go into a public bar and drink six beers. They are mean, malicious and envious . . .[5]

For Maugham, this new class of student is simply one of the most visible signs that the tectonic plates of society are shifting: that previously impregnable bastions of the class system in Britain are being assaulted, and have fallen, to a cadre of social inferiors (in the same review, he describes this new class of student as 'the white collar proletariat',[6] as though the only proper costuming for the working classes is a set of greasy overalls). This rising tide of scum (to use Maugham's own term) threatens not only the proper hierarchies of class, but the ordered succession of the generations:

> Some will doubtless sink back, perhaps with relief, into the modest class from which they emerged; some will take to drink,

some to crime and go to prison. Others will become school-masters and form the young, or journalists and mould public opinion. A few will go into parliament, become Cabinet minis-ters and rule the country. I look upon myself as fortunate that I will not live to see it.[7]

In this debate, Maugham is not alone. In speaking out against what he sees as the decay of British society and culture, he joins an august group of cultural elder statesmen (chief among them the novelist Evelyn Waugh, the playwright Noël Coward, and the poet, playwright and cultural critic T. S. Eliot) who have all set themselves against the post-Second World War British state. However, Amis is not alone either: around him is grouped a loose affiliation of writers who are given the purposely indefinite title of 'The Movement' – the poets Philip Larkin, Donald Davie and Thom Gunn and the novelist John Wain among them. These authors have varying political and cultural opinions; they are, however, united by an impatience with British society, which they see as stifling and oppressive.

So, when Tynan evokes Maugham at the beginning of his review, it is not just because Maugham provides him with a handy rhetorical *entrée*. Tynan praises *Look Back in Anger*, but he does not shy away from discussing what he sees as faults in the text (the play is twenty minutes too long; Tynan dislikes the 'painful whimsy'[8] of the ending). For him, the play is important, both because it marks the appearance of a striking new voice in British theatre, and because it could be the occasion for an assault on the old, damaging certainties of British society. By declaring himself on the side of the young, by gleefully describing *Look Back in Anger* as 'all scum and a mile wide', Tynan reasserts his own place in the cultural debates between (as he would see it) the establishment and the forces of change; and the lasting significance of the review is that, for the first time in the post-war period, a piece of new British theatre is enlisted to the radical cause. Within the review (itself a significant document in British theatre history) therefore, we find many of the elements that run through British playwriting in the 1950s: the idea of culture as a battlefield between the established and the radical (and, to a lesser extent, between the young and the old); the idea that theatre reflects a society in transition; and, over everything, an all-encompassing debate about Britain's identity – about how the nation could be defined, and could most usefully think of itself, in a world where the old certainties of imperial power no longer hold true. Precisely why these elements are so significant (and the role that they play in the development of the British stage, and British culture more generally) is something that I will explore in the rest of this section.

Britain 1945–60: managing the peace

> Mecklenburgh Square was a pretty sight when I [John Lehmann, a poet living in London] left it. Broken glass everywhere, half the garden scorched by incendiary bombs, and two houses of Byron Court on the east side nothing but a pile of rubble. Clouds of steam were pouring out of one side, firemen still clambering over it and ambulance and blood transfusion units standing by with ARP workers and police . . .[9]

Any account of the history of the 1950s has properly to begin here: with the Second World War, the Blitz, and with that period of the conflict where, as the mythology quickly erected around events would have it, Britain stands alone against what seems like an unstoppable German military machine. The key features of this myth are easily and quickly delineated. The plucky British stand their ground, while their allies capitulate or hesitate; the country pulls together to withstand the worst that Hitler can throw at them; and through a combination of bravery, stoicism and sheer bulldog cussedness (all traits embodied by the wartime premier, Winston Churchill), the indefatigable island nation wins through. At the war's end, it would be a brave (and a particularly objective) politician who would disagree publicly with the idea that Great Britain was a world superpower; the British have come through the war with their empire more or less intact and, alongside the USA and the USSR, is busy discussing the form and structure of the post-war world. All is well – or at least, after the country is rebuilt, rationing abolished, and a new deal worked out between the state and the British people, it soon would be.

However, beneath the undoubted achievements of the war, there are clear signs that the country is not doing quite as well as this. Britain's pre-eminent global position had been slipping slowly and steadily since the end of the nineteenth-century; those factors that conspire to boost the country in previous centuries (the raw materials and technology that enabled the British to lead the industrial revolution; the empire, which gave British firms a reliable market) now act as a drag on the British economy. Other countries, with larger or more productive workforces, could now compete with British firms on more than equal terms; and the cost of empire – a fiscal imposition that could be borne when the UK economy was doing well – becomes an insupportable burden when the economic climate changes. More immediately, Britain suffers badly through the Depression of the 1930s; and the sheer strain of conducting the war effort leaves the nation in debt. Although the country pulls together during the war, the memory of the 1930s – of mass unemployment, poverty and deprivation – is understandably still very strong; arguably, it is this that ensures that the election in 1945 is won, not by Churchill's Conservatives (the party most closely associated with the Depression), but by the Labour Party under Clement Attlee. Labour plays an active part in the wartime coalition government; and they are the party which manages to reflect most closely the post-war mood. Put simply, for a substantial part of the British electorate, the war represents a time when the country benefits from strong central planning; the government intervenes in British society and the British economy for the good of the nation as a whole. Labour, of all the post-war parties, seems most likely to carry the wartime mood of cooperation and intervention into the new, post-war world.

The Labour government (1945–51) can lay claim to being one of the most significant administrations of the past hundred years; certainly, it transforms British society, putting in place wide-ranging social reforms that are not seriously contested by the other political parties until the mid-1970s. By the time that Churchill and the Conservatives return to power, the country they rule has changed

– and they have little chance (and, it should be said, little inclination) to undo those changes. The reforms that Labour put into place were already outlined during the war: at the end of 1942 the coalition publishes a report, authored by William Beveridge, which outlines a new system of social insurance for British citizens. The report, which rapidly becomes much more famous than government reports normally do (either at the time or subsequently), proposes a radical reform of the provision of social care:

> Stripped to its core the Beveridge report was targeted on 'Five Giants on the Road to Recovery' which he identified in bold, capital letters – 'WANT, DISEASE, IGNORANCE, SQUALOR and IDLENESS'. To defeat them Beveridge designed a comprehensive welfare system . . . based on three assumptions: a free national health service, child allowances, [and] full employment . . .[10]

Although Beveridge himself disliked the term, his report lays the foundations for the post-war welfare state; the underlying philosophy behind the report (and behind many of the policies that Attlee's government carried out) is the idea that the state should provide a basic level of support for all citizens, regardless of class or income. There is to be no return to the suffering of the 1930s; the war has demonstrated that, when state and people work together, great things could be achieved. To vote Labour in these circumstances is not only a pragmatic choice, if you want to avoid the baleful influence of Beveridge's five giants: it is also a demonstration of faith in the best aspects of Britishness.

This is not to say that enthusiasm for Labour is universal: Noël Coward, gloomily surveying the 1945 election result, comments, 'I always felt that England would be bloody uncomfortable during the post-war period, and now it is almost a certainty that it will be so'.[11] It is, however, hard to question the result: on a turnout of 72.6 per cent, Labour polls nearly 49 per cent of the vote against the Conservatives' 41 per cent – a significant margin, given that there are far fewer voters willing to change their party allegiances than there have been in more recent contests. The new Labour administration quickly sets about putting in place the key elements of the new state: on 5 July 1948, the National Health Service is created; from 1946 to 1948, a number of parliamentary Acts increase the scope and number of benefits that the government provides for the British population; and the idea of universal secondary education is already established before Labour comes to power (in the Butler Act of 1944, which creates a tripartite system, with pupils attending either grammar, technical or secondary modern schools). Labour also takes key industries and businesses into public ownership (the public utilities – electricity, gas and coal – and the country's transport networks chief among them). These reforms, and others that the government puts in place, are intended to ensure that post-war Britain is fairer, more just and more equal; more fitted, in effect, to serve the needs of a generation that had just won a famous victory through the exercise of its communal will. Laudable though the reforms are, however, they are also expensive; and they have to be paid for at a time when the country would find it difficult to afford them. For one thing, as noted above, Britain is in debt; for another, the financial strain of maintaining an imperial presence around the globe (and of maintaining the military capability to police that presence) is crippling. The country is caught between two irreconcilable ideas of itself. It can either be Modern Britain, providing care for all of its inhabitants – or it can be Great Britain, a superpower measuring itself against the US and the USSR. It cannot be both. Many of the problems that the British government encounters from the late 1940s through to the early 1960s stem from the fact that it takes quite some time for this apparently simple fact to sink in.

Labour, after being returned to power in 1950 with a much-reduced majority, loses power to the Conservatives in the following year (owing to the vagaries of the British electoral system, they lose even though they gain more votes than the Tories). The incoming Conservative administration, however, largely accepts the idea that it is the government's job to provide for its citizens and intervene in the workings of the economy; they are, though, as much in thrall to the idea of Britain's pre-eminent position in the world as the Labour government they replace. To say this is not to dismiss successive Labour and Conservative administrations as deluded or wilfully ignorant: it would have been hard for any government to accept, either in public or in private, the fact that Britain's influence in the world is substantially less than it had been. It would have been even more difficult for politicians of both parties to predict just how quickly and decisively that influence would wane. It is also understandable that British governments of both parties should spend money and effort on those traditional industries – coal, steel, shipbuilding and the like – that had served the country well for much of the previous 150 years.

This blindness is undoubtedly harmful; it means that a lot of time, effort and money are spent in a desperate attempt to defend a global position that in practice simply cannot be sustained. It is, however, understandable. A generation of British politicians have been raised in a world where Britain is powerful; it is no wonder that they have trouble adjusting to a changed international situation. They could contemplate divesting themselves of some of their imperial burdens; for example, India is partitioned and granted independence in 1947 (arguably, the precipitate speed of the handover, and the botched nature of the partition, contributes to the bloody sectarian conflict that breaks out between Hindus and Muslims, caught up in the reorganisation of their country). However, no politician seriously undertakes a study of the costs and benefits of maintaining an empire until Harold Macmillan in the late 1950s. Similarly, both Labour and Conservative governments think it vital that Britain should have its own nuclear deterrent – for reasons that have far more to do with international status than military necessity. Aneurin Bevan (on the left of the Labour Party), and Winston Churchill (who regains the premiership when the Conservatives take power in 1951) might not agree on much, but they both support the idea of a British nuclear weapon. Bevan famously dismays many of his own supporters when, in 1957, he tells the Labour Party conference that unilateral nuclear disarmament would send a future British foreign minister 'naked into the conference chamber'.[12] During Churchill's last spell as prime minister, his chiefs of staff prepare a briefing paper for the cabinet on nuclear weapons; in part, it argues that 'Our scientific and technological capacity to produce the hydrogen weapon puts within our grasp the ability to be on terms with the United States and Russia'.[13] Neither Churchill nor Bevan likes the thought of nuclear warfare, but they are clear about the implications for Britain's global identity if the country stays out of the arms race: no one would take Britain seriously as a force in world politics. Much the same thinking keeps the country aloof from the negotiations that eventually lead to the formation of the European Coal and Steel Community (the forerunner of the European Union) in 1951. The countries in the Union – France, Germany, Italy, Belgium, the Netherlands and Luxembourg – had either lost the war, or had been conquered; for Britain to enter into partnership with them would be a clear signal that the British accept their reduced place in the world.

The Conservatives manage to stay in power from 1951 until their eventual defeat by Harold Wilson's Labour Party in 1964. During this time, the party is led, in succession, by Churchill (1951–55); Anthony Eden (1955–57); Harold Macmillan (1957–63); and Alec Douglas-Home (1963–64). Although in practice they are as variable as any set of prime ministers, they were all part of a generation that found it easier to think of Britain as Great rather than Modern. Of the four, arguably only Macmillan accepts the new international realities, and then only in part; both Churchill and Eden are hamstrung by their desire to keep Britain unambiguously Great (Churchill over the question of nuclear weapons; Eden, far more seriously, over the botched invasion of Suez – see below). On other matters, they and the party they lead accept the new, post-war world. All four accept the idea that the government should provide for and support the population as a whole; none attempts to roll back the boundaries of the welfare state that Labour had created. In 1954, Norman Macrae, a journalist writing for *The Economist*, dubs the economic policies of both parties 'Butskellism' – a composite name, taken from the then Conservative chancellor 'Rab' Butler, and his Labour shadow, Hugh Gaitskell. 'Butskellism' is, moreover, shorthand for a wider consensus between the two parties:

> Butler and Gaitskell had their differences, of course, but they also had a shared commitment to Keynesian management and moderate, professional administration. The parallels between

them were widely thought to reflect the wider affinities between the two parties and, beyond that, the mood of the country as a whole. There was no Conservative backlash against the welfare state, while on the Labour benches the verses of the Red Flag were sung with nostalgic reverie rather than with socialist fervour. 'Party differences,' Churchill said, 'are now in practice largely those of emphasis' . . . .[14]

Economically at least, the 1950s is a settled decade. The government has its share of financial crises (caused by Britain's troubled trading relations with the rest of the world; the value of the pound against other currencies; and the need to support the cost of the empire, the nuclear deterrent and the welfare state) but life for most of the population improves. Rationing, of many staple foodstuffs and other items such as clothing, which had been imposed during the war (with the exception of bread, which is rationed for a short while between 1946 and 1948) is finally abolished in 1954. There is full employment: new consumer goods (washing machines, televisions, vacuum cleaners) begin to appear – and what is more, are priced to appeal even to the working classes (which accounts for just over 70 per cent of the British population). When Macmillan, months after becoming prime minister, makes a speech about the state of the British economy, his words – or a version of them – soon pass into the folklore of the time:

> Let's be frank about it: most of our people have never had it so good. Go around the country, go to the industrial towns, go to the farms, and you will see a state of prosperity such as we have never had in my lifetime – nor indeed ever in the history of this country. What is worrying some of us is 'Is it too good to be true?' or perhaps I should say 'Is it too good to last?'[15]

In the popular imagination, Macmillan's point emerges in a simplified form, as 'You've never had it so good' – a phrase so resonant that it has served as the title of two of the histories of the period.[16] This simplification is understandable and entirely forgivable; in terms of living standards, job security, healthcare and state support, it is true.

As the full quotation demonstrates, though, Macmillan is making a rather more tentative point. His speech is targeted at those people who have not been able to take advantage of the rising tide of prosperity in the decade; and his nervousness about the duration of the economic and social good times is based on a shrewd assessment of the forces that are buoying Britain up. British manufacturing industry is not as productive or as competitive as the booming economies in Europe, and it lags behind the economic powerhouse of the US; improved living standards in Britain are more to do with the stability and profitability of Western economies as a whole than they are because of anything that British manufacturers were doing. This in itself is a sign of Britain's changing status: rather than being one of the world's economic leaders, the country is now slipstreaming behind other, more successful countries. And balancing the economic successes of the decade, there are a series of international defeats and reverses, all of which contribute to the notion that Britain is a country in inexorable decline. For one thing, successive prime ministers are left in little doubt that, when they deal with the US, they are dealing with their global superiors: even Churchill, who takes his seat alongside Roosevelt and Stalin at Yalta in 1945 to discuss the nature of the post-war world, is not immune:

> I [Evelyn Shuckburgh, Anthony Eden's private secretary] attended most of the meetings with Truman . . . He was quite abrupt on one or two occasions with poor old Winston and had a tendency, after one of the old man's powerful and emotional declarations of faith in Anglo-American co-operation, to cut it off with a 'Thank you, Mr Prime Minister. We might pass that to be worked out by our advisers.' A little wounding. It was impossible not to be conscious that we are playing second fiddle.[17]

This is galling, as is the success of the nascent European Economic Community (especially when, at the end of the decade, the government's tentative overtures to the EEC are rebuffed by President De Gaulle of France). The empire is also a source of concern; Indian independence is followed by a rising tide of national rebellion in many colonies. Although the pace of imperial retreat does not really pick up until the second half of the 1950s, the forces that determine Britain's retreat from empire are gathering well before 1939. Uprisings, such as the Mau Mau rebellion in Kenya from 1952 to 1956, and the unrest in Malaysia which continued from 1948 to 1960, stretch the country's already over-committed resources; and the fear of losing imperial prestige lies behind what must rank as the government's most controversial and damaging foreign adventure – the attempt to retake the Suez Canal in 1956.

The whole sorry episode stems in large part from Britain's uncertain sense of its place in the new world. The prime minister of the time, Anthony Eden, serves successfully as foreign secretary under Churchill (he also, famously, takes a principled stand against attempts to appease Hitler in the late 1930s). However, by the time he becomes prime minister his health is failing; and those around him in the early 1950s are unconvinced, to say the least, that he is suited for the job. Churchill tells his principal private secretary (and close friend) Jock Colville, 'I don't believe Anthony can do it'.[18] Eden gets off to a good start: he calls a quick election in 1955, and the Conservatives are returned with an increased majority. After the election, he begins to run into trouble: the economy falters, and his control over the party he leads seems less than secure. It is at this time that a long-simmering dispute over the ownership of the Suez Canal erupts. This vital trade route (through which, at the time, some 80 per cent of Western Europe's supplies travelled) is effectively owned by Britain, under a complicated series of international agreements, since 1888; Egypt's new president, Abdel Nasser, a convinced Arab nationalist, seeks to take the canal back under Egyptian control since 1951 (when he repudiates previous agreements over its ownership). For Eden, and for Britain as a whole, losing Suez means more than losing power over a vital trade route; it is a sign of the ebbing of British power. If the president of a country like Egypt could dictate terms to Great Britain, the imperial game is up; and if Nasser is (as he seems to be at the time) becoming more and more dependent on the Soviet Union, then the loss of the Canal would shift the balance of power in the region away from the Americans – and away from Britain, their allies.

In July 1956, Egyptian troops seize control of the Suez Canal. Eden's immediate response is to retaliate; but this is difficult, for a number of reasons. First, the company that owns the Canal is registered in Egypt; any attack to regain the Canal would therefore be legally problematic – the British government could not simply claim that Egypt is attacking British territory. Second, the support of the American government is crucial; but the US president, Eisenhower, is standing for election that year – and is understandably wary of committing himself or his country in a potential conflict. Unsurprisingly, the British response is initially hesitant; military plans chop and change, and diplomatic discussions over the Canal's future soon get bogged down. An increasingly frustrated Eden, determined that Nasser should not be allowed to control the Canal, finally acquiesces to a plan, initially proposed by the French government (who are worried about Nasser's role in fomenting nationalist sentiment in Algeria – one of their colonies) and the Israelis. The plan runs thus. Israel will invade Egypt, and Britain and France will then step in, apparently to halt the conflict, but in effect, to regain control of the Canal area. The plan is legally dubious, and diplomatically very risky; it is also bound to be exposed (indeed, the Americans seem to have been aware of collusion between the three countries almost immediately).

On 29 October, the Israelis invade, and on the 31st, the British military operation begins. Public opinion in Britain is split between those who wish to avoid conflict and those who see Nasser as another dictator who needs to be taught a lesson. When fighting breaks out, opinion swings in favour of supporting British troops; but the international reaction is immediate – and damning. On 2 November, the United Nations overwhelmingly supports an American resolution calling for an instant ceasefire, Eisenhower orders the US 6th Fleet into the area and, decisively, the US puts the British economy under severe financial pressure. Eden, determined until the last moment to follow through with the plan he had agreed with the French and the Israelis, is given no option but to cave in. A ceasefire is announced on 6 November – and, as if the country is not humiliated enough, British forces are excluded from the UN security taskforce that takes control of the Canal. Eden's announcement of the ceasefire in the House of

Commons that afternoon is his last appearance as prime minister, and his last speech to the House. His health broken, he is soon replaced by Harold Macmillan (who, as chancellor, is the bearer of the bad economic news that brings the invasion to a close). It is not that Suez starts the process of British imperial decline: rather, it confirms just how far that decline had gone. Britain is now, it seems, an American client state, able to exercise power only if the US agrees; it is also unable to hold on to its colonies, if those colonies mounted a determined resistance. More than this, Suez undermines Britain in a less easily quantifiable, but none the less significant way:

> It was not so much that the affair marked the end of Britain as a Great Power: it marked our end as a good power, one that could normally be expected to act honourably. It was for me what Munich had been for a slightly older generation and Iraq would be for a younger: but whereas Munich and Iraq were understandable if deplorable acts of realpolitik, the sheer irrationality of the Suez adventure still fills me with melancholy amazement.[19]

The shame that accrues to the British action in Suez is made worse by the fact that, at the same time, the Soviet Union invades Hungary (where a reforming socialist government is trying to move away from the kind of dictatorial communism practised in Russia). There is some evidence[20] that the Russians choose their time carefully – only invading Hungary when international attention was focused on Suez.

This year 1956, in retrospect, marks the end of Britain's idea of itself as a world power. Harold Macmillan is quick to accept that the US now is the most important Western nation; in a famous simile, he likens Britain to ancient Greece, and the US to imperial Rome – with the clear implication that Britain could exert a civilising influence on those more powerful than itself. It also, again in retrospect, spurs on other changes. Britain at the end of the 1950s is a markedly less deferential society than it had been at the beginning of the decade – and materially the country was certainly more comfortable than it had been. Macmillan, a far cannier politician than Eden (and a far more subtle political operator) is able for a time to make political capital from these changes; so much so that he manages to steer his party to another decisive victory in 1959. At a time when the economy seems to be delivering substantial improvements in people's lifestyles, and new social forces seem to be reshaping the country, Macmillan is a reassuringly calm, avuncular figure. He presides over an accelerating consumer boom; he manages to speed up the process through which Britain sheds its empire; but even he cannot fully accommodate himself to the idea that Britain is a nation in decline. Even though Britain could no longer justifiably claim it is a superpower, the behavioural habits associated with the country's previous status are still in place. In December 1957, the chancellor, Peter Thorneycroft (with whom Macmillan falls out in early 1958), gives the prime minister a sober assessment of where Britain stood in the late 1950s:

> With relatively few assets and large debts, we continue to live on the scale of a great power. We have the most expensive defence forces in Europe. We have joined the nuclear 'club'. We claim at the same time a very high standard of life. We seek to lead the world in the social services we provide.[21]

In other words, as the 1950s turns into the 1960s, Britain is still trying desperately to be both Great and Modern: and the contradiction is as unsustainable at the end of the decade as it was at the beginning.

Britain 1945–60: culture and society

> That is what has happened in the Fifties – a generation suddenly made up its mind. Not so much to rebel against the old order of authority and standards, but to refuse to vote for it . . .[22]

In 1956, a piece of new writing from a previously unknown, and very young, author is hailed as a landmark in British cultural life. The author's name is Colin Wilson: his debut publication, *The Outsider*, comes garlanded with the kind of publisher's blurb that most authors would sell their souls to attain:

> . . . Considered merely as a survey of some of the most important literary figures of the last century or so, and as a summary of their ideas, the book would be extremely worth reading. But it is more than that. It is scarcely too much to describe it as a blueprint of the malaise of the soul of mankind in the mid-20th century. It represents a challenge to every thinking person. The author of this remarkable book is only twenty-four.[23]

This is a striking endorsement; even more so, because it comes from a reputable publishing house (Gollancz published, among others, Kingsley Amis). Press reaction to *The Outsider* is equally effusive: two months after it appears, the *Daily Mail* comments that it had received '. . . the most rapturous reception of any book since the war'.[24] Respected cultural commentators (Cyril Connolly, in an article for the *Sunday Times*, and Philip Toynbee in the *Observer*) hail the work as a masterpiece – and Wilson, who as the papers are keen to point out had been sleeping rough on Hampstead Heath, and who composed his masterpiece in the reading room of the British Museum, is rumoured to have made £20,000 in the year following the book's publication. *The Outsider* (an examination, as Wilson would have it, of one of the key figures of the modern age: the man who rejects all forms of social control in the name of a rather poorly defined idea of freedom) has not proved as durable as *Look Back in Anger*. On closer examination, even those who endorse it on its first publication find problems with the book. Wilson, for one thing, makes extensive use of other texts, which he comprehensively misquotes; for another, the central argument of the book is, frankly, incoherent. It is also fair to say that Wilson himself plays a key role in the decline of his reputation, which is as swift and sudden as its rise. He endorses the ideas of the pre-war leader of the British Union of Fascists, Oswald Mosley; his public statements display an increasingly messianic sense of his own importance; and he is embroiled in a public scandal (the father of Wilson's girlfriend threatens him with a horsewhip, after reading apparently pornographic sections of Wilson's diary). More damagingly, Wilson hands his diary over to the *Daily Mail*, in a misguided attempt to clear his name. The *Mail* gleefully publishes extracts, in which Wilson declares 'I *am* the major literary genius of our century . . . the most serious man of our age'.[25] No wonder, given this, that when his second book, *Religion and the Rebel* (1957) is published, the same literary figures who had supported him now revise their opinion of his merits; Toynbee says of the new work, 'No quotation can do justice to the flaccid banality of Mr Wilson's writing style . . . or . . . to . . . the grandiloquence of his claims'.[26] By the decade's end, Wilson's brief time in the limelight passes; still convinced of his own intellectual prowess, he slides back into obscurity as fast as he had climbed to fame.

Wilson's story is an instructive one, and takes us to the heart of the social and cultural atmosphere of the time. Arguably, Wilson would not have had the fleeting impact that he had were it not for a number of competing forces which transform British life. Some of these have already been referred to: Britain moves from rationing and austerity to full employment and relative plenty, but at the same time the country has to readjust its idea of itself as a force in the world. At the same time, and as noted above, patterns of consumption are changing. This in turn breeds a new set of cultural anxieties for a number of commentators, both old and new, and from various parts of the political spectrum. On the one hand, a generation of established artists find themselves out of step with a post-war world where the old social structures and traditions are in decline; on the other hand, newer commentators, such as Colin Wilson from the political Right and Richard Hoggart from the Left, argue that post-war comfort breeds a kind of rootless conformity. Hoggart in particular is scathing about the impact that new patterns of consumption have on previously stable and secure working-class communities. In a much-quoted passage from his 1957 book *The Uses of Literacy*, Hoggart anatomises the teenagers who made use of a peculiarly post-war phenomenon, the coffee bar:

> Compared even with the pub around the corner, this is all a
> peculiarly thin and pallid form of dissipation, a sort of spiritual

dry-rot amid the odour of boiled milk. Many of the customers – their clothes, their hair-styles, their facial expressions all indicate – are living to a large extent in a myth-world compounded of a few simple elements which they take to be those of American life.[27]

Hoggart, in the book's introduction, is commendably clear about his strong emotional attachment to the old working class; however, the concerns voiced in this and other sections of the book (that British culture is in danger of being swamped by a vapid, conformist, Americanised mass art, targeted at the lowest common denominator of public taste) are widely shared.

At bottom, these various reactions to the social trends of the decade have the same cause. Britain is changing rapidly: it isn't simply that the country is no longer as powerful as it used to be – the very fabric of an apparently stable society seems to be under threat. In part, this is due to the increasing affluence of the time; as Stephen Lacey has noted:

> The statistics are certainly impressive: between 1951 and 1964 total [industrial] production increased by 40 per cent; the number of cars increased from just over 2 million to 8 million and the number of TV sets from 1 million to 13 million. Average earnings in the period increased by 110 per cent and the average standard of living rose, in real terms, by 30 per cent. Consumer expenditure as a whole doubled in that time and share prices trebled in the 1950s alone. Expressing this in another way, Eric Hobsbawm wrote that by the early 1960s '91 per cent of British households had acquired electric irons, 82 per cent television sets, 72 per cent vacuum cleaners, 45 per cent washing machines and 30 per cent refrigerators'.[28]

Lacey points out – and it is worth remembering – that these economic benefits are not evenly distributed: the north of Britain lags behind the south (a pattern which persists, with some variations, up to the present). For those members of the artistic and cultural establishment living through such a period of profound transformation, the problem isn't the uneven distribution of the country's newfound affluence; nor is it the fact that increased comfort masks other, more painful realities (such as the status of women within British society, the racism encountered by immigrants from the West Indies and elsewhere, and the increasingly desperate rearguard action fought by some members of the legal establishment against the decriminalisation of homosexuality). The problem, rather, is wealth itself. Evelyn Waugh, for example, views the new, post-war world with what can only be described as curmudgeonly disdain; his 1946 novel *Brideshead Revisited* traces the inexorable decline of the elegantly aristocratic Flyte family – a decline caused by the equally inexorable rise of the newly powerful and affluent middle and lower classes. Other figures, less reactionary than Waugh, voice similar concerns. After visiting the USA in 1954, the novelist and playwright J. B. Priestley coins the term *admass*, to describe a new type of society in which 'people would cheerfully exchange their last glimpse of freedom for a new car, a refrigerator, and a TV screen'.[29] This concern – that a superficial consumer society would destroy older, more deeply rooted forms of social organisation – lies behind Hoggart's disparaging picture of the 1950s coffee bar; concern over the impact of affluence on British life is as liable to be expressed on the Left of politics as it was on the Right.

Other people are, on the surface at least, happier with the direction Britain is taking. For one thing, memories of the deprivation that many people suffered in the 1930s are still strong; and the relatively protracted end to rationing means that, for everyone growing up in the 1950s, the new prosperity seems to promise not only comfort, but also a measure of freedom. The mass unemployment of the Depression disappears; Arthur Seaton, the working-class protagonist of Alan Sillitoe's first novel *Saturday Night and Sunday Morning* (1958), knows that times are better for him than they were for his father, and he revels in the change:

> No more short term [work] like before the war, or getting the sack if you stood ten minutes in the lavatory reading your Football Post – if the gaffer got on to you now you could always

tell him where to put the job and go somewhere else. And no more running out at dinnertime for a penny bag of chips to eat with your bread. Now, and about time too, you got fair wages if you worked your backbone to a string of conkers on your work, and there was a big canteen where you could get a hot dinner for two-bob. With the wages you got you could save up for a motor-bike or even an old car, or you could go on a ten-day binge and get rid of all you saved.[30]

This sense of newfound possibility also animates the work of artists whose subject matter comes from further up the social scale. In their cases, though, that sense of new potential is not simply caused by a change in the economic situation; it is also profoundly shaped by developments in the popular culture of the time. John Osborne, for example, points out that

A lot of my generation . . . were very influenced by jazz . . . It was a special voice that we all latched on to, because it was exotic and it was powerful, and it was completely different from the kind of voice that we knew at the time.[31]

Osborne's taste in jazz is indeed shared by many of his contemporaries (in particular by Kingsley Amis and Philip Larkin); it is also part of a wider attitude to culture – an attitude which sets out to attack and overturn previously existing ideas of what is artistically significant, and what can comfortably be ignored. The new writers of the 1950s are, to a greater or lesser extent, unwilling to accept the idea that popular culture – jazz, Hollywood movies, supposedly non-literary genres such as detective and science fiction – should be ignored or despised. Famously, the hero of Amis's *Lucky Jim* refers slightingly to 'filthy Mozart';[32] one can imagine that this is the kind of comment which angers Somerset Maugham. What writers like Amis prize about the popular culture of the time is its immediacy. It does not demand specialised knowledge; it does not need to be decoded before it can be enjoyed; it speaks directly to the experiences and the aspirations of its audience. Moreover, coming as much of it does from the United States, it speaks to Osborne and his contemporaries of a world which is less constrained, more dynamic and far more exciting than anything that Britain has to offer.

British social structures, however, do not change nearly as rapidly. Although some of the more apocalyptic pronouncements made by Waugh, Noël Coward or John Betjeman might suggest that the old forms of British life are disappearing as rapidly as snow in the sun, the problem – at least as many of the younger authors and cultural commentators would have it – is that Britain remains stubbornly unchanged. In 1955, the Conservative journalist Henry Fairlie picks up a term coined by the historian A. J. P. Taylor to describe the operation of power in British life; on 23 September (significantly, the day after another threat is made to the established order of things; on the 22nd, a new commercial TV station – ITV – broadcasts for the first time) Fairlie publishes an article describing the operations of an amorphous group of powerful people that he describes as the 'Establishment':

> By the 'Establishment' I do not mean only the centres of official power – though they are certainly part of it – but rather the whole matrix of official and social relations within which power is exercised. The exercise of power in Britain (more specifically, in England) cannot be understood unless it is recognised that it is exercised socially. Anyone who has at any point been close to the exercise of power will know what I mean when I say that the 'Establishment' can be seen at work in the activities of, not only the Prime Minister, the Archbishop of Canterbury and the Earl Marshall, but of such lesser mortals as the Chairman of the Arts Council, the Director-General of the BBC, and even the editor of the *Times Literary Supplement* . . .[33]

As a descriptive term, the 'Establishment' is usefully vague. Fairlie does not mean to suggest that he is describing a coherent organisation; rather, he wants to draw attention to the fact that, in terms of class and education, those who rule the country are a remarkably cohesive group. As Dominic Sandbrook points out:

> Between 1948 and 1956, no less than half of the recruits to the higher levels of the civil service had been to Oxford, and a further third had been to Cambridge. Half of all the new appointments had studied classics or history; just one in a hundred had studied science . . . Not only were the two major universities disproportionately favoured, but certain colleges within them were especially successful at sending their boys to fill senior positions in the civil service. Between 1956 and 1961, for example, twenty-seven senior positions were filled by graduates of New College, Oxford; twenty-six by men from King's, Cambridge; and twenty-five by Balliol men. During the same period, precisely one position went to a man who had been educated at a comprehensive secondary modern school.[34]

Especially in the wake of Suez (see above), the idea that Britain is effectively ruled by a self-perpetuating, self-selecting elite, impervious to new ideas and new social movements, becomes part of the common currency of discussions of the future direction of the nation. Anthony Eden is, after all, the exemplar of the establishment; well connected (the son of a baronet); educated appropriately (Eton and Christ Church, Oxford); and fatally out of touch with the post-war world. The struggle against entrenched, established power, in fact, becomes one of the key themes of the decade. In episode after episode of the surreal radio comedy *The Goons* (first broadcast in 1951), establishment figures are mocked; the programme's resident villain, Hercules Grytpype-Thynne, has an impeccably upper-class accent, and one of the regular buffoons, Major Bloodnok, is an equally well-spoken (and equally untrustworthy) representative of the British army's officer class. In one of the decade's iconic TV serials, *Quatermass II* (1955), the intrepid, dynamic scientist Bernard Quatermass finds it difficult to gain governmental support for a proposal to establish manned bases on the Moon; as the serial unfolds, he finds that the establishment has been infiltrated by aliens. Those in power, the serial suggests, are quite simply a different species.

Even here, though, there are ambiguities. The idea of a full-scale revolt against the powers-that-be does not have much purchase, either in British society as a whole or in the culture of the time. The country is living in the aftermath of the cataclysm of the Second World War; understandably, there is little appetite for further radical change – especially given that things seem to be getting generally better. Also, those who seem to be in revolt against the old order are themselves largely products of that order. Amis, Wain and Larkin have been to Oxford; George Devine, who becomes the figurehead for new theatre writing during his tenure at the Royal Court (see below), knows, and has worked with, most of the key figures of the contemporary British stage. Viewed uncharitably, their criticisms of 1950s society might seem rather more like grumbles from the inside of the establishment, rather than attacks from the outside. So, if the cultural conflicts of the 1950s can't be seen in the same light as those in the 1960s (a decade in which new, rather more radical ways of organising public and personal life are matters of public debate) how can they be best discussed?

A clue comes from one of the founder members of The Movement (if such a phrase can be used of such a loose collection of individuals). John Wain, a young novelist and poet (and a near contemporary of Amis and Larkin at Oxford), presents a series called *First Readings* on BBC radio in 1953. For the opening broadcast, he selects a section from the as-yet-unpublished *Lucky Jim*; he also makes a statement that sums up, as well as anything could, the ambiguous nature of the cultural revolts of the time:

> Having got as far as the middle of the Twentieth Century, we ought to be looking both back and forward. Looking back, we see that we have passed through a period of frontier expansion. Daring pioneers, often proceeding by guesswork and with equipment they had designed and built themselves, pushed out into the unknown and established some kind of foothold there . . . But a period of expansion has to be followed by a period of consolidation . . . The question is no longer, 'how much further can we press on?' It is rather 'what shall we do now we are here?'[35]

Partly, this is a familiar plea for new work that addresses a new world; partly, though, it is rather conservative. Wain is looking back over a cultural scene that has, before the war, nurtured the modernist experiments of T. S. Eliot and James Joyce, the assault on representative art practised by the Cubists and the Surrealists, the exercises in experimental atonality in the music of Schoenberg (or the radical harmonies developed by Stravinsky). The last thing that Wain seems to want is more experimentation; now is the time, he suggests, to stand back, and to take stock. The *New Statesman*'s radio critic, Hugh Massingham, reviewing the show, might have drawn the conclusion that 'Mr Wain's implication [was] fairly clear. Our brave new world is over at last and the old fogies can be led off to the slaughterhouse',[36] but, from the tone of Wain's comments, it seems that something far less transformative is being proposed; something which will downplay the cultural guesswork of previous generations, in favour of art which is, if not more sober in content, then at least more down to earth in terms of form.

Anything more revolutionary would have seemed entirely out of place in 1953: as Stephen Lacey notes, this year marks the high point of the 1950s social and political consensus. That consensus proves difficult to sustain as the decade progresses. Suez is profoundly divisive. As might have been expected, once the conflict begins public opinion swings behind the troops: government policy, however, proves harder to accept – and some prominent voices are raised against the invasion (in particular, the *Observer*, Kenneth Tynan's newspaper, publishes an editorial condemning the conflict). Especially on the Left of British politics, a critique begins to emerge which questions both the cultural conservatism of the T. S. Eliots and the cautious revolts of the Amises; as Stefan Collini[37] argues, the main target of this critique is the apathy which, for Marxists like the historian E. P. Thompson, seems to have settled over British life in the earlier years of the decade (it is telling that, when a collection of Thompson's essays is published in 1960, it is titled *Out of Apathy*). Similarly, when Jimmy Porter rails against the state of the nation, it is the apathy of the British that he finds hardest to swallow; and when Beattie Bryant in Wesker's *Roots* harangues her family, it is their passive acceptance of their place in the world that is the main target of her attacks. However, those who attack the complacency of the country are apt to find themselves isolated; lost in angry impotence, like Jimmy Porter in Osborne's *Look Back in Anger*, Ronnie Kahn in Wesker's *Chicken Soup with Barley*, or Jean Rice in Osborne's *The Entertainer*, cut off from their culture, like Beattie in Wesker's *Roots*, or in a more extreme example, imprisoned and awaiting execution like Musgrave at the end of John Arden's *Serjeant Musgrave's Dance*.

The culture wars of the 1950s, then, cannot really be thought of as a simple confrontation between the old and the new: although some writers and artists of the pre-war generation (Coward, Maugham, Eliot, Waugh et al.) have undoubtedly embraced some very conservative attitudes which ensure that they are out of step with the new decade, some of them have also engaged in the radical transformation of their various art forms – transformations that the younger, post-war authors reject. At the same time, Amis and his generation seem to regard much of British society as stuffy, staid, hidebound, overly cosy and (the great target of much of Amis's fiction) profoundly dull. However, newer writers on the whole like the idea that literature and art should not experiment (or, at least, not experiment so radically). To do so is to run the risk of pretension, of exclusivity, and of producing art for the sake of art. These contradictions (alongside his own manifest inadequacies) help to explain Colin Wilson's swift ascent, and his equally swift descent; his approach to literature and philosophy might appeal to those who yearn for the experimental eclecticism of the 1920s and 1930s; the same people are liable to be put off by the youthful arrogance of his work. Similarly, the very writers who might be on Wilson's side (the new generation, publishing for the first time in the 1950s) find themselves largely out of sympathy with him; not because his work is inadequate or poorly argued, but because it is pretentious and, by their lights, disturbingly foreign. When Amis discusses a spat with Wilson in a letter to the poet and historian Robert Conquest (caused by Amis's scathing review of *The Outsider*), he finds it remarkably easy to pretend that Wilson is French; 'Had an incredible letter from Capitaine C. Wilson of the Légion Etrangère', the letter runs.[38]

Perhaps the closest that the new writers of the 1950s get to a unified summary of their aims and world-view is in *Declaration*, a collection of polemical essays published in 1957. The collection, edited by Tom Maschler, brings together contributions from a number of the key figures of the decade: John Osborne, Kenneth Tynan, Doris Lessing, John Wain, Lindsay Anderson and Colin Wilson (alongside two of his closest intellectual acolytes, Stuart Holroyd and Bill Hopkins). The volume attracts a fair amount of attention at the time (not least because it contains a spirited attack by Osborne on the Royal Family; the convention of the time is that the monarchy remains above public debate, and therefore above criticism). However, the collection as a whole falls short of the impact that Maschler wished to achieve. The book does not have a unifying theme; there is little in practice to link the quasi-fascism of Wilson, Holroyd and Hopkins with the various shades of left-wing opinion held by Anderson, Osborne, Tynan and others; moreover, some notable figures – Iris Murdoch and Kingsley Amis in particular – refuse to contribute. Amis signals his dissatisfaction in characteristically robust terms: in a letter to Maschler, declining to take part in the collection, he said, 'I hate all this pharasaical twittering about the "state of our civilisation", and I suspect anyone who wants to buttonhole me about my "role in society". This book is likely to prove a valuable addition to the cult of the Solemn Young Man.'[39] (Maschler goes ahead and publishes the letter in the introduction.) Even the book's launch is rather fraught: it was due to take place in the Royal Court, but the theatre's ruling council (prone, as Philip Roberts points out, to expressing a great deal of unease at the apparently left-leaning slant of many of the plays staged in the theatre) do not allow the event to take place in the theatre (the volume is eventually launched, rather less impressively, at a drinking club in the King's Road). Maschler's title might have sounded bold and decisive; however (and typical of the cultural debates of the time), on closer examination the revolutionary transformation of British culture it seems to signal is far more uncertain and ambiguous. If the political establishment cannot decide whether Britain is Modern or Great, then it could be said that the artistic and cultural establishment, and those who seem to be dead set against it, are equally uncertain – this time over the relative merits (and also the very definition) of what is Old and what is New.

CHAPTER 1
THE BRITISH THEATRE 1945–60

In 1959, the playwright John Whiting published an article in *Encore*, a journal which, since its inception in 1954, had been a determined advocate for new forms of drama. The opening paragraph of the article has been much quoted, because it casts the events of the previous few years in an appropriately revolutionary light:

> The main engagement took place in Sloane Square. There was a complementary action, in the Far East, at Stratford. These separate forms were never co-ordinated. The east relied very much on mercenaries recruited from another country. The west, although at one time there was an uneasy and shortlisted alliance with France, employed the natives. The west once occupied the Palace and the Comedy, but these were not held. At this moment the east has taken Wyndhams and the Criterion . . .[1]

The ironically apocalyptic tone of the paragraph is rather more than an exercise in authorial whimsy. It does not stretch the facts too far to say that during the 1950s a battle was waged for the soul of the British theatre (and that at least some of those involved in the battle would have talked about the struggle in such fundamental terms). From a broader historical perspective, Whiting's description of the struggle, in which the new forces of the Royal Court (working from Chelsea) and Joan Littlewood's Theatre Workshop (working in Stratford, in the East End of London) take on the might of the commercial West End, chimes with the political and cultural debates outlined above. These narratives, though, as I have said, proved to be much more complex – and Whiting's article is valuable, because it catches that sense of complexity, of confusion and of a situation which seemed so clear-cut descending into something far more difficult to define and understand:

. . . The situation is now confused. What exactly is written on that banner which the winds of expediency will so irritatingly fold? What are those charming businessmen doing on this side of the barricades? Is it true that some of the insurgents have been decorated by the enemy? They say that the social-realists and the experimentalists have fallen out. There are ugly rumours of unholy alliances. Even the citadel itself, the curiously named Royal Court, is threatened.[2]

The situation at the end of the 1950s in British theatre might have been confused; but things were undoubtedly different. The nature of the theatre industry had changed markedly from the late 1940s onward; and even though the change was not as clear-cut as it sometimes appeared in hindsight, dramatists working in the early 1960s operated in a very different climate than their immediate predecessors.

The British stage 1945–60: the theatre industry

In some ways, it could be said that the British theatre had a good war. For some venues (most famously the Windmill Theatre – a variety theatre, specialising in nude tableaux) staying open through the worst of the Blitz had become a badge of honour; and although the worst of the bombing raids in 1940 had almost stopped theatrical activity in London, the state of the London stage had improved by 1945:

> Revues, light comedies, revivals of classics by noted actors including John Gielgud, Laurence Olivier and Ralph Richardson, and the occasionally highly successful new work, such as Noël Coward's *Blithe Spirit* (1941), had all proved an appealing mix for audiences. By July 1945, for example, *Blithe Spirit* had achieved 1,716 consecutive performances, *Charley's Aunt* 1,466 and *Arsenic and Old Lace* 1,057.[3]

However, as Shellard notes, this apparent recovery was rather fragile. At the war's end, the number of theatres in the West End had shrunk by 12 per cent; fewer stages meant greater congestion, as long-running productions refused to give way to new work; and the theatre faced increased competition from cinema, which had enjoyed an entirely understandable surge of popularity. In terms of new writing for the overcrowded London stages, the future looked rather bleak. In shaming contrast to the theatre in other countries, British theatre had no distinctive theatrical voices of its own. In other words, well before the inception of the English Stage Company at the Royal Court, influential voices were calling for a revolution in British playwriting; by the time of *Look Back in Anger*'s first production, the ground had been extensively prepared.

In 1947, the author and dramatist J. B. Priestley, at the time a more influential voice than Hobson, published a broadside at the current state of the British theatre industry:

> Theatre at present is not controlled by dramatists, actors, producers or managers, but chiefly by theatre owners, men of property who may or may not have a taste for the drama. The owners . . . take too much out of the theatre . . . [It] is not that the owners are purely 'commercial', but that they cannot help satisfying their own particular tastes . . . What I condemn is the property system that allows public amenities and a communal art to be controlled by persons who happen to be rich enough to acquire playhouses.[4]

Priestley, in effect, called for the British theatre to be put on the same footing as the new National Health Service (which was to come into being in 1948); a communal service should be brought under public ownership for the communal good of the British people. Unlikely though his recommendations might have seemed at the time, Priestley's argument was based on a clear perception of the current organisation of the stage. The British post-war stage was almost entirely a commercial proposition. There were some significant amateur companies (the left-wing Unity Theatre Movement, formed in the 1930s, being perhaps the most important),[5] but the larger stages of the West End – the showcase for theatre in Britain – were controlled by entrepreneurial management groups, the most famous being H. M. Tennent Ltd. Tennent was managed by Hugh Beaumont (universally known by his nickname, 'Binkie'); at the end of the war, the company was responsible for twelve productions, running in eight theatres in the West End. Over the next few years, the company bankrolled some of the most significant productions on the London stage: new plays by Terence Rattigan, who came to be regarded as Tennent's house dramatist; Rodgers and Hammerstein's innovative musical *Oklahoma!* in 1947; the first British production of Tennessee Williams's *A Streetcar Named Desire* (1949), which contained a memorable performance by Vivien Leigh as Blanche Du Bois; Christopher Fry's translation of Jean Anouilh's *Ring Around the Moon* (1950).

What makes the picture even more complicated is the fact that the financial arrangements underpinning theatre production in the period are bafflingly labyrinthine. Tennent was only one of a number of such companies; Prince Littler's Consolidated Trust – known commonly as 'The Group' – held a sizeable stake in Tennent and many other companies in the field, and exercised control over more than 50 per cent of the theatre seats in London, as well as dominating the number-one touring circuit of large regional theatres. As Dan Rebellato has pointed out, it is easy to overestimate the power of organisations like 'The Group', and to see their command of the most important stages as more harmfully monolithic than it actually was. However, there is no doubt that the concentration of power in the hands of a relatively small group of owners was increasingly perceived as a problem, both by other, less influential and successful commercial managements, and by key figures and groups inside and outside of the theatre industry:

> The criticisms were exclusively and precisely directed toward the structures of ownership. The TUC conference in 1944 called for the monopoly tendency in the entertainment industry to be broken up. Over the next four years, several prominent figures urged some kind of statutory intervention. Sybil Thorndike, and Freda Jackson called for theatre buildings to be nationalised, and Llewellyn Rees urged the managers to

see that 'their policy is creating a situation in which nationalisation may prove to be the only solution'. J. B. Priestley's proposal that the state regulate theatre buildings, was echoed by Basil Dean, Robert Morley and Peter Ustinov.[6]

These calls were not heeded (at least not directly); but they chime interestingly with wider developments in British society. At the end of the people's war, the theatre, like many other aspects of British life, seemed ripe for public ownership.

The state and the theatre

Such a radical transformation of the theatrical landscape was never likely to happen immediately. However, this did not stop those who wished for such a change from organising a conference on the future of British theatre in 1948; and it did not stop theatre managers from reacting to the ideas the conference proposed with mingled horror and disgust. The conference was co-organised by two journals (*New Theatre* and *Theatre Newsletter*); and the organising committee originally included representatives from the Theatre Management Association (who represented the major commercial producers). The TMA, however, pulled out before the conference itself, alarmed at what they saw as its left-leaning, anti-commercial bias. When the conference took place, it drew representatives from across the theatre world (for example the actors Ralph Richardson and Sybil Thorndike, the playwrights James Bridie and J. B. Priestley – who had called for the conference in the first place – and the director Tyrone Guthrie); the delegates were also addressed by Sir Stafford Cripps, the Labour chancellor. Looking at the proposals passed by the conference, it is easy to understand the managers' reaction. There were proposals for the control of theatre rents, and for local authorities to spend money on new theatres, as part of a programme of civic development. Needless to say, these policies were never enacted; and even the period's most decisive change in the state's relationship with the arts – the formation of the Arts Council in 1945 – did not immediately threaten the supremacy of 'The Group' and companies like it.

The Arts Council had grown from the wartime organisation

CEMA (the Council for the Encouragement of Music and the Arts). CEMA's role had been to support high cultural activity in Britain (its counterpart, ENSA – the Entertainments National Service Association, nicknamed 'Every Night Something Awful', because of the variable quality of the work it produced – dealt with more obviously popular forms of entertainment). CEMA's chairman, interestingly, was John Maynard Keynes – the economist whose ideas underpinned the political consensus of the 1950s; when CEMA, after the end of the war, was formally re-created as the Arts Council, it must have seemed to the producing companies who organised the British theatre that a full-scale reorganisation of arts provision, along the lines of the transformation of healthcare under the new National Health Service, was about to happen.

Certainly, the tone of some of the Council's statements seemed to suggest as much. Bill Williams, the Council's secretary general in the early 1950s, delivered a speech in Liverpool in 1953. His view of the organisation of the London stage was clear and unequivocal:

> The theatre in London is dominated by show business organised on strict commercial lines. There are some specially obnoxious features about the London theatre. One is the profiteering in bricks and mortar by speculators ... The consequence ... is that any show which does not reveal immediate signs of a long run is whipped off at once. The twin mottoes of the London theatre are: long run or sudden death.[7]

However, the impact of the new Council on the arts during the 1950s was not as far-reaching. For one thing, the amount of money from central government was never enough to enable the Council to do more than fund a relatively small number of companies and artists; and for another, the Council had a rather paternalistic (not to say dismissive) attitude to theatre outside of London, and to theatre that didn't fit a rather narrow definition of worthiness. Amateur theatre, for example, was dismissed; and some companies – most notoriously Joan Littlewood's Theatre Workshop – had a fraught relationship with the Council throughout the 1950s (see below). The Council's role in funding new forces in British theatre in the 1950s was crucial – the early history of the Royal Court would have been very different without Council support – but its impact was not as great as in the 1960s (when an increase in government funding and the decline of the commercial stage conspired to make the council's role more prominent).

Both 'The Group' and the Arts Council, although their philosophies were very different, shared one key notion: that London was the theatrical showcase of the nation. This is still undoubtedly a fact of theatrical life, but in the 1950s, London dominated absolutely. Commercial companies such as H. M. Tennent knew that the biggest openings, the longest runs and the greatest profits came from the West End, and structured their productions accordingly (with successful London plays sold to the main provincial theatres owned by the big production companies as the latest West End hit). The Arts Council, too, was more likely to give support to ventures in the capital; that was, after all, where the heart of the industry was. Even given this, and the constraints imposed by the Council's limited funds, it is true to say that something approaching nationalisation began to happen in the infrastructure of British theatre during the 1950s. The Council did fund new initiatives in London (like the Royal Court); and Council money, backed by increased levels of investment from local government, slowly started to transform the theatrical infrastructure across the country.

Repertory theatre in the 1950s

Repertory theatre felt the force of this transformation most keenly. Regional repertory theatres began to organise themselves into a cohesive group in the mid-1940s. In 1944, the Conference of Repertory Theatres first met; and the conference became a formal council in 1950. In 1948, the first festival of British repertory theatre was held in London. The reps (as they were known, sometimes with a rather grudging affection) were a significant part of the post-war British theatrical landscape: according to Rowell and Jackson[8] in 1952 there were over a hundred repertory companies in Britain. Most of the companies were weekly reps, which, as the name suggests, meant that the playbill changed each week; during the performance season, actors were effectively on a treadmill:

> We started at 9.30 in the morning, and if you were half a minute late you had to apologise to the company, and on you went. I expect you've heard this before but you had the five days' rehearsal. You had the read-through on the Tuesday, you had Act I on the Wednesday, Act II on the Thursday, Act III in the morning on a Friday and did Act I and II in the afternoon and then all through the play on Saturday morning and then you went back and had dress rehearsal on Monday and the whole routine started again . . .[9]

There were advantages to this style of production; actors learned their craft very quickly, and got used to adapting to a constantly changing schedule. It was also a good training ground for some of the emerging playwrights of the 1950s. Both John Osborne and Harold Pinter served their time in rep companies; and although Osborne in particular had some characteristically acerbic things to say about the system, both he and Pinter imbibed lessons about play construction from the various thrillers and comedies in which they appeared. Michael Billington, in his biography of Pinter,[10] makes the interesting point that *The Birthday Party* (1958) is solidly constructed along the same lines as a standard rep thriller – the kind of thrillers that Pinter himself appeared in during the early 1950s.

The system's disadvantages, though, were inseparable from the punishing production schedule. The diet of shows was limited (Robert Aldous, quoted below, describes the standard repertoire as consisting of 'light comedies and thrillers *ad nauseam*'). Although everyone involved learned their craft quickly, rep itself gave few opportunities for actors, directors or technicians to develop; everything was geared towards the next week's show – which meant, for example, that the actor who could remember his or her part was prized as much as (if not more than) the actor with greater skill but a weaker memory. Lastly, the audience for weekly rep was in decline. Robert Aldous, who acted in a weekly rep in the 1950s, watched the audiences drift away:

What was so interesting about the period, television had just started in people's homes because that all started with the Coronation, and people were seeing the basic diet of repertory theatres – doing light comedies and thrillers ad nauseam, which was what you had to do – but they were seeing them suddenly better done on television. So theatres started to close because people weren't going out any more . . .[11]

As Rowell and Jackson point out, the audience for weekly rep thought of the theatres as part of their social lives; and when other media and forms of entertainment came along to occupy the same cultural position, the audiences gravitated towards them. TV kept people at home, and both theatre and cinema suffered; and for the elderly, who formed a significant part of the rep audience, bingo became the reason to gather together in the evening. The number of reps was declining; by 1954 there were sixty rep companies, falling to fifty-five the following year. Overwhelmingly, the reps that were closing were those whose operations were entirely commercial; the theatres that survived were those who had secured funding from the Arts Council and from local government. As Michael Billington notes,[12] this change began almost immediately after the war ended; for example, the Arts Council supported the reopening of the Theatre Royal in Bristol in 1946 – the first of a steadily growing number of investments in the larger provincial stages. These theatres were able to mount plays for longer; they were able to rehearse the texts for longer; they were able to give more thought to the fine details of directing and design than the weekly reps ever could. Lastly, and as a matter of civic pride, local authorities were keen to work with the Arts Council in a programme of new theatre building. The first of these was the Belgrade Theatre, which opened in Coventry in 1958; over the next decade, a further twenty such theatres were built.

The theatre of the 1950s was, therefore, in a period of transition. The elements of the theatre infrastructure that we are familiar with had yet to emerge fully; neither the National Theatre nor the Royal Shakespeare Company existed (both were formally created in the early 1960s). The commercial theatre, although still a major force on the

British stage, was loosening its grip; new theatres, publicly funded, were growing in number and influence – chief among these was the Royal Court. As the 1950s moved into the 1960s (and especially after the incoming Labour government, elected in 1963, began to pump money into the Arts Council), the trends that began in the post-war period took on a greater speed and urgency – until, by the end of the 1960s, the publicly funded stage was undoubtedly the most important and influential part of the British theatrical environment.

The British stage 1945–60: the writers' revolution

On 18 November 1956, a symposium on the state of the British theatre was held at the Royal Court; the discussions were carefully (and extensively) reported in *Encore*. Arthur Miller, who was at that time one of the most successful and significant playwrights in America, was responsible for the most famous (and the most damning) quote of the day; in terms that echo Harold Hobson's 1952 judgement, Miller commented, 'I sense that the British stage is hermetically sealed against the way that society moves'.[13] The only production that Miller exempted from this sweeping judgement was the play that the Court had just staged:

> *Look Back in Anger* to me is the only modern English play that I have seen. Modern in the sense that the basic attention in the play was toward the passionate idea of the man involved, and not toward the surface glitter and amusement that the situation might throw off. That play – and I'm not judging it now in terms of aesthetic fact – seems to me to be an intellectual play . . . and yet it seems to have no reflection elsewhere in the theatre.[14]

The cultural subtext of this quote is interesting, and very revealing. The rest of the world (or at least those parts of the world most accessible and interesting to theatre critics and practitioners) seemed to be winning the peace. America produced incisive pieces of dramatic social commentary, and large-scale, exciting, glitzy musicals; Continental Europe, recently ravaged by the war, was the home of the theatrically innovative and excitingly experimental. In both places, the theatre seemed at the heart of culture; whereas, in Britain, the theatre was at best a gaudy distraction, at worst a complete irrelevance.

This view has been subjected to extensive and incisive critique (most notably by Rebellato); and it would be hard to find any commentators in the early years of the twenty-first-century being so dismissive of, say, the work of Terence Rattigan (work which seems to provide a version of the type of incisive social commentary that Miller implicitly calls for). Also, to dismiss the theatre of the late 1940s and early 1950s is to downplay the impact and influence of companies and theatres such as the Old Vic (under the joint leadership of Olivier and Richardson) and Joan Littlewood's Theatre Workshop (which moved into a permanent home in the Theatre Royal Stratford East in the spring of 1953). It is also to lose the sense of a theatre which was diverse, and in some areas at least open to the same influences that were shaping performance in Europe and the States. David Rabey's summary catches some of the complexity of the period:

> English theatre of the 1940s was led by actors rather than dramatists. Olivier, Gielgud, Ashcroft, Redgrave, Edith Evans played in Shakespeare, Ibsen, Chekov. As the forties turned into the fifties, there as a vogue for French drama as purveyed by Anouilh (perhaps the leading example of Highbrow theatre at the time, as championed by the Francophile critic Harold Hobson), Giraudoux and Betti; in the mid-1950s, the London debuts of Beckett, Brecht, Genet and Ionesco claimed attention, and directors such as Brook and Hall made their names. The theatre which toured English regions relied heavily on author-based revivals (Shakespeare, early Shaw, adaptations of Bronte and Dickens) or domestic plays that could serve as star vehicles . . .[15]

With the considerable benefit of hindsight, perhaps the worst that can be said of the theatre of the early post-war years was that it was a fallow period. If new British writing for the stage was not strong (with a few notable exceptions – Rattigan, Eliot, John Whiting and the baroque poetic dramas of Christopher Fry: see below), other aspects of performance, like acting, design and the first stirrings of an indigenous British director's theatre, were either far more robust, or at least very promising. There was also something entirely positive in the fact that the British theatre was so open to plays and authors from other countries; it could not be said that the stage had retreated, post-1945, into insular parochialism.

And yet, at the time, the theatre did not seem in anywhere near good health – at least not for the influential generation of writers, critics and directors who flocked to contribute to *Encore*, or for influential critics like Hobson or the tyro Kenneth Tynan. Partly, their sense that theatre in Britain was stagnating was an understandable response, not only to the state of the theatre, but also to the state of the nation. The idea that post-war British society was suffering a period of stagnation was shared by cultural commentators, artists and writers generally. As I have noted above, Britain was slipping: and in the first few years after the end of the war, it was hard to tell where the cultural regeneration of the country was going to come from. Even when the seeds of that regeneration did emerge, the stage seemed to lag behind other art forms, such as the novel and poetry.

Censors and critics

There were two overarching forces which seemed to constrain the stage in the early 1950s. For *Encore*'s contributors, theatre did not seem to be capable of mounting a response to the changing realities of British life, both because it was in thrall to the commercial pressures decried by Priestley, and because it was more formally constrained by the Lord Chamberlain's Office, which exercised control over what could and could not be performed in theatres across the United Kingdom. The Lord Chamberlain's Office had been an unavoidable part of the theatrical landscape in Britain since the passing of the Theatre Licensing Act in 1737. By 1945, however, the office was not as powerful as it had once been; as Steve Nicholson has pointed out:

Although the walls of the old structure of [of theatrical censorship] may still have been standing when a new monarch and a new Lord Chamberlain took office in 1952, beneath the surface the foundations had been rattled. Indeed, it was possibly more apparent to the staff at St James's Palace [The offices of the Lord Chamberlain] than to most outsiders that their days were numbered. Like the colonised nations of the Empire, the theatre wanted its independence, and the question could not be 'whether' but only 'when'. The task for the Lords Chamberlain was to find a way to beat a dignified retreat.[11]

However, the retreat was to be a long one. The Lord Chamberlain's powers were not revoked until 1968, and throughout the 1950s the office still exercised a considerable influence on what could be performed on the British stage. Some of the office's decisions were rather inconsistent. The American author Lillian Hellman's *The Children's Hour*, which included a lesbian character, was banned, as was Shirley Cox's *The Gingerbread House*; Jean-Paul Sartre's *Huis Clos* had to be produced privately (in 1946, in a production directed by the young Peter Brook). In contrast, William Douglas-Home's 1947 play *Now Barabbas*, a play set in a prison, and including a character who was clearly homosexual, was granted a licence.

Other decisions were equally illogical. To give one example from many: despite the international success of *Waiting for Godot*, Samuel Beckett found it difficult to secure a theatrical home for his next play, *Fin de Partie (Endgame)*. George Devine, a passionate admirer of Beckett's work, stepped in – and the play was first performed, in French, at the Royal Court in London in 1957. When the English version was passed to the Lord Chamberlain for a performance licence in 1958, the Lord Chamberlain told Devine (who both directed the production and played Hamm) that the play would be refused a licence. Beckett agreed to remove some words that the censor found troubling ('balls', 'arse', 'I'd like to pee'); but he categorically refused to remove a reference to God ('The bastard! He doesn't exist!'). Reasonably, Devine pointed out that the line had already been performed, albeit in French, on the London stage. When he staged a rehearsed reading of the play for the Lord Chamberlain's representative (the impressively titled Lieutenant-Colonel Sir St Vincent Troubridge) he tried to sneak the line through as surreptitiously as possible, but to little effect:

> Besides reading Hamm, Devine was giving the stage directions *sotto voce*, and when he reached the offending passage he threw it away in the same undertone. However, the effort was wasted on St Vincent who sat through the meeting like a graven idol with his convictions unshaken. 'It's because it's in English', Devine told Ann Jellicoe afterwards, 'you can get away with much more in French. Think what you could get away with in Japanese!'[17]

Eventually, Beckett himself suggested a compromise; the line could be changed to 'The swine! He doesn't exist!' This was acceptable, and the play was staged later that year.

Unsurprisingly, when faced with such an unpredictable organisation, many writers, directors and producers exercised self-censorship as a matter of course. Most famously, Terence Rattigan altered the text of his 1954 double-bill *Separate Tables* to remove the suggestion that one of the male characters (the Major, in 'Table Number Seven', the second of the two plays) had been accused of 'persistently importuning'[18] another man. Rattigan's decision was in part a reaction to the light this cast on his own sexual orientation: as a gay man in the 1950s, he faced imprisonment if his lifestyle were made public. However, the decision was as much a pragmatic response to the likely opinion of the Lord Chamberlain. As Rattigan put it:

> It is literally true that when I began the play . . . I had already reached the point where the Major's offence was to be revealed before I realised that, if I were to get the play done in the West End at all, I would have to find a way round the Lord Chamberlain's present objection to any mention of this particular subject.[19]

When the nature of the character's offence was changed (in the revised version, he was convicted and fined for the impeccably heterosexual offence of importuning young women in darkened cinemas, rather than young men in darkened streets) the Lord Chamberlain was happy to license the script; the Lord Chamberlain's reader called 'Table Number Seven' 'a little masterpiece'.[20]

For those arguing for a more directly relevant theatre, the commercial organisation of the stage and the presence of the Lord Chamberlain were powerful restraining influences; more than this, they were the visible presence of the establishment on the British stage. The Chamberlain policed language and subject matter of individual productions; so the British theatre as a whole learned to play it safe. Organisations like 'The Group' (and, it was argued, individuals like Binkie Beaumont) had the final say on plays produced on the main London and regional stages; British theatre as a whole gravitated towards the predictable, or the star-studded, or the commercially proven, or the opulent. Arguably, though, both the Lord Chamberlain and 'The Group' were useful, too; they gave other powerful, influential voices a clearly defined target – something on which to pin all the manifest failures and inadequacies of the time. These voices grew in number and volume as the decade progressed: chief among them (although pursuing very different agendas) were the critics Harold Hobson (who wrote for the *Sunday Times* from 1947 through to the 1970s) and Kenneth Tynan (whose most influential reviews were published when he was the drama critic of the *Observer* from 1954 to 1963). At a time when newspapers enjoyed large circulations, theatre critics were important trend-setters and taste definers; and the critics for the Sunday papers could be assured not only of a wide readership, but also that their readers would look to them for something more considered than a quick impression of the previous night's performance, delivered to meet the dailies' deadlines. Hobson and Tynan used what were very privileged positions to comment magisterially on the week's new performances. Both were deeply unhappy with the type of play routinely produced in British theatres; both looked outside of the country for new theatrical inspiration. They were responsible for the critical recuperation of *Waiting for Godot* in 1955, after the daily critics had savaged the first British production; Tynan in particular was instrumental in the creation of the *Look Back in Anger* myth (although it is not true that the play had received entirely negative reviews before Tynan weighed in); and, towards the end of the decade, Hobson spotted the incipient theatrical genius in Harold Pinter's first full-length play, *The Birthday Party* (1958), when everyone else – even Tynan – had missed it.

On other matters, though, the critics were sharply different. Hobson was religious (he had been a practising Christian Scientist since childhood); although he was a keen supporter of avant-garde theatre, championing Auden and Isherwood before the war, and Absurdist drama in the late 1940s and 1950s, he was profoundly antipathetic to Brechtian theatre, calling it 'the negation of everything which [was] most valuable in humanity'.[21] Tynan on the other hand was considerably younger (at the time of *Godot*'s first production, Hobson was fifty-one; Tynan was twenty-eight) and determinedly iconoclastic; he routinely praised Sir Laurence Olivier, the most popular actor of the time – but equally routinely he attacked Olivier's wife, Vivien Leigh, in the most amusingly damning of terms (of Leigh's 1951 performance alongside her husband in the title roles of *Antony and Cleopatra*, Tynan said, 'she picks at the part with the daintiness of a debutante called upon to dismember a stag').[22] Hobson supported French drama, an important force on the immediate post-war stage; Tynan, rather later in the decade, championed new writing from the US and Germany, and in particular Brecht. Hobson's dislike of the German dramatist was equalled in intensity by Tynan's distrust of Beckett and Ionesco (with whom he conducted a literary feud towards the end of the decade). Their reviewing styles also diverged. Hobson was unfailingly elegant and measured; for example, while Tynan celebrated the youthfulness of *Look Back in Anger*, Hobson discerned, behind a play that seemed to be all about Jimmy Porter, another play which 'is sketched into the margin of the first, and consists of hardly any words at all, but is controlled by a fine and sympathetic imagination, and is superbly played, in long passages of pain and silence, by Mary Ure [who played Alison in the original production]'.[23] In sharp contrast, Tynan delivered reviews which sometimes seemed performances in themselves. Alongside the pin-sharp descriptions, the fulsome praise and the equally unsparing attacks, Tynan had a gift for parody; reviewing a double-bill of Beckett's plays in 1958 (the first English productions of *Endgame* – mentioned above – and *Krapp's Last Tape*), he crafted a mock playscript, a dialogue between Slamm (a critic) and Seck (his secretary), that expertly caught the tone and rhythm of Beckett's writing:

> **Seck** . . . Item: Krapp's Last Tape, Krapp being a myopic not to say deaf not to say emetical eater of one and one-half bananas listening and cackling as he listens to a tape-recording of twenty years' antiquity made of a day, the one far gone day, when he laid his hand on a girl on a boat and it worked, as it worked for Molly Bloom in the long ago . . .[24]

Ultimately, the divide between Hobson and Tynan was generational. The rather more socially conservative Hobson was not well placed to become the cheerleader for a theatrical revolution. Tynan, on the other hand, was the right age; he had the right left-of-centre politics; and he used his position on the *Observer* to agitate for a radical transformation in the conduct and subject matter of the British stage. Given this, it is unsurprising that Tynan should become the journalistic standard-bearer for the new theatre; and that Hobson should be dismissed by the equally radical *Encore* ('It would be unfair to suggest that one of the most characteristic sounds of the English Sunday is the sound of Harold Hobson barking up the wrong tree').[25]

Before the revolution: 1945–56

Despite their temperamental and ideological differences, both Tynan and Hobson were united in identifying the main problem that bedevilled British theatre in the early and mid-1950s. It was that the theatre lacked a new generation of playwrights eager to anatomise the post-war world. Hobson paid a visit to France in 1952; on his return, he wrote despairingly:

> I came back [from Paris] to a country whose newspapers are mainly filled with tidings of war, insurrection, industrial unrest,

political controversy, and parliamentary misbehaviour, and to a
theatre from which it seems to me, in the first shock of reac-
quaintance, that all echoes of these things is shut off as by
sound-proof walls . . .[26]

Tynan, characteristically, was more forthright:

> Last week I welcomed a young Frenchwoman engaged in
> writing a thesis on contemporary English drama. We talked
> hopefully of John Whiting; but before long embarrassment
> moved me to ask why she had not chosen her own theatre as a
> subject for study. She smiled wryly. 'Paris is in decline,' she
> said. 'Aside from Sartre, Anouilh, Camus, Cocteau, Ayme,
> Claudel, Beckett, and Salacrou, we have almost nobody.'[27]

The article from which this quote is taken has become rather famous
because within it Tynan described a type of script that, in his opinion,
had come to dominate and ruin the British stage. He dubbed it the
Loamshire play:

> Its setting is a country house in what used to be called
> Loamshire but is now, as a heroic tribute to realism, called
> Berkshire. Except when someone must sneeze, or be murdered,
> the sun invariably shines. The inhabitants belong to a social
> class derived partly from romantic novels and partly from the
> playwright's vision of the leisured life he will lead after the play
> is a success – this being the only effort of imagination he is
> called upon to make. Joys and sorrows are giggles and whim-
> pers: the crash of denunciation dwindles into 'Oh, stuff,
> Mummy!' and 'Oh, really, Daddy!' and so grim is the conti-
> nuity of these things that the foregoing paragraph could have
> been written at any time during the last thirty years.[28]

Loamshire was the place, in other words, where British drama went to
die. It was not simply that commercial and social pressures forced
playwrights to bend their work into pre-existing, stale, tired shapes.
The influence of Loamshire spread, like damp, across every aspect of

the stage. It encouraged actors to be lazy; and, most damagingly, it crippled both directors and designers; why bother exploring the possibilities opening up on Continental stages, or in America, if they could not be applied to the average new British play? Tynan, of course, was engaged in hyperbolic exaggeration: he had a point to make – that almost everyone then working in the theatre was guilty of a collective failure of will and imagination, and an equally dangerous cultural and political timidity. It is, however, true that, with a few notable exceptions, most writing for the stage in the late 1940s and the early 1950s was unadventurous; and that, because of this, the theatre was perceived as lagging behind other branches of literature and art. Tynan finished his article with the anxious claim that a young, intelligent, questioning audience could (and did) go elsewhere for stimulation (the example he used was the cinema); and that only new, dynamic, socially engaged plays would 'lure them home'[29] to the theatre.

Tynan's hyperbole presented the readers of the *Observer* with a necessarily simplified version of the theatrical reality of the time. The truth was that the revival which seemed to spark so quickly into life in 1956 had been prepared for over most of the previous decade – and that the forces that shaped it had been more complex than the sudden appearance of a new generation of disgruntled, socially aware playwrights. The roots of the 1950s revival stretch back to the final days of the Second World War; and to incremental changes in the theatrical infrastructure, caused as much by actors, directors and designers as by writers. Indeed, part of the revolution that Tynan was calling for stemmed from some of the productions mounted by Binkie Beaumont, H. M. Tennent and 'The Group' – the very organisation that Tynan, *Encore* and the other voices calling for a transformation of the theatre blamed for its current parlous state.

The roots of the Royal Court, for example, could be found in the post-war Old Vic. From 1944 the old London theatre came under the joint leadership of two theatrical stars – Laurence Olivier and Ralph Richardson; although their time as joint Artistic Directors was brief (they were effectively manoeuvred out of their roles by the theatre's management – Richardson in 1948, Olivier a year later) their tenure was remarkably productive. They mounted a series of productions which still stand out as landmarks of the twentieth-century British stage (*Richard III*, *Henry IV Parts 1 and 2*, *Oedipus Rex*, played alongside Sheridan's *The Critic* with Olivier taking major roles in both, *Uncle Vanya*, the premiere of J. B. Priestley's *An Inspector Calls*). The Old Vic, however, was not simply a demonstration of what could be achieved by a repertory troupe of actors, given enough rehearsal time and accomplished artistic leadership. In 1946, the company drew up plans for the expansion of their operations: these plans bore fruit in the Theatre Centre (an umbrella title, covering the formation of a theatre school, a company for children – christened the Young Vic – and a stage for experimental drama). The trio placed in charge of this new development had impressive pedigrees: Glen Byam Shaw had worked with John Gielgud before the war; Michel Saint-Denis, the nephew of the influential theorist of acting Jacques Copeau, was an acclaimed director who had already founded the London Theatre Studio; lastly, George Devine was an actor and director who had worked with Denis, and who was familiar with the methods of acting training that Denis employed. Actors who passed through the Old Vic's training school were exposed to a wider range of styles and techniques than the general run of performers at the time; and although the Theatre Centre did not long survive Olivier's departure, the experience had served to further convince Devine that what Britain needed was a radically new theatre; as he put it in 1948, 'Productions must be up to date – methods must change. The producer must know his time and be in touch with it.'[30] Almost immediately after leaving the Young Vic in 1953, Devine met the young director Tony Richardson, and the pair began to draw up plans for what would become, within a few years, the English Stage Company.

As Billington[31] notes, the work done at the Old Vic might seem to be the polar opposite of the productions mounted by H. M. Tennent and the other commercial production companies. Tennent, in particular, had a reputation for star-studded and elaborately ornamental productions – the theatrical equivalent of the most nakedly commercial Hollywood film. As noted above, Binkie Beaumont was seen by some at the time as the absolute antithesis of the true theatre artist; although there were other theatre producers engaged in the same commercial operations, by the early 1950s Beaumont had come to be considered the figurehead for a type of theatre that was driven by profit, and which was therefore guaranteed to be safe, frothy and inconsequential. As Rebellato[32] also points out, Beaumont was considered suspect for another reason; as a homosexual, albeit a discreet homosexual, his very prominence in the commercial British stage could be held against him. At a time when the terms 'gay' and 'theatrical' were almost interchangeable,[33] it was far too easy for those commentators demanding a new theatre to contrast the virile new drama they wished to see with the effete, unmanly theatre produced under the aegis of H. M. Tennent (see, especially, J. B. Priestley – whose call for a new theatre in *Theatre Outlook* is couched in almost exactly those terms). And yet H. M. Tennent, and the other commercial production companies, were responsible for some of the most striking and influential productions of the late 1940s and early 1950s. Tennents supported the 1949 production of Tennessee Williams's *A Streetcar Named Desire*, directed by Laurence Olivier and containing an impassioned performance by Vivien Leigh as Blanche Du Bois. They and the other commercial managements were responsible for many of the foreign plays produced in London (mounting productions of plays by Anouilh, Sartre and Jean Cocteau); it supported the work of tyro directors (in 1956, for example, they produced a version of *Hamlet*, starring Paul Scofield and directed by the young Peter Brook) and they supported the relatively short-lived trend for verse drama, which flourished for a time in the late 1940s and early 1950s. Finally, it should always be remembered that the commercial sector supported Terence Rattigan; although he was condemned by supporters of the new drama for bowing to the commercial and social pressures of the time, the work produced by Rattigan on the West End stage was arguably as quietly radical as any other body of work of the period (see the essay on Rattigan below).

Verse drama

The fact that some playwrights chose to write in verse in the years following the war is on the surface rather surprising – a further move away from the idea that drama's business was to represent, discuss and analyse the real world. However, for one of its most important practitioners, the idea that verse drama moved away from surface reality was exactly the point:

> A verse play is not a play done into verse, but a different type of play; in a way more realistic than 'naturalistic drama'. Because instead of clothing nature in poetry, it should remove the surface of things, expose the underneath or the inside of the natural surface appearance. It may allow the characters to behave inconsistently, but only with respect to a deeper consistency . . .[34]

The vogue for poetic drama was sparked initially by the unexpected success of Ronald Duncan's *The Way to the Tomb* in 1945 (Duncan's play – first performed at the Mercury theatre in 1945, ran for over a year, and such was the demand that it transferred to the Garrick in the West End for matinee performances). The play – a slight satire on, among other things, the commercialisation of religion, depicted a contemporary society that was hungry for faith, but unsure about how to achieve it.

This idea – that people at the end of the war inhabited a spiritual wasteland, and could be redeemed by faith – ran through the work of the two most successful verse dramatists of the period. It animates T. S. Eliot's most commercially successful play, *The Cocktail Party* (first staged at the Edinburgh Festival in 1949, before a successful transfer to the West End; the play also ran for a year on Broadway); and, as David Rabey notes, it also echoes through the work of Christopher Fry (who was, for a short time, the most successful new dramatist of the period). Fry is largely forgotten now; but at the time his verbal dexterity and wit (not to mention the fact that his plays are, as Rabey puts it, 'predicated on a sense of spiritually benign playfulness')[35] chimed with the theatregoing audiences of the early 1950s. Verse drama never threatened to become a dominant theatrical form; but the upsurge is interesting, for two reasons. First of all, because it is an indication that the desire to move away from simple, formulaic dramas and light comedies existed well before the Royal Court revolution – even though it was manifested in a strikingly different form. Second, it was one of the few indications that theatre might be able to gain the kind of cultural prestige that was the province of the novel, or of poetry; after all, T. S. Eliot wrote plays – and his cultural stock was at its highest in the post-war years. (Eliot's work is dealt with in a separate essay below.)

Priestley and Coward

Other writers found themselves coming to a more or less easy accommodation with a changing world. J. B. Priestley's *An Inspector Calls* (first produced at the Old Vic in 1946) couched a plea of moral responsibility and social equality in quasi-spiritual terms. Inspector Goole, who comes to the household of a rich, contented family – the Birlings – to quiz them about their role in the suicide of a young, poor woman, performs the same function as the psychiatrist, Sir Henry Harcourt-Reilly, in Eliot's *The Cocktail Party* (although from a radically different political perspective); he acts as a semi-divine messenger, reminding the other characters that beneath the mundane reality of their lives, there are underlying eternal truths that simply cannot be ignored. His next play, *The Linden Tree*, is rather more directly connected to the late 1940s; its central character, an idealistic professor of history, fighting enforced retirement, mounts a passionate defence of the Labour Party's record in office:

> Call us drab and dismal if you like, and tell us we don't know how to cook and wear our clothes but for Heaven's sake recognise that we're trying to do something that is as extraordinary and wonderful as it is difficult – to have a revolution for once without looting mobs and secret police, sudden arrests, mass suicides and executions, without setting in motion the vast pendulum of violence which can take decimate three generations before it comes to a standstill. We're fighting in the last ditch of civilisation. If we win through, everyone wins through.[36]

Priestley's oddly mystical version of socialism placed him more or less at the ideological heart of the late 1940s; the same could not be said for Noël Coward. Priestley celebrated the victory of Labour in 1945: Coward, as noted above, was horrified. Before and during the war, his work had either celebrated the heartless glitter of polite society, or had presented a rather cosy view of a basically stable and contented nation – see *This Happy Breed* (1942), for example. The new post-war world suited him not at all; the plays he wrote during the period mixed a yearning for what he considered the old certainties, and direct attacks on the new socialist world. He went so far as to suggest, in *Peace in Our Time* (staged in 1947) that it might have been better for the Nazis to have won the war; at least their victory would have allowed the English to rediscover their essential selves. Coward, like Priestley's Professor Linden, thought that he was fighting in the last ditch for civilisation – but he fought on the other side; contrast Linden's speech with this, from Crestwell, the profoundly conservative butler at the end of Coward's 1951 play *Relative Values*. The family Crestwell serves has just beaten off the unwelcome advances of a social-climbing film star (who just happens to be the sister of the family maid); at the play's end, Crestwell invites the maid (and by implication, the audience) to raise a glass:

> **Crestwell**   I drink solemnly to you and me in our humble, but on the whole honourable, calling. I drink to her Ladyship and to his Lordship, groaning beneath the weight of privilege but managing to keep their pecker up all the same. Above all, I drink to the final inglorious disintegration of the most unlikely dream that ever troubled the foolish heart of Man – Social Equality.[37]

Crestwell delivered this speech for the first time in the year when the Conservatives took over from Labour: however, the passing of the old order continued apace – and Coward found himself marginalised.

Priestley and Coward were coming towards the end of their careers as successful dramatists (although in Coward's case, the end was protracted and rather painful, as it would be for Terence Rattigan later). Other writers managed to ride out most of the decade by producing work which seemed to offer more than the standard plot devices that Tynan so derided: N. C. Hunter managed to attract star performers (for example, *A Day by the Sea* in 1954 starred John Gielgud, Lewis Casson, Sybil Thorndike, Ralph Richardson and Irene Worth – a commercially unimpeachable cast) for plays which loosely echoed Chekhov. Edith Bagnold's comedy *The Chalk Garden* (1956), produced at the Haymarket at the heart of the West End, even received a glowing review from Tynan (albeit as an example of the West End's 'Glorious Sunset').[38] However, before the mid-1950s, newer dramatists – or at least those who did not want to produce work according to the commercially successful templates of the time – found it hard to establish themselves.

Ackland and Whiting

The varied experiences of Rodney Ackland and John Whiting – two otherwise contrasting writers – show just how difficult it could be to get anything controversial or different on stage. Ackland's *The Pink Room* was staged by the Lyric Hammersmith in 1952. The omens for the production seemed good; Terence Rattigan had invested in the production, which was directed by Frith Banbury (who came to the play fresh from working on Rattigan's latest success, *The Deep Blue Sea*). The play, though, did not quite strike the right moral tone for the times. Rattigan had to finance the production after Binkie Beaumont refused it, calling the script 'a libel on the British people'.[39] Ackland set his play in a West End drinking club, and peopled this illusory safe haven with characters that were in various ways trying to escape a reality that was too bleak or too threatening. They are spectacularly ill-equipped to deal either with the reality of the war or the new, post-war Britain; one character, a young aristocrat, pledges herself to work with those displaced by the war, only to be put off by pictures of the Holocaust; another, a writer, uses the club as a means of escaping the decline of his powers and the slow death of his career. The play got past the Lord Chamberlain (even though the reader for the Chamberlain's office worried about the references to homosexuality in the text). It did not escape from the critics, however: Hobson's reaction was typical ('On Wednesday evening the audience at Hammersmith had the impression of being present, if not at the death of a talent, at least of its very serious illness').[40] Afterwards, Rattigan broke off relations with Ackland; devastated by the reviews, Ackland did not write for the stage again for decades. It was not until 1988, when a rewritten version of the text (titled *Absolute Hell*) was performed at the Orange Tree theatre in London that the play was given the recognition that it deserved.

Whiting, on the other hand, managed to sustain some kind of a reputation; never popular – his most successful play, *The Devils* (1961), is now remembered more for Ken Russell's hysterical 1971 film version – he did at least manage to attract some significant attention and support. Both Tyrone Guthrie and Peter Brook, for example, wrote letters to *The Times* in his defence, after his first full-length play, *Saint's Day* (1951), was attacked in the press. For other emerging talents, Whiting's work was a talisman – showing that, even in the apparently moribund early 1950s, new forms of drama were possible. Writing at the end of the 1970s, Peter Hall (whose long and influential career in the British theatre was to start in 1955, when he directed the first production of *Waiting for Godot*) said:

> I remember the shock of meeting *Saint's Day* in the Arts Theatre in the summer of 1951 . . . I was twenty and a stage struck student, yet it was the first truly modern play I had seen in my life . . . Looking back now, Whiting seems a passionate and ironic evangelist, preparing the way for Beckett, for Pinter, for Arden, and for Bond.[41]

Saint's Day, which won a competition for new writing run by the actor Alec Clunes, was a formally adventurous text. It describes the increasing tension between the inhabitants of a dilapidated country house (an elderly poet, his granddaughter and her artist husband) and the poverty-stricken local villagers. The arrival of another poet, Robert Procathren, exacerbates this tension (both between the house and those outside, and between the inhabitants of the house); the situation is rendered worse by the news that some soldiers have escaped from a detention camp, and are looting the village. When violence erupts, it does so in a manner that seems unpredictable, random and uncontainable; it leaves the village burned and the house's inhabitants dead. The play certainly prefigures Bond (the minutely observed delineation of the roots of violence), and even Sarah Kane (like *Blasted*, the play visits warlike violence on an ostensibly normal British location). It is also very much of its time: the decaying old house, run by an equally decaying representative of a passing order, who finds it impossible to reconcile himself with the shifting world outside; a world in which apparent peace co-exists with both the memory and the threat of war. Whiting, however, couches his story in heightened language; the play is determinedly symbolic – and it was this that the critics found hardest to take. Just like *The Pink Room*, *Saint's Day* was attacked – not, this time, for immorality, but for obscurity (as this review, from the *Daily Express*, attests):

> I do not understand a word of the plot . . . I did not under-stand the violent shootings, a village fire and the hanging of the three principals by three lunatic soldiers . . . and finally, I did not understand why the audience – which included Tyrone Guthrie and Christopher Fry – were so patient with it all.[42]

The prominent support of these theatrical luminaries at least allowed Whiting to sustain a career; *Saint's Day* was followed by another three full-length plays before his early death in 1963. However, like Ackland, but for different reasons, Whiting found it difficult to fit in to the culture of the 1950s – even though, it could be argued, the tensions his work explored were intimately bound up in the culture of the decade. He never commanded a large audience; his elliptical, heightened dramas were not a good commercial proposition – and he began his career too soon, before the Royal Court provided a home for new drama, and before the influence of some new trends and approaches to theatre, developing in Continental Europe, had percolated through to the British stage.

The main engagement 1955–60: Beckett and Brecht

Beckett

By the middle of the decade, that process was well under way: French drama was already established as a major force on the British stage, and American theatre (both drama and musicals) seemed to provide a much more dynamic experience than anything produced in the UK. It could be said that dramas from other countries were not seen as exotic imports. They had attracted the attention of commercial producers, like Tennent, and successful British authors like Christopher Fry (who translated Anouilh). Even the more experimental forms of European drama had found a place on the London stage: Ionesco's *The Lesson* was produced in 1955. Even before the most decisive intervention from abroad, the British stage was very well used to looking to Europe and elsewhere for inspiration.

That intervention happened later in the year that *The Lesson* was produced. *Waiting for Godot*, first performed in 1953 at the Théâtre de Babylone in Paris, had tested even the patience of Parisian audiences; the first run was marked by walk-outs and confrontations between the play's supporters and its detractors. This, if anything, contributed to the play's success; audiences flooded the small theatre – even if only to see what all the fuss was about. This process was replicated across Europe over the next two years; and in 1955 the play, translated by Beckett, came to Britain. It took a little time to find a venue and cast. *Godot*'s growing reputation attracted the attention of some of the most famous actors of the day; Ralph Richardson and Alec Guinness were mooted for the first production, but negotiations over the play took so long that both actors and the first choice for director, Peter Glenville, had to pull out because of prior commitments (unsurprisingly, the Lord Chamberlain also demanded alterations to the text; and, as with *Endgame* later in the decade, dealing with his demands took time). This might have been a good thing; Beckett in particular found Richardson hard to deal with, because the actor

> . . . wanted the lowdown on Pozzo, his home address and curriculum vitae, and seemed to make the forthcoming of this

and similar information the condition of his condescending to illustrate the part of Vladimir. Too tired to give this satisfaction I told him that all I knew about Pozzo was in the text, and that if I had known more I would have said so I would have put it in the text, and that this was true also of the other characters. Which I trust puts an end to that star . . .[43]

Even though Richardson was not, in fact, put off, his rather strained encounter with the play's author demonstrated clearly the gap between the kind of work Richardson was used to doing, and the demands of a undeviatingly radical text.

To put an end to the uncertainty over the play's production, Donald Albery, the producer, opted to use a young director (Peter Hall, newly installed at the Arts Theatre Club in London) and rather less well-known performers. Hall read and was moved by the script; but his opening remarks to the cast betrayed his uncertainty over handling it effectively: '[I] really haven't the foggiest idea what some of it means . . . but if we stop and discuss every line we'll never open. I think it may be dramatically effective but there's no way of finding out till the first night.'[44] The first night, though, nearly proved too much for at least some of the cast. Peter Bull, who played Pozzo (and who never warmed to Beckett's play) talked of 'waves of hostility'[45] from the first-night audience flooding over the footlights; the cast ended the performance convinced that the play would have a short stage life. When the Sunday reviews appeared, however, the picture changed: both Hobson and Tynan came out in support of the play. Tynan's review included the prescient comment, 'It forced me to re-examine the rules which have hitherto governed the drama; and having done so, to pronounce them not elastic enough'.[46] The play went on to run successfully, both in London and on tour, although the audiences remained profoundly split over its significance. Some saw it as an example of foreign obscurity and pretension (amusingly, Knowlson records an audience member's despairing cry – 'This is why we lost the colonies!'). Peter Bull found the play's supporters equally disturbing:

[They] either sat spellbound in respectful silence or laughed their heads off in such a sinister way that the actors used to think they'd forgotten to adjust their costumes. It was the worst when they came round to the dressing-room after the play to tell us what it all meant. It was far too late for that anyhow, and it was disconcerting to hear that the character I'd been portraying for months represented Fascism, Communism, Lord Beaverbrook [an influential newspaper proprietor], Hollywood, James Joyce, or, rather surprisingly, Humpty Dumpty.[47]

John Bull[48] has called the first British production of *Waiting for Godot* 'the real starting point of the new wave of the 1950s', and it is easy to see why. It is a radical experiment with theatre form; it polarised its audience, creating a cultural flashpoint around which wider debates about the role of the artistic avant-garde could circulate; and, in doing so, it proved that even the apparently moribund, backward-looking British theatre could support radically new work.

Brecht

As John Bull also notes in the same chapter, the influence of the other major Continental intervention of the period was less immediate, and took longer to work its way into the British theatrical mainstream. Brecht had been a name to conjure with for some theatre practitioners in Britain since the 1930s. The BBC broadcast the cantatas *Lindberg's Flight* and the *Baden-Baden Lesson on Consent* in 1930, and *The Threepenny Opera* in 1935; Unity Theatre, an amateur socialist theatre company formed in London in 1936, was the first to put his work on stage (*Señora Carrar's Rifles*, in 1938. In addition to Brecht, the company was also influenced by other German theatre practitioners; a production mounted in the same year, *Busmen*, incorporated techniques first developed by Erwin Piscator). Joan Littlewood remembered discussing Brecht with Ewan MacColl, the first time they met.[49] After the war's end, Brecht's reputation, already established in Britain, grew as news of the work produced by his company, the Berliner Ensemble, gradually reached the country. Eric Bentley, who had met Brecht for the first time during Brecht's exile in California, ran a series of seminars on the playwright's work in 1950; Kenneth

Tynan attended, and became an increasingly zealous convert. He was not alone. Before the English Stage Company's first season at the Royal Court, George Devine took the company to East Germany to study both the Berliner Ensemble and the theatre they occupied; and Joan Littlewood, although retaining strong reservations about Brecht's work, was responsible for the first production of *Mother Courage* in Britain. The production was first assembled for the Devon Festival in 1955, and Littlewood herself played the title role (unsuccessfully, as it turned out – she took the part late in rehearsal, at Brecht's insistence).

Brecht's influence took a while to reach its fullest extent (Bull argues, convincingly, that it was only in the 1960s and 1970s that British theatre produced work that could be called Brechtian). In the 1950s, he was arguably more important as a point around which supporters of a new socially engaged drama could congregate, even if they denied his direct influence (as both Osborne and John Arden did). The Berliner Ensemble toured Britain for the first time in 1956, just after Brecht's death (their presence, alongside *Look Back in Anger*, helped cement the idea that 1956 was a watershed year in British theatre). Their arrival was greeted with delight by Tynan and the contributors to *Encore*; it wasn't simply that Brecht's theatre was determinedly political – it was also that the company displayed a discipline and commitment to their art that seemed entirely opposed to the pressures of commercial theatre:

> The Ensemble is clearly sustained by a strong artistic conception. Behind the simplicity, and the beauty of the decor and the costumes, every aspect of the production had been studied and worked on until it was absolutely polished. Brecht often rehearses his plays for months, and if, when the time comes, another production is not ready, another play in the repertory is substituted until it is ready . . .[50]

Tynan, reviewing the Ensemble in London in 1956, made the same points in a more effusive fashion:

> As Eric Bentley said, 'Brecht does not believe in an inner reality, a higher reality, or a deeper reality, but simply in reality.' It is

something for which we have lost the taste: raised on a diet of gin and goulash, we call Brecht naive when he gives us bread and wine. He wrote morality plays and directed them as such; and if we of the West End and Broadway find them as tiresome as religion, we are in a shrinking minority. There is a world elsewhere. 'I was bored to death,' said a bright Chelsea girl after *Mother Courage*. 'Bored to life' would have been apter.[51]

Devine's comparison is implicit; Tynan's is explicit. Brechtian theatre, simple, beautiful, committed and artistically satisfying, is held up as the necessary corrective for a theatre that is run in the interests of profit – a theatre which is over-elaborate, overly reliant on stars, more concerned with safely predictable plots and gaudy design. To support Brecht was to oppose H. M. Tennent, 'The Group' and the economic structure of British theatre.

The main engagement 1955–60: new British theatres

The English Stage Company

Events like the staging of *Godot*, and the seeping influence of companies like the Berliner Ensemble, did not seem to have a British counterpart in the early and mid-1950s (this view was not entirely fair – see below). Tynan, Hobson and the team who edited *Encore* might be the ones who called most loudly and insistently for a British company who could produce work that stood comparison with the best of the European competition; but their voices were merely the most prominent. In 1956, a new company, operating in a historically significant venue, seemed to offer those who wanted a new approach to the British theatre some hope. When the English Stage Company (ESC) began work at the Royal Court, it did so with a heavy weight of expectation on its shoulders; as a *Times* article made clear, a generation of potential and actual playwrights were willing the success of the new venture:

On Monday, the English Stage Company opens at the Royal Court Theatre, under the direction of Mr George Devine, and despairing young playwrights must have rubbed their eyes in astonishment when they read what are to be the aims of the new enterprise. 'Ours is not to be a producer's theatre, nor an actor's theatre,' Mr Devine announces, 'it is to be a writer's theatre.'[52]

As noted above, the new venture also chimed in with the priorities of the Arts Council; and it brought together a number of already proven and established theatre professionals.

The original idea had come from a number of places. Devine met the young director Tony Richardson in 1953, and they started to draft plans for the type of theatre that the ESC later became. In the same year, Devine met the playwright Ronald Duncan, who had been running a drama festival in Devon (the same festival to which Joan Littlewood's Theatre Workshop took *Mother Courage* in 1955); Duncan was also interested in establishing a company, which would tour non-commercial plays (and, also, Duncan's own work – a point of tension later on). In 1955, Duncan teamed up with the theatre producer Oscar Lewenstein (a socialist who had strong links with Littlewood and Theatre Workshop) and Alfred Esdaile, a former music-hall comic who owned the lease of the Royal Court Theatre in Sloane Square. Devine had investigated the possibility of basing a company at the Royal Court earlier in the decade: the venue had the right historical associations – in the first decade of the twentieth-century, the theatre, managed by Harley Granville-Barker and J. E. Vedrenne, had mounted seasons of new drama (giving a home to the work of George Bernard Shaw and John Galsworthy). In 1956, after a protracted and rather tangled series of negotiations, in which another London theatre (the Kingsway) seemed likely to be the home for the new venture, the ESC launched itself at Devine's theatre of choice; the refurbishment of the Court was made possible by a grant of £7,000 from the Arts Council – a strong gesture of institutional support for the fledgling company.

The story of the Royal Court under Devine's leadership (which lasted until his death from a heart attack in 1966) has been told in detail elsewhere.[53] The idea that the Court's productions, in its first two or three years of life, transformed the British stage wholesale (an impression left by earlier studies – in particular by John Russell Taylor's *Anger and After*)[54] has been replaced by a rather more nuanced discussion of its place in the theatrical infrastructure of the time. Certain key features of the *Look Back in Anger* myth have also been revised: the play did give the Court the kind of success that could be used, both as a way of promoting the new theatre, and as a way of defining the kind of performances that it would support. It is not true, however, that Tynan's review saved Osborne's play (and by extension the whole Court venture) after both had experienced distinctly shaky starts; the Arts Council had put their weight behind the new theatre, after all, and the reviews for Osborne's play were rather more mixed, with a number of critics finding something to praise in the text. It is also not true that the play had the full backing of the company; before the first season began, Richardson and Lewenstein were convinced that the most successful play would be Arthur Miller's *The Crucible*, and that *Look Back in Anger* would be lucky to cover its costs.

Nor is it the case that Devine led a company that had a clear sense of what forms the new drama should take. For one thing, Devine was answerable to the ESC Council – and that council was not always happy with the direction that the company took. Ronald Duncan had helped to form the company because he hoped that it would serve as an outlet for his work: however, Devine was unimpressed by Duncan's writing, and tried to prevent productions of it at the Court. When the first Writers' Group was established at the theatre in 1958 (a significant date for the development of writing in Britain – but one whose full impact took time to emerge) Devine told the ESC's chairman, Neville Blond, 'I am particularly anxious not to ask Ronnie Duncan'.[55] In his turn, Duncan lobbied Blond for Devine's removal. Also, I have already pointed out above that the Court's management was rather nervous about any strong association with politically difficult events (the rescheduled launch of *Declaration* was a telling example of the ESC board's unwillingness to court controversy (see Introduction).

Having said this, though, the presence of the Court (and in particular the fact that a key production occurred so early in the company's history) did change the theatrical atmosphere. From the beginning,

Devine insisted that the Court should not gain a reputation for simply producing one type of play. He identified two lines of development in 1950s British theatre, one deriving from the type of new drama being imported from the Continent and elsewhere, and the other home-grown, and exemplified by *Look Back in Anger*. Devine committed the Court to representing them both:

> [When] we had a success with the Osborne, I said I am not going to pursue that line exclusively. I am going to introduce this other line, the line of Brecht and Ionesco and all that, because I believe that the truth lies somewhere between these two points. So I took a kind of dialectic and educative attitude towards the thing. From the audience's point of view it is not so easy because . . . one minute it is Beckett, the next minute it is Osborne, the next Arden, then Jellicoe, then Brecht . . .[56]

If one looks at the number and type of productions mounted at the Court in its opening years, Devine's strategy is clearly apparent. The company staged Osborne, Brecht, Beckett, Arthur Miller and Ionesco; it provided a home for Ann Jellicoe's ritualistic and violent *The Sport of My Mad Mother* and Arnold Wesker's minutely realistic *The Kitchen*; it supported the home- grown absurdism of N. F. Simpson (*A Resounding Tinkle*, *One Way Pendulum*) and the plays of John Arden (a fascinating and rather neglected author, Arden's work drew on a rich variety of sources: folk tales, melodrama, Jacobean drama and popular culture); it also staged revivals of classic texts (Wycherley's *The Country Wife*, Shaw's *Major Barbara*). Many of these plays might very well have found a home, at some point, on the commercial stage, even if only in small-scale productions or in private theatre clubs; what the Court provided, which no other theatre in London did at the time, was a location where new dramatists could have their work supported – where they had the right to fail, a right that the commercial stage, by its very nature, could not extend. (It is worthwhile remembering, though, that some members of the ESC Council were not as convinced that the right to produce something that was commercially unsuccessful was a good thing.)

Alongside this varied programme, the company put in place an infrastructure that was designed to support developing writers. As noted above, the Writers' Group, as it was known, was set up first of all in 1958: this provided not only support in script development, but exposure to workshop techniques that were still new to the British stage. Keith Johnstone, at that time a play-reader and director at the Court, gave classes in improvisation (Johnstone later went on to write one of the most influential texts on improvisation), and Devine himself led sessions in mask-work. Writers were also given the opportunity to have their work performed without decor on Sunday nights on the main stage. This was useful, for a number of reasons. First, new directors could hone their craft without the pressure of a full production; Second, Sunday-night performances were paid for by supporters of the theatre; these supporters were grouped together in a theatre club, called the English Stage Society – and performances run by theatre clubs did not have to gain a licence from the Lord Chamberlain. Devine's aim was to integrate writers as closely as possible into the life of the theatre. To this end, playwrights associated with the Court could act as script-readers (for five shillings per script); they were allowed to attend rehearsals; and they were entitled to a 'playwright's pass' – access to free tickets for Court productions.

Lastly, Devine was keen to develop an aesthetic for the Court – a way of unifying the various productions mounted by the theatre, which would serve also to distance the Court from the commercial stage. He favoured a stage that was as uncluttered as possible; if 'The Group' were associated with the visually elaborate, the Court's performances were to adopt something of the spareness of Brecht's and Beckett's theatres. There was also a practical element to this: the Court's stage was small, and there was no wing-space to speak of. The early productions (until 1957) were played against a permanent surround, designed by Margaret Harris, in Brechtian fashion, to be a reminder that the world of the stage was constructed and unreal. The theatre's second in-house designer (and one of the most influential British theatre designers of the period) Jocelyn Herbert shared Devine's commitment to a simple stage (she was also Devine's partner until his death) As she put it:

George . . . wanted to get away from swamping the stage with decorative and naturalistic scenery; to let in light and air; to take the stage away from the director and designer and restore it to the actor and the text. This meant leaving space around the actors, and that meant the minimum of scenery and props . . . Along with this desire to clear away all the clutter went a deep respect for the text, a conviction instilled by George Devine . . . What we were there to do was to present the play as close as possible to what the author intended.[57]

Although other members of the company did not share Devine's ideas about design (Tony Richardson, in particular, preferred more elaborate settings; and he also liked to use the theatre's original system of traps), it is clear that Devine thought of it as an integral part of the ethos of the company. Design supported the actor and the text; and the institution existed to serve the playwright.

In a theatre environment where the lack of risk-taking new writing had been identified as a major problem, the Court seemed to provide the solution. Not only did it support the new author, but it subordinated everything else to the text; it also placed that text in a pantheon – alongside new writing from elsewhere, and revivals of already – hallowed older plays. No wonder the theatre drew the voluble support of Tynan and *Encore*; and no wonder, when Olivier was looking to ally himself with the new theatre, he should choose the Court, and an Osborne play (*The Entertainer*). The Court, after all, seemed everything that the modernisers of the British stage had been looking for; and it also contained enough traditional ballast, in the form of revivals and foreign work, not to seem wholly out of place in the London theatre of the time. In retrospect, Olivier's performance as Archie Rice was immediately acclaimed as the equal of any of the Shakespearean or classical roles that had defined his career up to that point; it was, perhaps, as significant for the history of the theatre as the premiere of *Look Back in Anger*. It showed, definitively, that this new, upstart venture could stand alongside the commercial stage; and conversely that the commercial stage could lend some of its lustre to the new drama. In the midst of the revolution, accommodation was not only possible, but also theatrically and commercially useful.

Theatre Workshop

Not everyone was so happy with the work coming out of the Royal Court. Beaumont, famously, walked out of *Look Back in Anger*, and Rattigan commented that Osborne's play seemed designed to set the younger dramatist up as Rattigan's polar opposite. Opposition also came from other sources, one of them perhaps rather surprising. Despite the fact that Oscar Lewenstein was closely associated with both companies, Theatre Workshop did not support the work of the Court:

> One day I thought we should start a war of the theatres, so halfway through the play [Brendan Behan's *The Hostage*], when the social worker and her fancy man have irritated everybody beyond endurance, I told Howard Goorney [who played the caretaker] to have them stowed in two dustbins to be labelled 'Return to the Royal Court', where they were currently performing Sam Beckett's *Endgame*. The Royal Court didn't respond. They were too soft-centred – very middle class and proper . . . George Devine. As for their John Osborne, 'Angry?' said Brendan. 'He's about as angry as Mrs Dale [the middle-class leading character in a radio soap opera of the decade].[58]

Some of this is, simply, jealousy; however, the idea of the Court's soft-centredness is less easy to defend. Devine was firmly linked to the theatrical and cultural establishment, and Osborne quickly embraced his new celebrity (establishing at least a social relationship with both Beaumont and Rattigan). Theatre Workshop remained firmly on the outside throughout the decade, partly through choice, and partly because of a definite (if largely unspoken) bias against the company and the work that it did. To translate this into crudely financial terms: in the year that the Arts Council offered £7,000 to the Royal Court, Theatre Workshop received £500 – even though the building they had occupied (the Theatre Royal Stratford East) could also have done with a full refurbishment.

Theatre Workshop had gained a permanent home in 1953; but the roots of the company went back to the 1930s, and the growth of agit-prop theatre companies during the Depression. Its founders, Ewan MacColl (a pseudonym; his real name was Jimmie Miller, from Salford) and Joan Littlewood (from Brixton in London; poor but bright, Littlewood had gained a scholarship to RADA but left, disillusioned and unhappy, before her studies finished), had worked together in a number of companies during the 1930s and 1940s – the Theatre of Action, the Theatre Union. In 1945, and with a great deal of experience in touring theatre behind them, they formed Theatre Workshop; from then until 1953 they toured extensively, both in Britain and Europe. By the time that they took up residence in the Theatre Royal, Theatre Workshop had evolved into a unique company, certainly when compared to the rest of the theatre in Britain at the time. Littlewood in particular drew on a comprehensive range of influences: Brecht, Stanislavsky, Meyerhold (a name more or less unknown on the British stage at the time), Jaques-Dalcroze's Eurhythmics, Laban's movement work, *commedia dell'arte*, Piscator, Eisenstein, Vakhtangov and Toller. She also brought to the company a thorough knowledge of theatre history – particularly of Elizabethan and Jacobean theatre, and the work of Molière. Ewan MacColl, for his part, gave the company a distinct group of plays which, as Robert Leach[59] has noted, stand comparison with Brecht. Together, they created a company which operated along the lines of a *commedia* troupe, or the Berliner Ensemble; actors were expected to participate in training which not only developed their analytical and characterisation skills, but which also developed the physical aspects of performance. They were also expected and encouraged to engage in improvisation – something that Littlewood used as a diagnostic tool when working on new plays later in the 1950s. As Leach points out, these elements did not exist separately; perhaps Littlewood's key achievement was in synthesising all of her influences into a coherent whole.

MacColl's departure coincided with the company's move to permanent premises: Littlewood regretted the move, saying in a BBC interview in 1994 that they only moved to Stratford East because 'it was the only place that we could get for twenty pounds a week'.[60]

However, in a theatrical environment which was centred on London to the exclusion of the rest of the country, a base in the capital meant one thing: Theatre Workshop came to the notice of the London critics. As a company who worked in a style that could be linked to Brecht (and as a company that had a direct link with the German playwright/director) they provided Tynan in particular with further ammunition with which to make a case for socially engaged theatre. However, the company struggled through the decade: support from the Arts Council was inconsistent, and relations between the company and the Council were fraught:

> If the Arts Council were ever to be associated with us, some of our actors would have to be replaced while the rest underwent a lengthy period of retraining. Learn to time bitchy lines while drinking tea? Drop your trousers while running in from one door and out through the other? We might even aspire to the high camp which passed for Shakespearean acting . . .[61]

Furthermore, the very fact that the company was now in London, and garnering good reviews, was in itself a source of tension:

> . . . the problem was, by this time, we were getting wonderful reviews from Harold Hobson and Kenneth Tynan. And Chelsea and Hampstead, if they say it was good, they would flock to the productions. And we sometimes earned £8 a week when they came. And we were having this . . . you know, it was a kind of crossover. And some said, 'Well look, we've got more money.' And Joan would say, 'Yes, but you're selling out to Binkie Beaumont [H. M. Tennent] and the Arts Council.' [laughs] And we said, 'No, we're not, they're nobody . . . they're not offering to buy us.'[62]

Also, the very nature of those good reviews sometimes displayed an ignorance of the way that the company worked. As noted above, the playwright was supposed to be the figure driving the development of a new British theatre; Theatre Workshop did not treat the writer with the same kind of veneration as the Court. In fact, when from the mid-1950s onwards the company came to focus on new writing, they treated texts as malleable, as raw material to be shaped in rehearsal, rather than as art works that should be respected. This approach was frequently extremely successful; the final shapes of Brendan Behan's *The Quare Fellow* (1956) and *The Hostage* (1958), and Shelagh Delaney's *A Taste of Honey* (1958) owe as much to Littlewood and the company as they do to the original material. Delaney's play (or, more correctly, the version of Delaney's script developed by Theatre Workshop) has been identified as a significant turning point in the representation of working-class, female and gay characters.[63] Its central character, Jo (a young girl unexpectedly pregnant after an encounter with a black sailor) is not condemned for her choices – she survives; Geoff, the art student who takes care of her, is gay – but he is neither transformed into a martyr nor condemned as a malign influence. Credit for shaping the production, as with Behan's work (although to a lesser extent), should have been given to Littlewood and the Theatre Workshop company; when Delaney's next play, *The Lion in Winter*, was produced at the Court, it was not given the same attention in rehearsal – and the play was the weaker for it.

This approach, though, was not common enough to be recognised at the time. In the 1970s, companies like Joint Stock would build on the Theatre Workshop approach, and would involve the writer in the creation of genuinely collaborative texts; in the 1950s, even Tynan had difficulty in accepting the fact that the productions he reviewed were the products of group effort rather than individual genius:

> [There] are, in this production [Behan's *The Hostage*], more than twenty songs, many of them blasphemously or lecherously gay . . . Authorship is shared by Mr Behan, his uncle and 'Trad'. Nor can one be sure how much of the dialogue is pure Behan and how much is gifted embroidery; for the whole production sounds spontaneous, a communal achievement based on Miss Littlewood's idea of theatre as a place where people talk to people . . .[64]

Tynan thought that *The Hostage* was Behan's best work, and one of the best productions that Theatre Workshop mounted; however, even in this positive review, one can clearly see that he draws a distinction between the text and the performance, between the 'pure Behan' and the 'embroidery' of Theatre Workshop. The idea that the two might have been so closely interwoven in rehearsal as to be inseparable does not seem, despite the review's positive tone, to have occurred to him. Theatre Workshop, in retrospect, suffered from the misapprehension of both their supporters and their detractors; their structure, their position and their political outlook did not endear them to the Arts Council; and their approach to theatre – and the collaborative, director-led ethos of the company – did not fit an era where, post-Osborne, the playwright was the new theatrical messiah.

The situation is confused: entering the 1960s

> When *Look Back in Anger* came out it was exciting, but already the working-class intellectual wisecracking at his wife's carica-tured Daddy is a stock character. We know the English are still snobbish about accents, we're not happy about the British Empire, suburban life is often dull and many middle-aged men are unfulfilled. We can't communicate with each other, have a lot of illusions and don't know what if anything life is about. All right. Where do we go from here?[65]

If any production signalled the changing of the theatrical guard, as the 1950s turned into the 1960s, it was *The Last Joke* – a play whose commercial pedigree would, earlier in the decade, have suggested a long run to appreciative audiences. The play (about the contested ownership of a portrait) was written by Edith Bagnold (responsible for solid West End hits such as *The Chalk Garden*); it starred John Gielgud, Ralph Richardson, Anna Massey, Ernest Thesiger and Robert Fleyming – a stellar cast, even by the standards of H. M. Tennent, who produced the play at the heart of the West End. However, far from being the kind of success that showed the continued resilience of the commercial theatre, the play was a notorious flop. The script had to be rewritten (fourteen versions of the text were produced – and even then, finally, the plot was incomprehensible), and when the reviews came in, they were uniformly negative: ('A meaningless jumble of pretentious whimsy' (*Sunday Dispatch*), 'a perfectly dreadful charade' (*Daily Mail*), 'a caravan of overblown nonsense' (*Evening Standard*). Kenneth Tynan's review ended by consigning the play, the production and the style of theatre to the past:

> Miss Bagnold's purpose may be to demonstrate that aristocratic patrons of art are spiritually preferable to bourgeois buyers who are motivated by spite and a desire to outbid their betters. A tenable conceit . . .; but in the modern world, it is little more than a *jeu d'esprit*, slim and soon exhausted. The walls are converging in on us, as in Edgar Allan Poe's story, and although there is room still for diamonds, there is none for costume jewellery . . .[66]

The play lasted all of two weeks before closing: Tennent never recovered from the failure – its time as a major producing house had come to an end. If one follows the logic of Tynan's argument, it is not only that the play was irredeemably bad; it was also antique – ineptly handled, certainly, but also simply out of time.

However, it would be wrong to suggest that such a devastating defeat for the old guard meant that the new wave had definitely won out. In October 1961 Tynan, coming to the end of his time as a newspaper critic, surveyed the West End – and was profoundly unhappy at what he saw:

> A decade ago, roughly two out of three London theatres were inhabited by detective stories, Pineroesque melodramas, quarter-witted farces, debutante comedies, overweight musicals and unreviewable revues; the same is true today. The accepted new playwrights were Fry, Eliot and Anouilh; of the threesome Anouilh is still represented on the playbills of London, and the other two have been replaced by Arnold Wesker (*The Kitchen*) and John Osborne (*Luther*). As for Theatre Workshop, it is almost as though it had never been . . .[67]

Partly, this is a familiar story. The *Look Back in Anger* myth masks the fact that, as with all moments of historical transition, change takes a long time and is never complete; and a theatrical revolution based primarily in only two venues was never likely to spread across the rest of the theatre overnight. As the John Whiting quote at the beginning of this section makes clear, by the end of the 1950s the battle for the future of the British stage (as the contributors to *Encore* on one side, and veterans like Noël Coward on the other would have it) was far from resolved. Coward (who wrote furiously about the new theatre in a series of articles, published in the *Sunday Times* in early 1961) saw the new drama as the result of a sector-wide conspiracy, led by critics, against established writers whose sole desire was to entertain the audience; Tom Milne, writing for *Encore*, saw the theatre revolution not as all-encompassing but as dangerously fragile. In an article ('Taking Stock at the Court', 1958) which begins with the ringing endorsement, 'God help the English Theatre if this company dies',[68] Milne looked rather more coolly at the type of work that the Court had actually produced in its two years of operation:

> An analysis of the plays presented at the Court, however, is both interesting and disturbing. Only seven of the nineteen plays presented were premieres (including [Osborne's] *Epitaph for George Dillon*, already produced non-professionally, and the one-acter *How Can We Save Father?*); three others had been previously produced in the provinces, seven were foreign plays, two were classics . . .[69]

Note the comment, 'three others had been previously produced in the provinces'; no matter what side of the battle the commentators were on, both sides shared the idea that for a play to count it had to be shown in London.

The truth lies somewhere between these two opposing poles. A change in British theatre was under way, and its influence stretched across a number of areas. There were clear signs of institutional change. In 1961, the Shakespeare Memorial Company, based at Stratford-upon-Avon under the leadership of Peter Hall, was relaunched under Royal Charter, as the Royal Shakespeare Company; and despite the throwaway sneer at provincial premieres in Milne's article, the new generation of regional reps had begun to change the theatrical landscape in Britain as a whole (one of the new reps – the Belgrade in Coventry – nurtured the early work of Arnold Wesker). New writing had a far higher profile, thanks initially to the Court; the success of *Waiting for Godot* had demonstrated that even the most theatrically experimental work could find a British audience; the fiasco over *The Last Joke* had demonstrated the growing weakness of the old commercial stage, at least in its current form; Theatre Workshop had provided a British equivalent to the Berliner Ensemble (although it took quite some time for its full influence to be felt).

However, to Tynan's despair, the West End had not succumbed to the forces of the new revolution. George Devine at the Royal Court could point to some successes, but other dramatists – John Arden, in particular – failed to attract an audience; and, as noted above, Devine had to spend part of his time dealing with the internal politics of his institution. The Arts Council's financial support was crucial to ventures like the Court; the financial support it provided meant that Devine's policy of accepting commercial failure in the name of artistic development could be supported; but the Council did not have much money to spend – so its influence over the commercial pressures felt by many in the theatre was limited. Theatre Workshop, perhaps the most radical innovation in British theatre (in its organisation, its ideology, its openness to influences from mainland Europe and its approach to the text) had stuttered through the decade; it never managed to secure Arts Council funding, it lost actors (like Harry H. Corbett) and writers (like Shelagh Delaney) to other London stages, and its very success, in the environment of the time, made sustaining a coherent company very difficult. In 1961 Littlewood, understandably exhausted by the demands of keeping the company going, quit; even though she returned a couple of years later to stage the extremely successful *Oh, What a Lovely War!* (1963), the company never regained the coherence it had enjoyed in the 1950s. Finally, the Lord Chamberlain had steadily lost power through the decade, but at the turn of the 1960s the office was still there; it was to be another eight years before censorship was no longer exercised routinely on new British theatre texts.

So, at the end of the decade, the picture was mixed. New writers had made an undoubted impact; and in the wake of Osborne's success, the theatre could be placed alongside those other art forms whose relevance to contemporary British society had already been proven. However, the place of more challenging types of new work was less secure. Ann Jellicoe's *The Sport of My Mad Mother* (1958) flopped at the Court, even though it had won joint third place in an *Observer* new play competition (the other third-placed play, N. F. Simpson's *A Resounding Tinkle*, was rather more successful). Jellicoe, although grateful to the Court for their support, was nevertheless aware that, as a woman, she was a marginal figure (it is indicative that, even given this, for most of the 1960s Jellicoe was the most produced woman playwright on the British stage). As Maggie Gale noted, Jellicoe's relative isolation was shared by the few other women play-wrights who worked in the theatre in the 1950s – particularly those who wished to write about the lives of poorer women: 'During the 1950s there were a number of plays where the lives of single working-class women and mothers were foregrounded. These were, however, few and far between. The West End was still largely domi-nated by the concerns of the middle and ruling classes . . .'[70] In other words, it was easier to be Edith Bagnold (whose plays reflected those concerns) than it was to be Sylvia Rayman, whose play about the plight of single mothers (*Woven of Twilight*, 1957) appears in retro-spect to be a pioneering text; but the fact that, after Rayman's work was produced, it became slightly easier to produce more realistic images of women does not change the fact that it was difficult for a new woman playwright to make a lasting impact. Rayman's play is largely forgotten; and the other famous woman dramatists first produced in the 1950s are mainly associated with one play each: Shelagh Delaney with *A Taste of Honey* (1958), and Ann Jellicoe with *The Knack* (1962).

Other writers whose work was celebrated in the 1960s found the 1950s a more difficult proposition. As noted above, John Arden's plays regularly failed to attract audiences at the Court. Harold Pinter

– probably the most significant British dramatist of the 1960s (if not of the whole post-war era) – saw his first full-length play flop; not even a glowing review by Hobson could save *The Birthday Party* from an early closure. Even Arnold Wesker, who had to some extent inherited Osborne's mantle as spokesman for the disaffected poor, initially found it difficult to convince the Court that his work was worth staging; although some of the ESC (William Gaskill and Lindsay Anderson) were enthusiastic about *Chicken Soup with Barley*, Devine was unconvinced – and suggested that the play be first produced in Coventry rather than London (although both it and *Roots*, the next play in the trilogy, played at the Court soon after their runs began) – see the essay on Wesker below. None of the other dramatists of the late 1950s – Bernard Kops, David Cregan, James Saunders, Keith Johnstone, Christopher Logue, Barry Reckford, et al. managed to sustain a long career, partly because the infrastructure couldn't support them; later in the 1960s, not only would increased Arts Council support bolster the number of venues that could take writers, but a network of touring companies and arts centres would be hungry for new writing (John McGrath, just beginning his writing career in the late 1950s, would benefit greatly from this new development – as would Caryl Chuchill in the 1970s). At the end of the 1950s, though, these changes could not have been anticipated; and at the end of a decade where a revolution in British playwriting had been much anticipated, and then loudly hailed, the success of that revolution was not assured. It could be said that, in this, paradoxically, the 1950s British stage was a true mirror of its time: like British society, British theatre was subject to an incomplete transformation – and uncertain how far, and how fast, the changes that began during the decade would go. John Whiting's summary of the decade, quoted above, seemed worryingly apt: at the end of the decade, the clear lines of conflict that had opened up in the mid-1950s had blurred – and the situation was very confused indeed.

CHAPTER 2
INTRODUCING THE PLAYWRIGHTS

Introduction

As pointed out in Chapter 1, the political, cultural and theatrical climate of the 1950s was rather complex and difficult, and the political realities that the country had to deal with were new and troubling. Culturally, Britain was coming to terms both with a decline in international influence and with global shifts which threatened to destabilise its sense of identity; and the theatre, at least at the beginning of the decade, seemed particularly badly placed to deal with the profound changes that were shaping British society. It was censored; it obeyed, for the most part, commercial dictates; and during the first part of the period, it had the reputation of lagging behind other art forms. The four writers whose work will be dealt with in the following sections all found themselves in various ways caught up in the changing nature of the time; and all of them found themselves involved, directly or indirectly, in a wider argument about the nature of theatre. Whether, as it was for Eliot, theatre was the place to air and disseminate spiritual truths; or whether, as for Rattigan, theatre was ostensibly a place for entertainment, and not for ideas; or whether, as it was for both Osborne and Wesker, the theatre was a place where the state of Britain could be anatomised, each took up a position which reflected wider currents running through the stage from the end of the war to the beginning of the 1960s.

Their routes into theatre also reflect something of the position that the stage held during the decade. Eliot came to the stage because he saw it, not as a high cultural form which was artistically credible enough to carry complexity, but because of its popularity. Rattigan, from the time of his first big success, operated at the heart of the commercial London stage, while Osborne operated on its fringes, as a jobbing repertory actor. Wesker did not have a background in the theatre (although he had been an amateur actor), but came to the form because he was enthused by the possibilities that *Look Back in Anger* seemed to have opened up. Between them, Eliot, Rattigan, Osborne and Wesker defined a theatrical territory that was riven by the same divides that operated in British society. There is little to link the poetic drawing-room comedy of *The Cocktail Party*, the painful quietness of *The Deep Blue Sea*, the loose vitality of *The Entertainer* and the broad historical sweep of *Chicken Soup with Barley*; and that perhaps is the point. The sheer variety of these texts in itself is a sign of a theatrical environment which was changing radically; and, moreover, one in which the idea of what theatre was for – its place in culture, and in British life generally – was undergoing profound and fundamental re-evaluation.

T. S. Eliot (1888–1949): faith, fragmentation and tradition

T. S. Eliot was born in St Louis, Missouri, in 1888: his family originally came from New England and were wealthy, and well connected. Eliot was the last of seven children; his parents were in their forties by the time of his birth, and this, his father's encroaching deafness, and the family's insistence on instilling modes of correct behaviour in their children (and the fact that Eliot himself was born with a medical condition – a congenital double hernia – that meant he had to wear a truss from an early age) seems to have contributed to the formation of a character that was reserved, careful and rather distanced from the world in which he grew up. The family had strong links with the Unitarian church – a Puritan Protestant denomination (Eliot's grandfather founded the Unitarian Church in St Louis); and the person to whom Eliot seems to have been closest in his childhood, his Irish nurse Annie Dunne, sometimes took him to the Catholic masses in the city.

His home city furnished him with images to which he returned throughout his life; even though the family was rich, the part of St Louis in which they lived was run-down, and images of poverty exist side by side with anatomisations of polite society in his earliest poems.

The Mississippi, and the climate of the area, also provided the young Eliot with a store of images; of powerful rivers, of mud and fog. However, even though he continually returned to these images, he never seems to have felt at home in St Louis – nor in New England and Boston, an area with which his family retained close contact. In 1906, Eliot, as was almost inevitable given his upbringing, social standing and intelligence, went to Harvard; there, he impressed his contemporaries as clever, well-read, capable of wit but at the same time rather detached and solitary. Eliot initially did not shine at Harvard; but he did find intellectual material that shaped his thinking, and which helped him develop an original poetic voice. He found some members of the Harvard staff particularly influential; in particular, Irving Babbitt, who taught Eliot during his final year, argued against the idea of egalitarianism, and emphasised the importance of order and authority – ideas that the young Eliot found very congenial. Also at Harvard, Eliot encountered symbolist poetry (through Arthur Symonds's 1895 book on the subject); he later said that Symonds's book influenced the course of his life. The symbolists created poetry from obscure but resonant images; in particular, Eliot was drawn to the work of Jules Laforgue, in whose ironic, satirical and distanced writing he found a model for his early verse.

Even though he had been involved in Harvard's literary circle (joining the board of the university's literary magazine, *The Advocate*), the course of Eliot's life was not decided by the time of his graduation. He moved to Paris in 1910 for a year of postgraduate study; a potential career as an academic philosopher was one of the options open to him. In Paris, Eliot attended lectures given by the philosopher Henri Bergson, whose ideas on the evolution of consciousness and the subjective experience of time appealed to him; he was also exposed to the profoundly conservative, Catholic and authoritarian writing of Charles Maurras – an encounter which was to prove lastingly influential. In general, Eliot immersed himself in the artistic and philosophical life of the city; the full range of his studies – alongside images and associations culled from his earlier life – found expression in the startlingly original poems that he wrote between 1910 and 1911. These poems – 'The Love Song of J. Alfred Prufrock', 'Portrait of a Lady', 'Rhapsody on a Windy Night' and others – formed the heart of his first collection (*Prufrock and Other Observations*, published in 1917). They mixed the striking images of symbolism (and Laforgue's alienated satire) with a strongly dramatic use of tone of voice; in Eliot's early poetry, the reader is frequently aware of a speaker – and very frequently of a character whose thoughts and impressions the poet records.

Over the next few years, Eliot oscillated between philosophy and literature; he went back to Harvard, and worked on a thesis on F. H. Bradley, a critic of Bergson's philosophy (the thesis was completed in 1916, but Eliot was never examined). In 1914, after a summer in Germany, he moved to Oxford to continue his studies. Later the same year, a mutual friend brought Eliot's verse to the attention of the American poet Ezra Pound, who was living in England; intrigued, the more famous Pound sought Eliot out, and spent the next few years strongly advocating Eliot's poetry. The following year, Eliot was introduced to Vivienne Haigh-Wood; attracted by what then appeared to him as her frankness and impulsiveness, he married her in June 1915. Eliot's family were shocked and upset – even more so when they discovered (as Eliot himself had) that Vivien had a history of nervous illness. There are conflicting accounts of Eliot's first marriage (with Carole Seymour-Jones's 2003 biography *Painted Shadow* making the case against Eliot as a husband, and other biographers such as Peter Ackroyd providing a more balanced perspective). Whatever the truth of it, the relationship between Eliot and his first wife was uniquely poisonous: Eliot's own mental health was fragile, and although the two seem to have had periods of relative stability (chiefly when one was taking care of the other), her volatility and his reserve (and, it has been suggested, his fear of sexuality) meant that the marriage was frequently difficult – and occasionally traumatic. To support himself and his wife, Eliot took a job at Lloyd's Bank in 1917; this provided the young couple with financial security, but the strain of the job added to the strain of his marriage – and Eliot took on a number of other commitments for various literary magazines (most important, and most taxing, he was the founding editor of the influential *Criterion* magazine from 1922). His breakdown in 1921 was as much to do with the pressure of overwork as it was to do with the strains of his marriage.

Prufrock did not attract many readers, but Pound continued to champion Eliot's verse; a second volume, *Poems 1920*, an anthology of his verse up to this point (*Ara Vos Prec*), and the publication of a collection of essays (*The Sacred Wood*) served to raise his profile. The essays helped to provide the critical framework against which Eliot's poetry was judged; taken together, they began to establish the idea that Eliot was not simply a poet, but a cultural force. Surprisingly, though, given the innovative nature of the poems, the Eliot of the essays talked approvingly of the role of tradition in the work of the individual artist (tradition helped establish an ideal order of art works, within which new work necessarily found its place, and to which the individual artist should surrender). From the early 1920s onwards, a significant strand of Eliot's theoretical writings concerned the theatre; in essays such as 'Four Elizabethan Dramatists', he began to formulate a theoretical response to what he saw as the inadequacies of theatrical realism:

> In a play of Aeschylus, we do not find that certain passages are literature and other passages drama; every style of utterance in the play bears a relation to the whole and because of this relation is dramatic in itself. The imitation of life is circumscribed, and the approaches to ordinary speech are not without relation or effect upon each other . . .[1]

In other words, realism in the theatre was inadequate: poetic drama was necessary, because it provided a formal structure – otherwise, life would simply be imitated (leading to, as Eliot described it in the same essay, 'the desert of exact likeness to the reality which is perceived by the most commonplace mind').[2]

With the publication of *The Waste Land* in 1922, Eliot's place at the forefront of modernist literature was assured. *The Waste Land* (written in bursts from 1919, and published in a final form that owed a great deal to Ezra Pound's editorial input) seemed to capture the sense of uncertainty and fragmentation that characterised the period after the First World War. Although Eliot provided apparently explanatory notes for the poem (notes which confuse as much as they elucidate), the power of the poem, arguably, comes from its fundamental incoherence; the idea of the contemporary world as a spiritual and cultural wasteland is conveyed most powerfully from the jumbling of images and registers within the poem – and from the sense it gives of a series of distinct, precisely captured voices, speaking over and across each other in a cacophonous dialogue. The poem as a whole is tied together by association, rather than by a coherent argument; and it gestures towards the absence of spirituality as a key factor in the aridity of modern life. Eliot's interest in spirituality was long-standing (and encompassed Buddhism as well as the Anglo-Catholic Christianity that he was soon to embrace); an important strand in *The Waste Land*, it was to come to the fore in subsequent poems, and in the drama that he was to write later in his life.

Eliot left his job at Lloyd's in 1925, for an editorial position at Faber. At the same time, he began the long process of distancing himself from his wife (he left Vivienne, finally, in 1934, and she was committed to an asylum in 1938); and he was baptised into the Church of England in 1927. In 1928, in the preface to *For Lancelot Andrewes*, he described himself as 'a classicist in literature, royalist in politics, and Anglo-Catholic in religion'.[3] His subsequent work, from the poem *Ash Wednesday* (1930) onwards, reflected this assertion. Sometimes Eliot's religious and social conservatism spilled over into outright (and sometimes offensive) reaction (as in *After Savage Gods*, published in 1934). Mostly, though, he presented himself as the upholder of tradition; and, as he became an increasingly public figure, he grew careful of his image. (*After Savage Gods*, for example, was suppressed: it contained material – some of it anti-Semitic – that did not sit well with Eliot's growing reputation.) His poetry became more meditative, and the clash of voices of *The Waste Land* was replaced by one voice – sonorous, grave, but still capable of moments of imagistic, associative beauty. His final major poetic work – the sequence of poems, begun in the 1930s, and published as *Four Quartets* in 1943 – asserted the importance of faith and tradition as bulwarks against a world sliding into war.

At the same time, Eliot's interest in the theatre began to bear fruit. He had worked on an experimental, ritualistic poetic drama in the 1920s (fragments of this incomplete project were published as *Sweeney Agonistes* in 1932). In the mid-1930s, he was commissioned to write a piece of theatre for Canterbury Cathedral; his response, *Murder in the Cathedral*, was first performed in 1935. A drama about the killing of Archbishop Thomas Becket in 1170, the play is arguably Eliot's most successful; it dramatises the murder through a set of shifting poetic registers which make use of the striking images of his early poetry, the measured gravity of his more recent work and, in the self-justifying speeches of the knights who kill Becket, his ear for the registers of different types of speech (in the knights' case, he catches the sinister blandness of governmental rhetoric uncomfortably well). *Murder in the Cathedral* echoed arguments that Eliot had made elsewhere (the death of spirituality, and the ruin that followed it); but the play made the argument public, in a way that his verse could not.

Eliot's subsequent dramas, as Sarah Bay-Cheng points out below, can be seen as attempts to intervene in a wider social debate about the nature of faith and forgiveness (although as she points out, this did not automatically mean an entirely Christian approach to the spiritual); and the models that he chose reflected his belief in the importance of tradition. *The Family Reunion* (1939) took the basic plot of Aeschylus' *Eumenides*, and applied it to an English country house murder mystery: its central character, Harry, Lord Monchensey – pursued by furies that only he, his servant and a spiritually perceptive family member, Agatha, can see – comes to embrace a religious vocation as a way of expiating the guilt over his wife's death. Eliot felt that the play (which closed after five weeks) was unsuccessful, because it did not integrate its classical plot and the contemporary setting particularly well; but it did set the template for the dramatic work that he was to produce after 1945 – at a time when work that contained the twin lures of faith and tradition would prove, at least temporarily, to be exactly what the theatre felt it needed.

Terence Rattigan (1911–46): the commercial stage

Terence Rattigan was born in 1911, the second of two boys, to a well-off family; his father, Frank, was a diplomat, and Rattigan benefited from the social position and influence that his father's job carried – at least for the first few years of his life. He was educated at a private school (Harrow) and went to Oxford; although he did not graduate, refusing to take his final exams, he did manage to make the contacts that were open to students at Oxford and Cambridge – contacts that were undeniably useful to him in later life. During his schooldays, Rattigan had developed a love of the theatre (and had begun to write plays – although, in a rather self-deprecating autobiographical note, written later in his life, he dismissed his early work as melodramatic). At Oxford, he wrote theatre reviews, submitted plays to the OUDS (the Oxford University Dramatic Society – run at that time, ironically, by George Devine), and played a small part in the OUDS production of *Romeo and Juliet*, which was directed by the new star of London's Old Vic theatre, John Gielgud. Rattigan cultivated Gielgud, and their friendship helped give the aspiring playwright access to the commercial theatre. Under the surface, though, Rattigan's life was not as comfortable. His parents were frequently absent, as his mother followed her husband in his various diplomatic postings. His father's diplomatic career came to an abrupt halt in 1922; he was fired both because he fell foul of shifts in British imperial policy, and because of a series of affairs – the last of these with Princess Elizabeth of Romania. When Elizabeth became Queen of Greece, Frank Rattigan's position became untenable, and he was retired on a small pension. For a while, he maintained the fiction that he was still employed; and he called himself by the military rank he had briefly held – styling himself 'Major Rattigan'.

At Harrow, Rattigan began to experiment sexually; according to a friend, quoted in Wansell's biography, he 'never for one moment questioned whether or not he was a homosexual. He just knew he was, and it did not disturb him in the least.'[4] For someone of Rattigan's class, to be homosexual in the 1920s and 1930s was to be part of a parallel society, which ran along the same class lines that divided the rest of the country; although rates of arrest for importuning (that is, approaching other men for sex) varied in the 1930s and 1940s, for someone like Rattigan, able (after his first significant successes) to own his own flat, it was possible to live reasonably securely – as long as one was private and discreet. The idea that at some point one might be held publicly accountable for private behaviour necessarily meant that a crucial part of Rattigan's life had to be kept private; however, it began to feature, in coded form, in the plays that he began to write. His first play, *Embryo* (later renamed *First Episode*), co-written with Philip Heimann, revolves around unspoken, unrequited and unacknowledged homosexual love; a complex series of affairs, between Tom (an Oxford undergraduate who produces plays), David (his best friend), Joan (his lover) and Margot (a visiting actress), is complicated further because of the close relation between David and Tom – a relationship which Margot labels 'degenerate'. The play is an uneasy mixture of the serious and the comic; but it does contain themes to which Rattigan returned: the idea of passion as a disruptive force, the tension between the characters' private lives and public morality (Margot gets David sent down from Oxford by telling the senior proctor that Joan had been in his room at an unsuitable hour). Tellingly, the play's oblique references to homosexuality were trimmed back further by the Lord Chamberlain's office, who ruled that it was 'unpleasant', but let it pass. After a short try-out in 1933 (during which Rattigan noted the audience's responses, rewriting the play accordingly), *First Episode* had a short run at the Comedy Theatre in the West End in 1934, and an equally small run on Broadway the same year.

Never mind that the play had failed, that it had failed to convince Rattigan's family that he had a career as a playwright and that it marked the end of his partnership with Heimann (to whom Rattigan was hopelessly attracted); Rattigan, at the age of twenty-two, had been produced on the West End stage. After a brief and unsatisfactory attempt to adapt *A Tale of Two Cities* for John Gielgud, Rattigan sent the text of a new play, *Gone Away*, to the theatre producer Bronson Albery. This was one of two plays that Rattigan had written (the other, *Black Forest*, was a more serious text, which had an ageing schoolmaster as its central character). His mother advised Rattigan to send *Gone Away* for sound commercial reasons; a comedy was more likely to attract an audience. Albery accepted the text; and, renamed *French without Tears*, the play was staged at the Criterion Theatre in November 1936. Rehearsals had not gone well, and Rattigan wasn't expecting a great deal from the production; its success took everyone by surprise. *French without Tears* is a light comedy (again, loosely based on Rattigan's own experience) in which a group of young men gather in a villa in the south of France to learn the language under the authoritarian tutelage of Monsieur Maingot. The young men – Brian, Alan and Kenneth – come to form an alliance with another pupil, Lt-Commander Rogers (an older man whom they originally treat with suspicion) against the sexually voracious Diana, who tries to seduce and manipulate each of them. At the end of the play, they manage to shake themselves free: and Lord Heybrook, the heir on whom she has set her sights, is revealed at the play's end to be a fifteen-year-old boy (in an early draft of the play, Heybrook was extravagantly homosexual). The play's comic impetus comes from the men's attraction to, and fear of, Diana; the sexuality that she embodies is both alluring, and also dangerous – and must be rejected if the men are to retain any pride in themselves.

French without Tears was a substantial hit, running for 1,030 performances: it catapulted Rattigan to stardom (and, along the way, made the concealment of his private life even more important). Commercial managements now took notice of him; and he was able to develop a parallel career in cinema, as a scriptwriter. In the theatre, though, it took some time for Rattigan to have a comparable success. *Follow My Leader*, a farce about the emergence of Hitler (co-written with his friend Tony Goldschmidt), was refused a licence by the Lord Chamberlain, because it might offend the Nazi government. The play was eventually licensed in 1940, when the playfulness of the satire (the dictator is called Zedesi – inevitably, his followers greet him with the salutation, 'Up, Zedesi!') seemed misplaced: the play only ran for eleven days. The second play written during this period, *After the Dance*, came as something of a surprise (to the Lord Chamberlain's office at least); a serious play, it follows the Bright Young Things of the 1920s and early 1930s into middle age, chronicling their attempts to hang on to the sense of freedom and possibility they had when they were younger. As Helen, one of the play's younger characters, tells David, the older married man with whom she is about to start an affair:

> You see, when you were eighteen you didn't have anybody of twenty-two or twenty-five or thirty or thirty-five to help you, because they'd been wiped out. And anyone over forty you wouldn't listen to, anyway. The spotlight was on you and you alone, and you weren't even young men; you were children.[5]

This generation – Noël Coward's generation – could act out their private lives in public, because there was no social pressure on them; as they get older, however, the world changes around them, but they do not change – and the pressure of maintaining the identities forged in a moment of freedom destroys them. Joan, Helen's wife, commits suicide – and at the end of the play David rejects Helen, staying on a path which will lead to his own death.

After the Dance opened in 1939, to good reviews; however, after a month, audiences began to dwindle (as Rebellato suggests, the darkening pre-war atmosphere of that year was not the best time to stage what is a very bleak play) and the production closed. The failure stung Rattigan: he did not include *After the Dance* in his collected plays. The public rejection of *After the Dance* plunged Rattigan into a bout of insecurity; to help allay this, he sought therapy from Dr Keith Newman, a manipulative and eccentric psychiatrist who, it has been argued, served as the model for Mr Miller in *The Deep Blue Sea* (see the essay on Rattigan below). On Newman's advice, Rattigan joined the RAF – and the experience helped, distancing him from the writer's block he was currently suffering, and providing him with the material for *Flare Path* (1942), the play that gave him his next hit, and which united him for the first time with Binkie Beaumont and the Tennent Group. *Flare Path* is set in a pub next to an airfield, and deals with the build-up to, and the aftermath of, an air-raid; although by no means a narrowly jingoistic play, it did stress the quiet heroism of the aircrews

– and, in doing so, managed to catch the public mood. *Flare Path* was the first in a line of hits: Rattigan followed it with *While the Sun Shines* (1943) in which servicemen of varying nationalities (American, French and British) compete for the love of a titled English girl, and *Love in Idleness* (1944), which, in successive drafts, took one of the central themes of *Hamlet* (the relation between Hamlet and his mother) and turned it into a cross-generational vehicle for two stars of the commercial theatre, Alfred Lunt and Lynn Fontainne. Rattigan finished the war with two successes running simultaneously in the West End, and with the reputation of being one of the commercial jewels in Tennent's crown; the left-leaning liberalism of his early work had moderated, and *Love in Idleness* in particular showed that he could present apparently conservative sentiments sympathetically. After the successes of the war years, Rattigan had the right to feel that he was a part of the theatrical establishment; the terms on which that success had been achieved – an acceptance of the commercial realities of the stage, and a willingness to accommodate his work to the demands of the audience – were the very factors that were to tell against him so heavily after 1956.

John Osborne (1929–56): the fatality of hatred

John Osborne was born in Fulham, London, in December 1929; he was not only from a different generation than Rattigan, but from an entirely different section of society. Whereas Rattigan's early life had been privileged (even after his father's disgrace), Osborne's view of the world was shaped by harsher circumstances. Writing about his upbringing in his 1981 autobiography, *A Better Class of Person*, Osborne was characteristically forthright about the place where he grew up:

> Fulham in the 1930s was a dismal district. It sprawled roughly across an area, at least as far as my territory was concerned, from Hammersmith to Chelsea to Walham Green . . . to Putney Bridge at the other end. It was full of pubs, convents,

second-hand clothes shops, bagwash laundries and pawnbro-
kers. Everything seemed very broken down.[6]

What is conveyed most strongly in Osborne's autobiography, when he
writes about the world in which he grew up, is a sense of constraint; of
being trapped, by the places in which he lived, by the circumstances
in which his family found itself and, most obviously, by his family.
Osborne was an only child (a sister, Faith, died from tuberculosis
when he was two). For much of his early life, his father and mother
lived apart; their rocky marriage was exacerbated by his father's illness
(Thomas Osborne suffered from TB too, and died when Osborne was
ten). Osborne, in his notebooks and his autobiography, paints a clear
and uncomfortable picture of his parents and the rest of his extended
family; his relatives are presented as a series of grotesques – although
he does not condemn all of them out of hand, there is the sense that
he did not feel part of either the Osbornes or the Groves (his mother's
side of the family).

His relationship with his parents, however, was both more immediate and more fraught. He came to idolise, and to an extent to
romanticise, his father as a man of almost saintlike weakness. Thomas
Osborne, who came to London from south Wales, worked for an
advertising firm; however, his illness forced him out of work at the age
of thirty-eight. Osborne's image of his father was, necessarily,
constructed at a distance; Thomas's TB was contagious, and Osborne's
mother, understandably, was terrified that her son might catch the
illness that had claimed his sister. This distance helps to explain the
rather idealised figure his father cuts in Osborne's autobiography; as
his own biographer, John Heilpern, puts it, 'Osborne's life-long
lament for his father was for a man he barely knew'.[7] If his father was
idealised and absent, his mother was demonised, and all too present.
In his autobiography, Osborne gives her no quarter. He refers to her
as 'Nellie Beatrice' as though to deny their relationship; he describes
her appearance in terms that are positively Dickensian; and he blames
her for what appeared to him to be her damaging indifference to his
father, and for isolating him (even her understandable attempts to
prevent her son from contracting the TB virus are blamed for making

Osborne wary of crowds). The relation between them, at least in Osborne's mind, is caught in the passage that describes returning to his home in the aftermath of his father's death:

> [My mother] was waiting excitedly for me and at once insisted that I go into my father's bedroom to look at him in his coffin. The smell in the room was strong and strange and, in his shroud, he was unrecognizable. As I looked down at him, she said 'Of course, this room's got to be fumigated, you know that, don't you? Fumigated.' Frumigated was how she pronounced it. With my father's body lying in the bedroom across the landing, I had been obliged to share my briefing room with my mother, who spent hour upon hour reading last Sunday's *News of the World*, the bright light overhead, rustling the pages in my ear and sighing heavily. For the first time I felt the fatality of hatred.[8]

Osborne always associated his lifelong battle against depression with his father's death; and the anger directed at his mother in this account of his past became a characteristic defence mechanism against the rest of the world.

Osborne himself was sickly as a child; when he was twelve, he spent a year in bed with rheumatic fever, and suffered at various times from migraines, a twisted appendix, boils, blisters and a very serious bout of peritonitis. These illnesses helped to contribute to the sense that Osborne felt himself to be alone; from an early age, he seems to have lived at a distance from the rest of the world, and the sense of being an outsider stayed with him for the rest of his life. It certainly governed his attitude to his schooling. At the age of fourteen, he was sent to a minor boarding school, St Michael's in Devon, 'to make up for my non-existent education', as he put it;[9] the fees were paid for out of a fund that his father had opened before his death. Osborne, however, did not last long there: he was expelled for punching the headmaster during his second year. The headmaster had caught him smuggling cider into the school, and had slapped Osborne at assembly the next day, in front of the whole school. As he did when bullied by anyone, Osborne hit back.

In 1947, Osborne was employed for a while as a journalist (on the trade paper *Gas World*); but, although he had talent as a writer (which he was beginning to exercise), journalism as a career did not appeal to him. He also spent a great deal of time watching theatre in the West End, further developing a love of performance that stretched back to his childhood. Osborne's performative tastes were wide and inclusive; alongside the legitimate theatre, he loved the music hall and cinema. Getting involved in the theatre, as he did at this time, gave him an outlet for this enthusiasm; and, after a brief period performing in an amateur company, he turned professional – and, like Harold Pinter, learned the craft of theatre in a series of rep productions, in theatre up and down the country. His life as an actor gave him a means of escape from his mother; it gave him a chance to express the dandyish, bohemian side of his character (for Osborne, this was another link to his father, who had the same character traits); and it gave him a practical understanding of the business of performance – what worked and, crucially, what to react against.

This practical experience was soon applied to his first dramatic experiments. Osborne began to write for the theatre at eighteen – very soon after he became an actor. Encouraged by an older actress, Stella Linden (with whom he was having an affair, and with whom he attempted to write), he studied conventional plot construction, but found the type of well-made play that repertory theatres habitually staged to be mechanical and constricting. The plots were artificial; the need to provide predictable plot reversals and strong moments at the end of the first and second acts was limiting; and it was a given that the audience should not be offended: 'Above all, no character who was unsympathetic could ever dominate a play. It was a point to be made to me endlessly ... The playmaker's manual had no entry for "Walking out" ...'[10] This was anathema to Osborne, who later in life took a perverse pleasure in testing the audience's patience and tolerance. These early experiments were failures: only one, *The Devil Inside*, had a production (in Huddersfield in 1951), but they did at least give the young Osborne a grounding in the craft of playwriting – and it helped him decide that, for him, the problem with the well-made play was that it was not excessive enough; it did not capture the passion and the messiness of experience.

Osborne met his first wife, the actress Pamela Lane, through the theatre; they married in 1951, against her family's wishes (it seems likely that Jimmy Porter's description of Alison's family owes something to Osborne's treatment by Pamela's parents). The marriage did not last; the life of a jobbing actor was not one that fitted marriage, and Osborne throughout his life had trouble sustaining relationships with women. Pamela had an affair, the rows between them occasionally became violent and the marriage came to an acrimonious end in 1954. By the mid-1950s Osborne had both the failure of his marriage and the growing awareness that he was a failure as an actor to contend with; he was also penniless, and living on a riverboat with Anthony Creighton, a gay friend with whom he had tried to set up a touring theatre company. As he had with Stella Linden, Osborne formed a writing partnership with Creighton; the most successful collaboration, *Epitaph for George Dillon*, was staged by the Royal Court in 1958. *Epitaph* is an interesting play; although in some ways it is unconvincing (the minor characters are not well-defined, for example), the central character, George Dillon, is the first identifiable anti-hero in Osborne's work. An actor-dramatist, critical and dismissive of the lower-middle-class family with whom he lives, Dillon engages in the kind of lacerating rhetoric that would, in the mouth of Jimmy Porter, seem to herald a change in the nature of British theatre. Talking of the family he lives with, George rails:

> Tell me, have you ever heard any of them, even once, laugh? I mean really laugh – not make that choked, edgy sound that people make all the time. Or, to put it more intelligibly: I don't mean that breaking wind people make somewhere between their eyebrows and their navels, when they hear about the old lady's most embarrassing moment. I mean the real thing – the sound of the very wit of being alive . . .[11]

In passages like this, Osborne finds his voice – the characteristic rhythms and cadences through which his later protagonists would channel their passion, their rage and their disgust.

While living on the houseboat with Creighton in 1955, Osborne wrote the play that was to define the era, and which defined him. *Look Back in Anger* was written in response to the advert that the English Stage Company took out in *The Stage*, requesting work from new dramatists. When Devine read the play, he was sufficiently excited to search the writer out; the second volume of Osborne's autobiography, *Almost a Gentleman*, begins with a lively account of Devine's visit to the boat. The play was accepted and produced; Osborne experienced the same, sudden fame that had found Rattigan after *French without Tears*; and, rather ironically, a play which draws on some intensely private material (Osborne's memory of his dying father; the tension in his first marriage; his anger and his sense of incipient, all-pervading failure) became one of the key public documents of the age.

Arnold Wesker (1932–58): 'I could add to what was happening'

Arnold Wesker was born in east London in 1932: he was the son of Jewish immigrants – his father was originally from Russia, his mother from Hungary. His parents met at work (both were tailor's machinists: his mother later went on to work as a cook), and, as Wesker notes in his autobiography, both sang together in a socialist Zionist organisation called Poale Zion; as *Chicken Soup with Barley* would suggest, the young Wesker grew up in a family that was both closely embedded in a particular community, and deeply political. Wesker was one of two children (a third child, Mervin, died from meningitis a few weeks after his birth). Wesker's parents did not have a happy marriage; and Wesker remembers being periodically raised, in his early years, by two spinster aunts. Partly, this happened during times when his parents had separated; but it also happened when both his mother and father had to go out to work to support the family. Temperamentally, his father and mother were incompatible; Wesker described the difference between them in a way that indicated their relative places in the society of his childhood: 'My mother was admired, esteemed, [my father] was charming and indulged.'[12]

Wesker's mother – the avowed model for Sarah in *Chicken Soup with Barley* – was a member of the Communist Party, and Wesker grew up in a politically engaged household. More than this, though, the world of the East End was, as Wesker puts it, 'swarming' with life:

> I would love to dwell on this swarming life in the East End, the interaction of groups, the coming together and splintering of political organisations, seeds laid here which sprouted there, the crossing of barriers, the interaction of lives, intellectual and cultural cross-fertilisation. It all fascinates me. Barnardo and Booth began here. The Whitechapel Library and Art Gallery belong in the same period as Toynbee Hall. Jack London [the communist novelist] came to the East End in 1902 and lived in a doss house in Thrawl Street, where Kossoff's the baker baked one of my birthday cakes. On the other side of the road the barber's plank across the chair to make little boys high enough to be reached with scissors. Dora Gaitskell came from those streets to be a Labour prime minister's wife [Wesker is misremembering; her husband – Hugh Gaitskell – was a leader of the opposition in the 1950s]; and Solomon, a pianist; Lew (Lord) Grade grew up in Brick Lane and founded a TV empire – ATV; Sydney (Lord) Bernstein's father owned silent movie houses there; Lionel Bart, Georgia Brown, Bernard Kops ran around in the area. Comedian Bud Flanagan, band leader Joe Loss, the poet Isaac Rosenberg, the painters Mark Gertler and David Bomberg all flowered in that maze of teeming streets.[13]

Wesker is almost exactly Osborne's contemporary; it is interesting to compare this portrait of a culturally rich, thriving environment with the bareness of Osborne's upbringing (even if that bareness is probably exaggerated in Osborne's memory). Wesker grew up in a culture which was both engaged, and which valued learning; Wesker, as he puts it, was 'unschooled', partly because his education was disrupted by the war; the young Weskers, like many of the children of the East End, were evacuated to rural safety (in Wesker's case, this meant Ely and, following that, Buckingham). However, this did not mean that Wesker came to adulthood without any sort of education; he was encouraged to write by one of the teachers at his school, and he read widely and voraciously (in his autobiography, he describes himself as an autodidact; but notes ruefully that he always felt inferior when confronted by those who had gone to university). The family moved from Stepney to a London County Council flat in Hackney in 1942; his father's increasing ill-health meant that Wesker's mother took on an ever greater responsibility for keeping the family going.

Wesker had been involved in amateur dramatics as a teenager (his first attempt at drama, *And After Today*, was written in 1950 for the Query Players, the amateur company with whom he had performed from his mid-teens). When he applied to RADA, he could not take up a place because LCC did not give grants for potential acting students. He was ambitious, though; he already thought of himself as an aspiring writer – he wrote poems and stories, and he had submitted an essay to the *New Statesman* in 1949. For much of the 1950s, Wesker's ambition and his circumstances clashed. He was called up for national service in the RAF in 1950; he found some of the training (in particular bayonet practice) unacceptable:

> The central dramatic moment for me during training was the unacceptable order to snap a bayonet into the end of our rifles and run screaming at a hanging sack of straw. After the stupid bullying, after the pain of marching and marching and about-turning and smashing feet hard on tarmac (I wrote poems about all that, too) I found I couldn't take any more. My being was offended – body, soul and intelligence.[14]

After a confrontation with the squadron leader, during which Wesker was told that if he didn't comply he would face a court-martial (a claim that the older Wesker realised was an empty threat), he complied – taking refuge in the thought that, when he stabbed the target, he was acting his part. While in the RAF, Wesker wrote a series of detailed letters about the experience, with the idea that he could, at some future point, turn them into a novel; they later formed the basis of his 1962 play *Chips with Everything*.

After the end of national service, Wesker took on a number of jobs; he moved to Norfolk, where his sister and her husband had set up a carpentry business, and at various times worked as a farm labourer, a freelance journalist and a kitchen porter. He also reapplied to RADA, but found, for the second time, that he could not get a grant. Over the next few years working in kitchens was to be his main source of employment – after fourteen months working as a porter, he returned to London to work as a pastry cook, and in 1956 he worked in a kitchen in Paris for nine months as a chef. In Norfolk in 1954 he met Doreen Bicker, a Norfolk girl he nicknamed Dusty, and they were married in 1957 (something of the dynamic of their early relationship is caught in *Roots*, whose central character is based on Dusty).

During this time Wesker continued to write; and this period of his life gave him a range of experiences that he mined in the plays from *The Kitchen* onwards. These experiences also, and understandably, influenced Wesker's view of the world. Although he had never followed his mother into the Communist Party (his membership, for a short time, of the Young Communist League was as close as he came) Wesker was a socialist, and his experiences in the 1950s honed and shaped his politics, as they honed and shaped his writing. However, as John Bull notes in the essay on Wesker later in this book, he was never a simple cheerleader for left-wing politics. Rather, his writing was born from a desire to make sense of, and to conduct an argument with, the circumstances in which he had grown up, and the responses of the people he knew to those circumstances. For example, *Chicken Soup with Barley* grew out of political arguments between Wesker (who classed himself, after the Soviet Union's invasion of Hungary, as a disappointed socialist) and his mother:

> My memory of how and why I wrote the play is clear. I had quarrelled with my mother over politics, raging at her continuing adherence to communism. We quarrelled constantly. I'm ashamed to remember how I rarely missed an opportunity to make a sarcastic observation about the misdemeanours of the Soviet Union or its satellites. 'There!' she'd say. 'He's attacking me again. Always criticising me.'[15]

Wesker returned to London from Paris to enter the London School of Film Technique in 1956. He saw *Look Back in Anger* when it toured in 1957:

> The impact cannot be understated [*sic*]. I have no record of a frontline reaction . . . but I remember four things: the energy of the dialogue, and the way it fused to the personality of Jimmy Porter who uttered it; the image of those dead Sunday bells ringing . . .; the ending which I thought at the time to be weak, . . . I've changed my mind since; and an exhilarated feeling that not only was theatre an activity where important things were happening but one where I could add to what was happening . . .[16]

Emboldened by the turn that the theatre was taking, Wesker sent two newly written playtexts – *Chicken Soup with Barley* and *The Kitchen* – to Lindsay Anderson, who was involved both with the London School of Film Technique and the Royal Court. Anderson responded positively to both texts, and showed them to George Devine. As noted in Chapter 1, Devine was wary about staging *Chicken Soup*; but Wesker's work had the voluble support of John Dexter (whom Wesker had met on the CND march to the Aldermaston nuclear base in 1958). Dexter directed many of the premieres of Wesker's work over the next few years. Fittingly, by the end of the decade, Wesker's work was playing on the London stage which seemed designed, more than any other, for his work; and it is a sign of how far things had changed in the decade that, alongside Eliot the already established cultural icon, Rattigan the star of the commercial stage, or even the rep-hardened Osborne, a working-class, Jewish Londoner could have his plays performed on what had become one of the most important stages of the time.

CHAPTER 3
PLAYWRIGHTS AND PLAYS

T. S. ELIOT: PLAYS OF THE 1950S
by Sarah Bay-Cheng

In a letter dated 19 August 1949, T. S. Eliot described his new play to fellow author and sometime playwright Djuna Barnes: '*The Cocktail Party* is the name of it, but that's only what I call it in order to entice the public – the esoteric name is *Upadhammam Samutpada*, but nobody would promote a play with a name like that. Well, we'll see.' Barnes never questioned the meaning of Eliot's 'esoteric' title and he offered no further explanation. To date, no mention of this title appears in criticism of the play (although various accounts cite 'One-Eyed Riley', a bawdy song included in the text, as an earlier title).[2] Given that the relationship between Eliot and Barnes was coloured by his role as her editor and mentor, it is tempting to think that he was simply playing Old Possum to a younger writer. Yet, this seemingly simple statement contains two elements central to understanding Eliot's intentions as a playwright during the 1950s: his deliberate efforts to create a simultaneously popular and poetic theatre, and his appropriation of mythical sources, including Buddhist philosophy and Greek drama as a framework for his theatre.

To understand Eliot's later plays, *The Cocktail Party* (1949), *The Confidential Clerk* (1953) and *The Elder Statesman* (1958), one must assess the unique function of poetry within the plays. As remarked upon by virtually every critic of the plays, Eliot's verse calls attention to its own highly formalised construction, without flagrantly violating a veneer of realism. For critics such as Michael Selmon, such formalised speech is an intentionally self-referential dramatic dialogue that foregrounds language. But others contend that Eliot's poetry is not exclusively verbal. Denis Donoghue, for example, argues that 'The "poetry" of poetic drama is not necessarily or solely a *verbal* construct; it inheres in the structure of the play as a whole.'[3] Particularly in the plays following *The Cocktail Party*, Eliot's director and collaborator E. Martin Browne noted that the 'poetry is not in the words but in the conception and the characterization'.[4] Despite his numerous critical arguments to the contrary, Eliot the playwright did not always believe that language should be the most prominent feature of a theatrical production. In 'Seneca in Elizabethan Tradition' (1927), he argued that the text was merely 'a shorthand . . . a very abbreviated shorthand indeed, for the acted and felt play, which is always *the real thing*',[5] and his attention to rewriting during rehearsals confirms this.[6]

Eliot's mention of the stage as 'the real thing' is deliberately ironic. On the stage, Eliot conflates physical reality – tangible props, actors' bodies and the box set – with spiritual ignorance of the unseen reality, experienced in faith and, potentially, a transcendental death. Poetry, in the form of oral speech, is an ephemeral element of the performance, suggesting a connection between the theatricality of the text and an inaccessible belief in the supernatural, which appears in his last three plays as both Buddhist enlightenment and as Greek dramatic irony. Both the 'mystery' of Buddhist thought and the initially unnoticed Greek allusions fit within Eliot's larger idea of the doubleness of poetic drama. In an early essay on the subject, 'Rhetoric and Poetic Drama' (1919), Eliot wrote that, 'The really fine rhetoric of Shakespeare occurs in situations where a character in the play *sees himself* in a dramatic light'.[7] Later in 'John Marston' (1934), he argued,

> It is possible that what distinguishes poetic drama from prosaic drama is a kind of doubleness in the action, as if it took place on two planes at once . . . In poetic drama a certain apparent irrelevance may be the symptom of this doubleness; or the drama has an under-pattern, less manifest than the theatrical one.[8]

Eliot's poetry, within what appears at first to be a realist, even naturalistic, *mise-en-scène*, highlights the philosophical division that all his characters confront: is the physical world real and finite, or are we merely playing at reality? This perhaps unanswerable question best explains Eliot's purposes in the theatre, and might further explain why a poet who readily embraced the solitary dictates of high modernism might turn to the popular stage. Eliot divides the theatrical space into two layers, the visible theatrical action and the poetic 'under-pattern'. For Eliot, then, realism in the theatre is necessary, but only as an illusion to be seen through. The social mechanics of the British drawing room are created for the audience, if not the characters, to transcend. To this end, nearly all of Eliot's characters become obsessed with their own sense of themselves as actors. In an early draft version of *The Confidential Clerk*, for example, the titular character explains his sense of displacement is akin to that of 'an actor who's walked on to the stage / And finds that he is in another theatre . . . You see, I haven't learned the words for my present part.'[9]

If Eliot's stage presents the world of illusion as theatrical reality, his language further disrupts the assumptions of realism, inviting the audience to transcend their own fantasies. The verse in his 1950s plays heightens not merely the audience's awareness of language, but their awareness of the world as illusory. This critique of the modern world as illusory continues themes expressed in Eliot's earlier poetry (*Prufrock* and *The Waste Land*) but the fact that he now treats this material dramatically renders the theme more tangible. In all three of the late plays, the theatre itself becomes a place where the illusions of social behaviour and identity, so often taken for reality, are exposed as empty performances.

By engaging with the popular stage, Eliot contradicts much of the received wisdom regarding his persona as a writer. Though often overlooked, Eliot's desire successfully to 'entice the public' is consistent with nearly all of his writings on theatre, which consistently favour the popular or lowbrow, such as the music hall, alongside Shakespeare, whom he saw both as an artistic genius and popular writer. As he wrote in 'The Possibility of a Poetic Drama' (1922), 'The Elizabethan drama was aimed at a public which wanted *entertainment* of a crude sort, but would stand a good deal of poetry; our problem should be to take a form of entertainment, and subject it to the process which would leave it a form of art'.[10]

The Cocktail Party

Eliot's use of the theatre as the realm of mistaken perceptions is perhaps clearest and most effectively conveyed in the first of his late comedies. It is clear that the Eliot, who renamed 'He Do the Police in Different Voices', 'Wanna Go Home Baby?' and 'All Aboard for Natchez, Cairo, and St. Louis' as *The Waste Land, Sweeney Agonistes* and *Ash-Wednesday*, had clearly reversed himself when he turned 'Upadhammam Samutpada' into *The Cocktail Party*. As he told Alan Downer in 1949, he intended to write plays 'until I can convince people that I know how to write a popular play'.[11]

By any objective standard, *The Cocktail Party* accomplished just that, at least at the time of its first production. Though a significant proportion of the play's critics reacted negatively to Eliot's work in the theatre, the play ran successfully both on Broadway and in the West End, won the Tony Award for Best Play in 1950, and appeared on the *New York Times* bestseller list. Perhaps more importantly, Eliot himself believed that he had solved the 'problem' of poetic drama. In his lecture 'Poetry and Drama' (published 1951), Eliot wrote that whereas *Murder in the Cathedral* (1934) was the work of a 'beginner' and *The Family Reunion* (1939) was 'defective', *The Cocktail Party* followed 'the aesthetic rule to avoid poetry which could not stand the test of strict dramatic utility'.[12]

Yet the play itself seemingly contradicts his claim. The characters in the play do very little, and almost nothing happens on stage. The play is set in two locations: the living room of Edward and Lavinia; and the office of Sir Henry Harcourt-Reilly, a kind of spiritual guide and psychotherapist. Such locales invite endless conversations that do little either to develop the characters, or to create dramatic action. Indeed, the characters are tormented by this lack of action. As Edward says, 'I see that my life was determined long ago / And that the struggle to escape from it / Is only a make-believe, a pretence'.[13] This lack of action prompted some critics to denounce the play as merely literature (and bad literature at that) on stage. Alan Dent wrote in 1950: 'The critic in me is alarmed that a play so deplorably weak in stagecraft should be hailed as a masterpiece.'[14]

Eliot's original 'esoteric' title suggests that the reason for the lack of overt action might contradict the received wisdom that the play is a Christian tale of conversion, filtered through Euripides' *Alcestis*. 'Upadhammam Samutpada' roughly translates as 'the coming into existence of the false law or doctrine'.[15] Upa typically refers to the lesser or the younger, while Dhamma (also translated as Dharma) is a multivalent term referring to law, religion, morality and duty, among many others. According to Buddhist tradition, Dhamma is predominantly a guide to the transformation by which a person lets go of the limiting delusions that cause attachment to the physical world (and thus suffering), thereby achieving enlightenment, or Nibbāna (Nirvāna). Henry Clarke Warren (Eliot's professor at Harvard) translated Dhamma as 'any established law, condition, or fact, either of nature or of human institutions. It is the word I render by Doctrine when it signifies the Buddha's teachings.'[16] Samutpada means sam (together)-ut (up)-pada (to be, become), thus 'to come into existence together'. Combined, the full translation suggests the coming into existence of the lesser, or false doctrine.

Since its first production, *The Cocktail Party* has been read in the light of Eliot's conversion and his early religious drama. William Arrowsmith carefully outlines the Christian allusions throughout the play, and Christopher Innes in *Modern British Drama: The Twentieth Century* subtitles the section on Eliot 'the drama of conversion'.[17] Innes argues that Eliot's drama was an extension of his critique of modern culture as expressed in poems like *The Waste Land*, and the 'practical expression of his Christian ideal of communion, extending outward in performance to create a community'.[18] Eliot himself suggested Greek myth as his source when he announced in his lecture 'Poetry and Drama' that 'no one of my acquaintance (and no dramatic critics) recognized the source of my story in the *Alcestis* of Euripides'.[19]

The Cocktail Party itself is fairly straightforward; a drawing-room comedy written in blank verse. As Clive Barnes wrote, 'the verse is deliberately flattened into the most prosaic poetry a great poet ever wrote'.[20] It opens in the London flat of Edward and Lavinia Chamberlayne, during a floundering cocktail party. Over the course of the first Act, the characters' rather petty conflicts are slowly revealed. Just before the party, Lavinia has apparently left Edward, and we see Edward's lame attempts to get rid of his guests before they discover the true reason for Lavinia's absence. Though the party eventually ends, the guests return one by one for intimate conversations with Edward. Through these conversations, we learn that Edward has just broken off his affair with the young Celia Coplestone and that she has broken the heart of equally young Peter Quilpe, who himself was also having an affair with the now absent Lavinia. Also in attendance are the Unidentified Guest – who mysteriously knows the location of Lavinia and later reveals himself to be her psychotherapist – and two friends, Julia Shuttlethwaite and Alexander MacColgie Gibbs, both of whom eagerly attempt to take care of the neglected Edward much against his will.

Much of the plot is simplistic at best. In the first Act, Edward bemoans the loss of his wife, only to regret her return in Act Two. Lavinia and Edward again part following their reunion, but are rather antagonistically reconciled by Sir Henry Harcourt-Reilly by the end of the second Act. Act Three returns the characters to the Chamburlaynes' flat two years later, more or less as each was before, but no more resigned to their fate. Even the conversation has not evolved. The play opens with Alex telling a story about his adventures with the Maharaja; in the third Act he tells a similar story about Celia's death in Kinkanja. In addition to the obvious rhyme and the orientalist 'foreign' sound of the subject, Alex also tells his stories in the same pattern. On both occasions he repeats to Julia that 'There are no tigers', an odd explanation since he claims never to have mentioned them. Despite Alex's claim in Act One that 'I never tell the same story twice' (p. 297), nearly all of his stories are indistinguishable, and almost all concern his adventures in what Julia calls a 'strange place' (p. 373). Fitting for a cocktail party that seems to go on indefinitely, all of Alex's stories are incomplete. In a rare moment of rhyme, Julia nearly repeats herself – 'It's such a nice party, I hate to leave it / It's such a nice party, I'd like to repeat it' (p. 302). Moreover, the dialogue of the play is full of internal repetitions; Edward offers whisky to the Unidentified Guest three times in response to repeated requests for gin. The exception is Celia, who in the second Act actively breaks the cycle of repetition and, consequently, is the only character not to return in Act Three.

In Act Two, the Uninvited Guest re-emerges as Sir Henry Harcourt-Reilly. He presides over two therapeutic meetings, the first with Lavinia and Edward, and the second with Celia. It is in this second meeting that the tenor of the play changes considerably. Up until now, the characters have appeared almost universally foolish, complaining of petty problems and involved in trivial relationships. Celia, however, complains that her world has become an illusion, and that this sense of unreality has become intolerable:

> For what happened is remembered like a dream
> In which one is exalted by intensity of loving . . .
> And if all that is meaningless, I want to be cured
> Of a craving for something I cannot find
> And of the shame of never finding it. (p. 363)

Celia has most often been interpreted as a Christian martyr, but her dramatic journey more closely follows the path to Buddhist enlightenment. Celia's desire to be cured of her romantic 'cravings' is consistent with the transcendence of suffering according to the four noble truths of Buddhism: suffering is universal; its cause is desire; when desire ceases, suffering ceases; and suffering ceases by following the eight-fold path.

If Celia follows the path of a Buddhist saint, then Edward, Lavinia and Peter Quilpe demonstrate an attachment to delusion and frustrated craving that takes them away from the eight-fold path. Sir Reilly attempts to enlighten Edward by convincing him to let go of his wife, repeating the Buddha's own allegory, that to give up attachment to desire is to be 'like a man who has given up his wife'.[21] When Edward complains that Reilly has left him in the dark, Reilly again tries to lead him to the paradoxical realisation that by admitting he knows nothing, he will gain knowledge: 'There is no purpose in remaining in the dark / Except long enough to clear from the mind / The illusion of having ever been in the light' (p. 309). But Reilly fails, and Edward agrees to the conditions by which Lavinia will return.

Most scholars read the return of Lavinia, and Reilly's effort to 'bring someone back from the dead' (p. 329) as paralleling Euripides' *Alcestis* (in which Admetus loses his wife and has her restored to him by Heracles). But the Alcestis myth is not the only myth at work here. When Edward objects to Reilly's characterisation of his wife as returning from the dead (she has, he argues, been gone for only one day), Reilly responds, 'we die to each other daily. / What we know of other people / Is only our memory of the moments / During which we know them. And they have changed since them' (p. 329). Compare this with Harvey's description of rebirth and karma, in which people 'are constantly changing, "reborn" as a "different" person according to our mood, the task we are involved in, or the people we are relating to'.[22] Edward and Lavinia's relationship is one of repetitive ignorance; they are reborn to each other, but each time they are unchanged.

Although hardly an ideal relationship, at least one can admit that the Chamberlaynes have tried to change, which is more than can be said for Peter Quilpe, literally the 'whelp' of the play. Whereas Celia is determined to see through the illusions of the world, Peter's goal is to re-create the world as illusion. Peter returns in Act Three as a location scout in search of the 'most decayed noble mansion in England' and 'typically English faces' (p. 377). His task confuses those at the cocktail reunion, especially Julia, who asks, 'If you're taking Boltwell [mansion] to California / Why can't you take me?' (p. 379). Peter tries to explain that the actual manor house will not be moved, but merely re-created, and that the English faces he is sent to find will be re-created by American actors. At best, Peter recognises his own futility, but to a lesser degree than the other characters. Whereas Celia is overwhelmed by the illusions of the world, and Edward frustrated by his own metaphysical inaction, Peter bemoans his lack of career success: 'I thought I had ideas to make a revolution / In the cinema, that no one could ignore – / But here I am, making a second-rate film!' (p. 382).

This view of the cinema is consistent with some of Eliot's own stated views on film, which he attacked in his 'Religious Drama: Mediæval and Modern' (1937): 'Mechanisation comes to kill local life: with the universal picture palace, you may travel the world over and be unable to avoid Shirley Temple.'[23] But Eliot's condemnation is not total. Surprisingly, he seems to suggest that the cinema may in fact be the key to Peter's enlightenment. As Julia says, 'You have learned to look at people, Peter, / When you looked at them with an eye for the films: / That is, when you're not concerned with yourself / But just being an eye' (p. 383). This loss of ego (an 'eye' for an 'I') seemingly stems from the Buddhist teaching of the 'not-self', a state in which 'a person comes to see *everything*, all *dhammas*, as not-self, thereby destroying all attachment and attaining *Nibbāna*'.[24] Such sight, becoming simply an eye, is valued throughout the play (in the name One-Eyed Reilly (taken from the song he sings), and Julia's pair of glasses with one lens missing). That Peter, as a filmmaker, should inherit this one-eyed insight is surprising, but logical. When looking through the camera, the filmmaker closes his extra eye, becoming one-eyed. The emphasis on the eye may further relate to the concept of the 'Dhamma-eye', with which the Buddhist sees beyond the illusion of the material world.

But Peter, despite his one-eyed view, gains no such enlightenment. Like the habitual film viewer, he remains in the dark, unaware even of his own ignorance. After his initial reaction to Celia's death, Peter remains silent for the remainder of the play, saying only brief goodbyes at the end. Eliot once claimed that Act Three could be seen as an epilogue to the play, and the last few moments certainly suggest this. Celia, the character most likely to achieve enlightenment, is absent, and the couple that might have been reborn demonstrates in the final moments that little, if anything, has changed. At the end, Edward cannot even pay Lavinia a satisfactory compliment. As if to mock their attempted resolution, the play ends with a beginning:

Edward   And now for the party.

Lavinia   Now for the party.

Edward   It will soon be over.

Lavinia   I wish it would begin.

Edward   There's the doorbell.

Lavinia   Oh, I'm glad. It's begun. (p. 387)

While the verse structure here might effectively connect Lavinia and Edward, Eliot has clipped the lines, so that the echo deadens the verse line. The caesura of the complete line (split between the two characters) dramatises the gulf between them. These are not lovers who finish each other's sentences, but emotional strangers, who endlessly repeat their empty exchanges, unable to see past them or to invent new ones.

To be sure, Eliot did not rely exclusively on the text's hidden religious references. Throughout the play, characters constantly negotiate and debate the 'real'. Sir Reilly attempts to help Edward learn what he 'really' is (p. 307); Peter tells Edward that he felt something 'real' with Celia but still wonders, 'What is the reality / Of experience between two unreal people' (p. 316); and Celia confesses to Edward that her dreams were better than reality, and 'if this is reality, it is very like a dream' (p. 324). Most characters lie, but this becomes an essential part of their interaction. As Lavinia tells Edward in a line highly reminiscent of Oscar Wilde, 'Nothing less than the truth could deceive Julia' (p. 337). People are described as projections (pp. 327, 342, 359) and their realness is constantly debated. Katherine Worth observes that 'Eliot's central characters suffer from a troubling sense of division between their real and their active selves'.[25] Given the constant lying, performing and pretending throughout the play, as well as Eliot's awareness of the doubleness of character and actor, it is difficult to discern what is real and what is merely performance. If the appearance of reality itself is an illusion, then to search a fictional play for a real self would be a symptom of the problem Eliot illuminates. In the theatre, every person on stage is a created character, made real in the actor's body, but having no other existence. The theatre suspends reality, and repeats its events in nightly performances, yet adopts the material substance of reality to create the theatrical illusion.

Eliot is no doubt aware of these semantic problems within theatrical representations, since he repeatedly juxtaposes the rhetoric of the real against self-reflexive comments on the theatre. The language of actors, roles and performances creates a steady current throughout the text. In addition to Peter's profession and Reilly's posing as an unknown stranger, Julia is identified as a mimic (p. 298), Edward is surrounded by actors (p. 307), Celia fades from Peter 'like a film effect'

(p. 315), and Lavinia tells Edward to find himself another part to play (p. 340), while he bemoans the role he feels Lavinia has imposed upon him (p. 349). To be liberated or enlightened, is to be beyond the realm of performance – as Julia calls it, to become 'transhumanised' (p. 367). At best, Edward and Lavinia can pretend to be comfortable in their roles (p. 367), while Celia has the opportunity to see beyond her previous roles and, most significantly, to act *outside the theatre*. It is surely no coincidence that Celia's death occurs off stage and between the Acts, well beyond the theatre space. She transcends the performance (even if the audience does not), and therefore concludes the play as a memory, an illusion. In a rare moment of insight, Lavinia recognises that Peter's memory of Celia is not authentic, but rather just an image (p. 382), and her observation might just as well apply to any sitting in the audience, for in fact, there never was a Celia, only an actress creating the image of the character.

Eliot's theatrical manipulations are not unique to *The Cocktail Party*. In *The Family Reunion*, he describes the uncomfortable relationship among the family members 'Like amateur actors in a dream where the curtain rises, / to find themselves dressed for a different play, or having rehearsed the wrong parts' (p. 231). In *Murder in the Cathedral*, Eliot repeatedly breaks the fourth wall of the performance, by having both Becket and the knights directly address the audience. But in *The Cocktail Party*, the metaphor of the theatre is critical to the dramatic action. In *The Cocktail Party*, the line between reality and representation is intentionally blurred, and character conflicts are almost always depicted in theatrical terms. Hugh Kenner in his *The Invisible Poet* summarised Eliot's dramatic method thus: 'we see only what is normally seen, and what is normally seen is an invention'.[26] In other words, while we may perceive reality in Eliot's theatre, these perceptions can only be illusions.

The Confidential Clerk

Perhaps emboldened by the success of *The Cocktail Party*, Eliot pursued links between the secular and the sublime in his next play,

The Confidential Clerk (1953). Eliot delivered this play to Browne not as notes (as with his previous play) but as a complete play draft, which Browne understood to reflect 'Eliot's greater self-confidence as a playwright, and also is conditioned by the fact that such a plot as he has chosen must be worked out to the end by a single mind'.[27] Eliot based *The Confidential Clerk* on Euripides' *Ion* (c. 414–12 BCE), a story of mistaken identity, repeated misidentifications and the ultimate reunion with a lost son. Euripides' play follows Apollo's rape of Creusa and her failed attempt to murder the resulting infant, Ion. Taken from his mother and raised in secret by the Pythian Priestess, Ion and Creusa are reunited many years later only to again mis-recognise each other. Adding to their confusion, Creusa's husband, Xuthus, receives a false prophecy and believes that the adult Ion is his own lost son. Both Ion and Xuthus believe in the prophecy, but jointly agree to keep it a secret. When a servant reveals this secret, Creusa attempts to murder Ion, only to fail again. Ion, in turn, vengefully pursues Creusa, who hides from him in the temple. It is there that Creusa and Ion discover the clues to their true relationship, confirmed by the revelations of Athena. They are happily united at the conclusion.

Eliot was not the first modernist poet to adapt this play; but whereas H.D. (the pen name of the American poet Hilda Doolittle) imagined Euripides' play as a modern tragedy suffused with feminist and maternal anxiety, Eliot recasts the play as a comedy. The central character, rather than the vengeful Creusa, is the mildly insulting Lady Elizabeth Mulhammer. Rather like Lady Bracknell in Wilde's *The Importance of Being Earnest* (1895), we are warned about Lady Elizabeth's temperament throughout the first scene. Sir Claude prepares his retiring secretary Eggerson for the appearance of Colby Simpkins, the confidential clerk (that is, a private secretary) of the title, and a man Sir Claude believes to be his long-lost son. Concerned that Lady Elizabeth might not accept Colby because of grief over her own missing child, the men – Sir Claude, Eggerson and eventually Simpkins as well – agree to keep Simpkins's true identity a secret until Lady Elizabeth can be brought around to the idea of Sir Claude's having a son.

When she appears on stage, however, Lady Elizabeth exhibits none of the qualities one might assume from the warning tones of the opening scene. She exhibits only relatively minor flaws: she mistakes the name of her husband's new secretary, calling him Mr Colby instead of Mr Simpkins, and threatens merely to bore him: 'I must explain to you, Mr Colby / That I am to share you with my husband. / You shall have tea with me tomorrow, / And then I shall tell you about my committees.'[28] Indeed, she is more akin to Miss Prism than Lady Bracknell; Lady Elizabeth has not simply lost her child, she has, as Sir Claude reports, 'mislaid' it. Even Eliot's language seems to echo the easy wit of Wilde's play. Sir Claude assures Simpkins that 'She has always lived in a world of make-believe, / And the best one can do is to guide her delusions / In the right direction' (p. 43). Like the characters of *The Cocktail Party*, however, Lady Elizabeth is not the only one living in a world of delusions.

Sir Claude's secret son is only the first of many secrets. Lucasta Angel, the fiancée of Sir Claude's business colleague B. Kaghan, is described as Sir Claude's ward and is rumoured to be his mistress, although she is in fact his illegitimate daughter. In the midst of an intimate scene at Simpkins's flat, Lucasta reveals her true relationship with Sir Claude, only to be disappointed when Simpkins reacts with shock at the revelation that she is his sister. Keeping his promise to conceal his own connection to Sir Claude, Simpkins admits only that his reaction is purely personal. Lucasta responds, 'I may be a bastard, but I have some self-respect' (p. 74) and returns to Kaghan. When Lady Elizabeth finally learns about Colby's adoptive family, she confirms Sir Claude's prediction, believing that he is her lost son. Colby's adoptive aunt, Mrs Guzzard, finally arrives in Act III to reveal that Lady Elizabeth's mislaid son Barnabas was raised by the Kaghan family and now goes by the name, B. Kaghan, who is engaged to Lucasta. Mrs Guzzard also confesses that Colby Simpkins is her own son. Because of her financial difficulties, Mrs Guzzard allowed Sir Claude to believe that Simpkins was his child, when in fact, both his unborn child and the mother, Mrs Guzzard's sister, died before childbirth.

With all the relationships now revealed, Simpkins follows Celia's path (although without the clear Buddhist references), choosing to have no family and to live without any pretence. Believing that Sir Claude will always regard him as a son, Simpkins agrees to renounce his position as clerk to become a parish organist, like his biological father. The play ends by renouncing deception. Colby leaves in search of his true calling, Mrs Guzzard returns to her home, while the remaining family members prepare for Kaghan and Lucasta's impending wedding and the familial reconciliations-cum-introductions. In the closing scene, Simpkins reveals what may be the play's intention: 'Now that I've abandoned *my* illusions and ambitions / All that's left is love' (p. 154), a theme Eliot would return to in *The Elder Statesman*.

As with *The Cocktail Party*, criticism has focused on the play's Christian themes. Lyndall Gordon argues that Colby's identity as an orphan allows him to reject the material concerns of family and individual desires in favour of a higher calling: 'He is a man in search of identity, abjuring father, mother, and the inviting Lucasta, so that he might fulfill a devotion to God alone.'[29] While Colby is remarkably similar in this aspect to *The Cocktail Party*'s Celia, Gordon nevertheless notes, 'None of Eliot's prospective saints is quite as humble as this second-rate organist whose very name, Simpkins, proclaims his nonidentity. To be God's instrument one must become nothing.'[30] Carol H. Smith also sees the work as a product of Eliot's spiritual message. 'He used the theme of the foundling child to express the Christian implications of the search for identity by insisting that discovering one's identity depends on discovering one's self to be a child of the heavenly Father.'[31] Colby's exit to pursue a career as an organist in Eggerson's church would seem to support this, as does the promise of familial reunion and new life in the marriage of Lucasta and Kaghan. Joyce M. Holland highlighted the reference to B. Kaghan's Christian name, Barnabas, the 'child of consolation' as indicative of a deeper meaning in the play. Juxtaposing Simpkins as a 'son of man' with Kaghan as the son of Lady Elizabeth, that is, a son of woman, Holland[32] argues that Eliot's plays map the creation of explicitly Christian communities. More recently, Carol H. Smith argues that 'the plays became for Eliot a public form in which to present, below the surface for those who could read it, a spiritual journey that he believed to be the defining meaning of his life'.[33]

This was also the widely accepted view at the time of the play's premiere. The director and Eliot's collaborator, E. Martin Browne, noted the trend. As he recollects in *The Making of T. S. Eliot's Plays*, *The Confidential Clerk* received a thorough Christian analysis when it played in Boston prior to its appearance on Broadway in 1954. According to Browne, a Harvard undergraduate student 'found the most elaborate Christian symbolism' in the play.[34] Browne notes that this became a dominant theme among the play's American reviews; he cites a review in the *Saturday Review* which saw 'obvious Trinitarian significance in Mr. Eliot's new work. According to them Act One is the Father, Act Two the Son, Act Three the Holy Ghost.'[35]

However, Browne, somewhat surprisingly, attributed this critical analysis not to Eliot's true intentions, nor to the play itself, but rather to what Browne characterised as 'the game of hunt-the-symbol' so 'dear to Americans'.[36] Browne suggested that Eliot's plays both contained and eluded such an analysis. Much in *The Confidential Clerk* would seem to suggest the desire for an elusive truth about the self, seen by Walter Kerr as a 'curious double image, like a Sunday comic strip in which the colours have slipped'.[37] Similarly, R. T. Davies argues in his 1953 review that 'No one should feel he is being got at, for at no point is the play in any respect a piece of Christian propaganda'.[38]

Contemporary critics have tended to cast *The Confidential Clerk* in more humanist terms. Robert A. Colby, for example, suggests that the play can be understood as a kind of social commentary, 'dramatizing the larger issue of alienation and kinship among human beings in general',[39] and Jeffrey M. Perl notes that the play can be understood as an exploration of group psychology in which Eliot staged ambivalence sequentially. Specifically, Perl notes that, 'the conflicting wishes of characters are all granted but, given the impossibility of doing so simultaneously, the wishes are granted in succession'.[40] For Perl, Eliot's doubleness in *The Confidential Clerk* is not to be found between the material and the spiritual, but within the divided experience of life itself. Christopher Innes, however, suggests that the mythic sources of Eliot's later plays had become totally subsumed by the naturalism of their construction: 'Eliot uses the stories of Oedipus or Orestes as analogues for a supernatural order unrecognized by the present.' Innes concludes that because these sources become completely 'integrated with the modern surface, in these last two plays the mythical level itself becomes unrecognizable'.[41]

If there is a link between *The Cocktail Party* and *The Confidential Clerk*, it is Eliot's repeated references to the theatre, illusions and play-acting as analogues for modern living. Lady Elizabeth lives in a world of illusions, but Sir Claude also longs for 'a world where the form is the reality, / Of which the substantial is only a shadow' (p. 47). In an earlier draft of the play, Simpkins described himself in explicitly theatrical terms, noting his failure to perform the role assigned to him: 'I'm like an actor who's walked on to the stage / And finds that he is in another theatre, / With a different setting and a different company / And a different play.'[42] As in *The Cocktail Party*, the world of illusion is often mistaken for reality. Sir Claude notes that 'make-believing makes it real' (p. 47) and Lucasta accuses Simpkins of living in an 'inner world – a world that's more real' (p. 63). As with Celia, who longs for something truer and less fantastic than the daily delusions of living, Colby Simpkins insists on clear boundaries between the realm of fantasy and reality, admitting that 'One can live on a fiction – but not on such a mixture / of fiction and fact' (p. 100).

Some of these references, no doubt, confirm Christian readings of the play. Sir Claude is a frustrated potter who attempts to create a son, an act akin to God's creation of Adam (whose Hebrew name means dirt or clay). Certainly, a garden theme runs through the play, both in Eggerson's romantic view of country life and Simpkins's confession, 'If I were religious, God would walk in my garden / And that would make the world outside it real / And acceptable, I think' (p. 65). The conclusion suggests a slippage between reality and fantasy, but this movement is animated not by God but by the desires of each character. Lady Elizabeth finds her son, Sir Claude confirms the existence of his son, only to have Simpkins then realise *his* desire to have no parents at all. This confusion of fantasy and fact, illusion and reality, stage realism and the reality outside the theatre may also suggests a link between Eliot's late plays and the more radical British drama to follow.

Eliot wrote in his introduction to S. L. Bethell's *Shakespeare and the Popular Dramatic Tradition* (1944), 'there is no illusion of actual life; but the audience are vividly aware of acting in progress, and the communication, through their cooperative good will, a work of dramatic art. If the one type of production is more realistic, the other is essentially more real.'[43] In response, Eric Salmon argues that the last three plays 'outwardly pretended to be drawing-room comedies . . . but inwardly wished themselves other and better'.[44] In his 1976 essay, Richard L. Homan makes an even more explicit claim: that Eliot's play as written radically altered the structure of Aristotelian causality such that *The Confidential Clerk* became a leading example of 'a truly antinaturalistic dramaturgy' more commonly associated with Harold Pinter.[45] Homan argues that Eliot's ending to the play engages a style akin to Eugene Ionesco's coincidental, existential joke between Mr and Mrs Martin (a couple who meet each other as if for the first time, only to discover through a series of truly marvellous coincidences that they share the same address, home and marriage bed) than to a Wildeian comedic resolution. Eliot replaces the neat reversals that bring *The Importance of Being Earnest* to a conclusion with a series of half-finishes and rather lame conclusions. B. Kaghan confesses that both he and Lucasta wish to be meaningful to Sir Claude and his wife. He concludes, oddly, 'And we'd take the responsibility of meaning it' (p. 59). What exactly does Kaghan mean? He appears to suggest that he and Lucasta will not only attempt to forge an emotional bond with their newly discovered biological parents but also that he and Lucasta will take the responsibility for determining what that bond will mean *to Sir Claude and Lady Elizabeth*. The play implies that all meanings in the play are not based on observations, empirical evidence, or what Simpkins calls 'a dead fact', but rather on the construction of reality by the characters themselves.

This emphasis on living fantasy over dead fact violates not only the causal structure of naturalism but also its positivism, and the systematic observational methods of psychology, sociology and anthropology. Eliot fundamentally violates both his play's comic-cum-realist veneer and its classical source material. Unlike *The Cocktail Party*, which suggests a hidden metaphysical reality beneath the façade of the stage illusion, *The Confidential Clerk* offers a world in which reality exists only in so far as those who live in it construct it. As Simpkins says of Lucasta's impression, 'You preferred it be one of your own creation / Rather than wait to see what happened' (p. 60). This is remarkably similar to Pinter's *The Homecoming*, as when Lenny describes his brutal beating of a prostitute. When Ruth, his brother's new wife asks, 'How did you know she was diseased,' Lenny replies, 'How did I know? / *Pause.* / I decided she was.'[46] The extended family of *The Confidential Clerk* does not discover life's deeper meanings; they determine them, or as Sir Claude accuses Mrs Guzzard, 'you are inventing this fiction / In response to what Colby said he wanted' (p. 149). This emphasis on reality as wilful construction is further reinforced in the play's repeated emphasis on names. Simpkins insists on referring to everyone by their formal titles, while Lady Elizabeth insists on calling people as she prefers, even inaccurately. It is only when she discovers that Barnabas Kaghan is her son that she (with some difficulty) agrees to call him by his chosen name, 'B', perhaps in recognition of his personally constructed self. As Eliot noted in an early draft, Sir Claude '*lived* himself into a role – squeezed himself into it with an effort'.[47] In this context, the fundamental question of the play is not, as some critics have suggested, 'Who am I?' but rather, 'Who do I want to be?'

This is a remarkable and almost unnoticed shift in Eliot's dramaturgy. Critics have noted the lack of overt poetry in his last two plays; even Browne observed that in *The Confidential Clerk* 'poetry is not in the words but in the conception and the characterization'.[48] Although this shift has been attributed to Eliot's desire to reach a wider audience, we might also see this change in language linked directly to his subject matter. If Eliot had wanted the audience to find the deeper meanings beneath the surface of *The Cocktail Party* and laid his poetry very subtly as his so-called 'under-pattern', then the lack of poetry in *The Confidential Clerk* reveals a distinct and very different sort of discovery for an audience. For the viewer looking for deeper meanings, this play offers nothing but its own emptiness: a flat, theatrical construction with little meaning other than what the audience constructs within the space of the play itself. This shift, akin to the ontological dramatic ruminations of Pinter and Beckett, suggests a continuum from Eliot's verse plays and the drama that follow. Eliot's penultimate play dramatises the condition of people who continue on without faith, without spiritual realisations and without further purpose. They construct their identities, forge relations among each other and attempt to create meanings from the superficial façade. However, like his lack of verse, Eliot's constructions are empty signs without any deeper, hidden meanings. Like the play's first American critics Eliot's own characters play hunt-the-symbol – but in vain.

The Elder Statesman

Set again among the lives of England's upper classes, *The Elder Statesman* in its earliest versions followed the spiritual ambitions of those, like Celia in *The Cocktail Party* and Colby Simpkins in *The Confidential Clerk*, who felt themselves out of place among the ordinary, material concerns of life. As Browne reports, Eliot had chosen *Oedipus at Colonus* as the model for 'providing one way of completing Harry's story [from *The Family Reunion*]'.[49] The choice of Sophocles' final play in his own familial trilogy – including *Oedipus Tyrranos* and *Antigone* – would suggest further the culmination of the spiritual and philosophical debates of Eliot's last three plays. Both plays focus on a central character at the end of his life, attempting reconciliation with their pasts.

In *Oedipus at Colonus* the blind, exiled King Oedipus arrives in a sacred grove where he is destined to die. Oedipus comes to terms with his tragic destiny and hears prophesised the unhappy fates of his children: his sons are warring against each other for control of Thebes and his daughters, devoted to Oedipus, will ultimately be punished for disobeying Creon. Substituting philosophical discussion for any real action, *Oedipus at Colonus* ends when Oedipus gains the strength to meet his death, described thus: 'We couldn't see the man – he was gone – nowhere! And the king [Theseus], alone, shielding his eyes, both hands spread out against his face as if – some terrible wonder flashed before his eyes and he, he could not bear to look.'[50] This moment is recognisable in Eliot's version. Reconciled with his daughter Monica and son Michael, Lord Claverton (the elder statesman of the title) leaves similarly unseen. As Monica's fiancé, Charles, observes, 'It's as if he had passed through some door unseen by us / And had turned and was looking back at us / With a glance of farewell.'[51]

In addition to again adapting a poetic play from a Greek model, Eliot also continues his dramatic obsession with role-playing, acting and multiple identities. Lord Claverton, for example, was originally Richard Ferry (also known as Dick Ferry), who took his wife's name, becoming first Mr Richard Claverton-Ferry and eventually Lord Claverton. Two characters emerge from his past, possessing very different names and identities: one, Federico Gomez, a respectable businessman from San Marco, was formerly Fred Culverwell, Claverton's Oxford classmate; and the other, Mrs John Carghill, formerly the actress known as Maisie Montjoy, actually named Maisie Batterson, was the young Richard Ferry's lover. Even the convalescent hospital where they meet is referred to as the 'hotel' Bagley Court, and the matron in charge insists that she too be called by a different name. The main plot recounts Lord Claverton's past mistakes, but unlike Oedipus, these are minor, even trivial affairs. After a romantic relationship with Maisie Batterson, Claverton had to pay damage for 'breach of promise' (p. 67). As Mrs. Carghill acknowledges, 'Men live by forgetting – women live on memories' (p. 66). But it is not only women. Gomez too returns to remind Claverton of the young Culverwell, who was allowed to take the blame when Ferry and Culverwell's car ran over an old man in the road. Claverton suspects them both of blackmail, but both Carghill and Gomez reveal that they want nothing more than to spend time with him. When Gomez becomes the newest resident at Bagley Court, it appears that Claverton has wandered into a farce akin to Sartre's *No Exit*, where hell is the people you used to know.

The perceived threats, however, are minor. The man in the road from young Ferry's accident was already dead and it is unclear what damage Mrs Carghill can do now that Claverton has retired from public life. Although it is tempting to think that Eliot identified with the ageing lord, both Carghill and Gomez are far more appealing than the stiff, immovable Claverton. Carghill is both charming and harmless and Gomez offers Claverton no real offence. The real consequences of Claverton's life may be seen in his impact upon his children, but these are not Oedipus' fateful burdens. Claverton's daughter, Monica, is happily engaged. His son, Michael, burdened by the expectations of his father, has had minor problems with schools and jobs and now longs to create a new identity away from his father. Following Gomez and encouraged by Mrs Carghill, Michael eventually leaves England for some kind of (undefined) work in San Marco. His choice is briefly seen as an existential threat: Claverton calls it 'a kind of suicide' (p. 117); and Monica, Claverton's daughter, asks her brother, 'But who will you be / When I see you again?' (p. 122). But the play makes clear the possible consequences are minor. Monica's fiancé, Charles, confirms that if anything happens, 'We shall be ready to welcome him / And give all the aid we can' (p. 127) and given Michael's difficulties in London and with his father, we are likely to agree with Mrs Carghill when she notes that 'A parent isn't always the right person, Richard, / to solve a son's problems' (p. 124). Compared with Oedipus, who must ruminate over a lifetime of patricide, incest, betrayal, the impending destruction of his adopted city and the death of his children, Claverton's reflections are petty. The only real consequence is that Claverton concludes the play more or less resolved: 'I feel at peace now. / It is the peace that ensues upon contrition / When contrition ensues upon knowledge of the truth' (p. 127). This is not an Oedipal catharsis, but an ordinary man's resigned acceptance.

Leo Aylen observes that in contrast to the 'ferocious pessimism of Sophocles, Eliot gives an atmosphere of reconciliation and peace',[52] Anthony S. Abbott calls the play 'a world without saints' with its central character 'an everyman',[53] and David E. Jones argues that the play differs from Eliot's others because 'there is no suggestion that the hero has an exceptional spiritual destiny'.[54] Among the earliest reviews in 1958, the critic for *Time* warned that 'To those who think of T. S. Eliot as clever, cynical, despairing, and enigmatic, his newest play . . . will seem disappointingly simple and much too full of the milk of human kindness'.[55] And certainly some were disappointed. As Kenneth Tynan wrote in his review, 'A new simplicity has certainly entered his style, but so has simplicity's half-wit brother, banality'.[56] More recent criticism has hardly been more favourable. Robin Grove accuses Eliot of ignoring a changing world:

> For the close of the 1950s, the plot could hardly be more old-fashioned. Europe may have torn itself apart, Hungary be crushed, Soviet and American empires threaten each other with destruction, Suez heap humiliation on top of dishonor, and Macmillan (1957) have come to power in a year of unprecedented industrial non-cooperation, but not a tremor from public events disturbs the protected *milieu* of the play.[57]

For Grove, who also hears the poetry of the play ring false – 'a style in which emotions are impersonated rather than expressed' – the simplicity of Eliot's final dramatic work is empty of meaning. What might have become a major theme of the play – the confrontation of a man with his past mistakes – becomes a rather empty plot as Eliot shifts his dramatic emphasis from contrition to romantic love.

As nearly every critic agrees, the play clearly highlights the value of love and acceptance. The ideal state in *The Elder Statesman* is no longer a kind of spiritual striving or a desire to find the deeper meaning in material life or individual quests, but rather to find contentment with the way things are. Some critics continued to read these themes of reconciliation and repentance as distinctly Christian. But, more often, contemporary critics have read the play through the lens of Eliot's engagement to Valerie Fletcher. As Browne reports, Eliot married Valerie in 1957, as he was revising Act III of the play. Shortly thereafter, Eliot added the final scene between the daughter Monica and her fiancé Charles as a culminating 'love duet'. In this final scene, Eliot gives way to the most indulgent kind of dialogue. As Charles declares to Monica:

> So that now we are conscious of a new person
> Who is you and me together.
>   Oh my dear,
> I love you to the limits of speech, and beyond.

It's strange that words are so inadequate.
Yet, like the asthmatic struggling for breath,
So the lover must struggle for words. (p. 131)

The major theme of the play – the confrontation of a man with his own past mistakes –becomes suddenly secondary. In an early draft, Monica, originally called Angela, even expressed love as the antithesis of much of Eliot's prior dramaturgtic argument. 'Perhaps,' she wonders, 'I have been living in a world of make-believe / With father. And the world of you and me, Charles, / The world I share with you, that is my real world.'[58] This reverses both *The Cocktail Party* and *The Confidential Clerk*, in which illusions of love kept one in an imperfect dream world. Here, it is love itself that liberates.

For contemporary critics, such as A. David Moody, such declarations of love and liberation are evidence of Eliot's own personal emotions, and the fulfilment of his longer dramatic project. Moody writes that, 'To bring home the unreality of what we ordinarily call reality – to effect a positive dis-illusionment – had always been an element in Eliot's work' and that in his final play, the purpose was to acknowledge the pleasures of romantic love.[59] Perhaps following his own admonition in *The Cocktail Party* to 'Resign yourself to the fool you are', Eliot in *The Elder Statesman* appears to relish the happiness, however superficial, of romantic affection. As he confirmed in a 1958 interview, 'At seventy I laugh at myself more than I did when I was young . . . and conversely I am less and less worried about making a fool of myself'.[60] In this way, Eliot seems to displace himself from the role of Claverton/Oedipus – the older man looking back – to the role of Charles, who looks forward to the future. So, in fact, the play's original subtitle may be the most accurate for Eliot himself – who has changed his name and his role.

Conclusion

In the years since Eliot's last play, most retrospectives of his play-writing regret that the young playwright of *Sweeney Agonistes* did not pursue his early poetic, expressionist style. Eliot's metadrama in *The Cocktail Party* and anti-naturalism in *The Confidential Clerk* suggest other potential directions for 'his dramatic vision. American experimental theatres pursued some of these directions. The Living Theatre, for instance, began their company with a production of Eliot's *Sweeney Agonistes* in 1949 and the Wooster Group integrated scenes from *The Cocktail Party* into their collage production *Nayatt School* in 1978. As Richard L. Homan has argued, connections can be drawn from Eliot to Pinter, although one must admit that such connections may be more constructed than discovered.

In hindsight, one can only conclude that Eliot's various dramatic attempts, though interesting, failed. While he managed to impress the audiences of his day, and has left behind moments of unquestionable poetic beauty on stage, his combined effort is largely without dramatic significance. His later full-length plays are almost never produced and when they are, it is usually through adaptation and manipulation. But this is not to say that his impact has not been felt on Anglo-American theatre. Poetic experiments continued on mid-twentieth-century stages in the subtle poetic inflections of Tennessee Williams's *The Glass Menagerie* (1944), the influence of Greek myth in Arthur Miller's tragedies of the common man and as pastiche in plays like Caryl Churchill's *Serious Money* (1987). But the poetic realisation Eliot calls for in 'Poetry and Drama' never emerged on stage. Instead, the experience of the world as illusion that Eliot hoped to articulate in his final plays surfaced on cinema screens (most notably in the French New Wave), while his 'condition of serenity, stillness, and reconciliation' and his advocacy of acceptance and love became rapidly incompatible with the post-war culture of the Cold War, television and nuclear weapons. Perhaps the real lesson of Eliot's drama is to question our faith in the theatre itself as transformative experience; an attachment and a desire for illusion that one may be better to live without, but that Eliot himself could not achieve.

TERENCE RATTIGAN: PRIVATE LIVES AND PUBLIC LIVES

Aunt Edna

[Let] us invent a character, a nice, respectable, middle-class, middle-aged, maiden lady, with time on her hands and the money to help her pass it. She enjoys pictures, books, music and the theatre and though to none of these arts (or rather, for consistency's sake, to none of these three arts and one craft) does she bring much knowledge or discernment, at least she is apt to tell her cronies, she 'does know what she likes'. Let us call her Aunt Edna . . .[1]

When Terence Rattigan, in his early forties, came to write the introductions for the first two volumes of his selected plays, he seemed, commercially at least, to be impregnable. Some recent works had been failures: *Who is Sylvia?* (1950), a play which contained a thinly veiled portrait of Rattigan's philandering father, had flopped – a second failure (as Rattigan saw it), after the closure of his previous play, *Adventure Story* (1949) after only 107 performances. However, *The Deep Blue Sea* (1952) seemed to have re-established his pre-eminence; and on the face of it, there was little in the theatrical world of the early 1950s to trouble him. The impact of deeper changes in British society and culture had yet to reach the theatre; and of the dramatists who had been successful in the 1930s, only Rattigan seemed to have retained his status. He had immediate access to Binkie Beaumont and the H. M. Tennent empire (even though Tennent did not automatically produce his work); and although he never achieved the success in the States that he wanted, his parallel career as a successful scriptwriter for the British film industry was partial compensation. He was interviewed, photographed and fêted. A new Rattigan play was news in itself; and his income and comfortable lifestyle were matters of public knowledge.

Privately, though, he was less happy. His father and brother both died in 1952; and there were clear signs of trouble in his professional life. In 1950, for example, Rattigan had published 'Concerning the Play of Ideas' in the *New Statesman*. This was in itself a calculated affront: Rattigan's article, which attacked the idea that theatre should be concerned with the dramatisation of current issues and concerns, seemed designed to stir up the journal's readership, who were wedded to the idea. The article, predictably, drew a storm of protest from a number of established writers such as Sean O'Casey and James Bridie, and from newer playwrights such as Peter Ustinov. Most damagingly, George Bernard Shaw dismissed Rattigan as 'an irrational genius'.[2]

When he came to write the prefaces, Rattigan was in a rather defensive mood. The introduction to the first of the two volumes hit back against those critics who had dismissed his initial successes as lucky accidents; and the second, which was based around a truth which might seem unarguable (that the playwright is vulnerable to the immediate response of an audience in the way that artists in other forms manage for the most part to avoid), made the mistake of characterising that audience in what seemed the most disparaging terms. Aunt Edna, the 'nice, respectable, middle-class, middle-aged, maiden lady' who represented the commercial theatre audience, was congenitally unable to appreciate the avant-garde (Rattigan called her a 'hopeless lowbrow'),[3] or indeed anything that engaged the mind rather than the emotions. Edna, for Rattigan, as not simply a representative British theatregoer; she was immortal – as likely to be found in the amphitheatres of Classical Athens as in the stalls of the Haymarket. Playwrights had at least to acknowledge her; and in Rattigan's case at least, this was not simply because Aunt Edna paid for her ticket (and therefore paid for his lifestyle):

> When I came . . . to try to reproduce, as a precocious playwright, the emotions that had been aroused in myself as a precocious member of an audience, the results, though no doubt ludicrous, were at least instinctively theatrical. It was by no cold and conscious exercise that I was able to act as audience to my own plays. I could not have written them otherwise. Aunt Edna, in fact, or at least her juvenile counterpart, was

inside my creative brain and in pleasing her I was only pleasing myself.[4]

Anyone writing for the stage, therefore, had to befriend Aunt Edna; Rattigan was clear, though, that this did not simply mean following her every whim. As he put it, this friendship 'should never become too close'.[5] As he gained more experience of writing for the stage, he had learned that 'although Aunt Edna must never be made mock of, or bored, or befuddled, she must equally not be wooed, or pandered to, or cosseted'.[6] However, even though she could be teased and bullied (in moderation, of course), Aunt Edna could not be ignored or gain-said; and perhaps the biggest of Rattigan's hostages to theatrical fortune was offered on the second last page of the preface, when he described Aunt Edna's response to the play of ideas:

> I . . . would merely, rather timidly, point out to the reader that, if these plays are not what are called 'plays of ideas', the reason is not necessarily that ideas do not interest me. It is merely, and let me here whisper in case any of these legendary beastly bullies overhear me, that I really don't think the theatre is the proper place to express them. That is not because I believe that Aunt Edna does not understand ideas – in fact she understands them much more readily than is usually supposed – but because, should she disagree with them, good manners must prevent her from answering back . . .[7]

The response to the *New Statesman* article was as nothing compared to the response to the preface. Aunt Edna, it is fair to say, passed from illustration to myth almost immediately; from a semi-comic portrait of the average audience member, she was trans-formed into a shorthand description of everything that was wrong with the British theatre. Even Rattigan's friends found themselves arguing with him.[8] Others were not so kind. Tynan, reviewing the double-bill *Separate Tables* in 1954, imagined a dialogue between Aunt Edna and a 'young perfectionist'.[9] Edna was initially dismayed when the young perfectionist (an entirely serious playgoer, who values the theatre as an art form rather than a commercial enterprise) claimed that both plays in the double-bill shared a common, sober theme – that love, whether indulged or suppressed, was a powerfully destructive force.[10] She could be soothed, though, by reassurances that her faithful friend Terence had not forgotten her:

> **YP** I agree that the principal characters, especially the journalist and the major, are original and disturbing creations. But there is also a tactful omniscient hoteliere, beautifully played by Beryl Measor. And what do you say to a comic Cockney maid?
>
> **AE** Ah![11]

Tynan's verdict ('**AE** Clearly, there is something here for both of us. **YP** yes, but not quite enough for either of us'[12]) was probably more damaging than a simple dismissal. In effect, it argued that Rattigan could not be taken seriously as an artist, not because his work was poor, but because it was fatally compromised. Whatever Rattigan wrote bore Edna's imprint; and Edna brought with her all the pressures of the commercial stage. In the theatrical debates of the time, Edna represented the ingrained, unthinking conservatism of the comfortable English middle classes: she was the goddess Apathy, comfily ensconced in the stalls, craving only the soporific and the comfortingly familiar.

The private and the public

In retrospect, Aunt Edna harmed Rattigan irreparably. By the beginning of the 1960s he was regarded both by critics and representatives of the new theatre as a man out of time. Osborne's characters raged; Wesker's argued; Brendan Behan's joked and sang; John Arden's did all four – what room was there for a writer whose work was characterised by an at times painful politeness? Moreover, Rattigan was linked to the commercial stage, and therefore to the theatrical establishment; his plays seemed rather ambivalent about the post-war settlement and the increased role of the British state. In *Harlequinade*, which followed

The Browning Version as the second part of the double-bill *Playbill*, the actress Edna Selby has to explain the facts of the new world to the theatrical *grande-dame* Dame Maud Gosport:

> **Edna**   ... Auntie Maud ... I don't think you quite understand the immense change that has come over the theatre in the last few years. You see, dear – I know it's difficult for you to grasp, but the theatre of today has at least acquired a social conscience, and a social purpose. Why else do you think we're opening at this rat-hole of a theatre instead of the Opera House Manchester?[13]

This is not quite on the same level as Coward's assault on the whole idea of social equality (see Chapter 1), but it seemed to place Rattigan on one side of the cultural divide, with the new Court dramatists on the other.

And yet perhaps it is this very ambivalence, given theatrical expression in Rattigan's plays in the late 1940s and 1950s, which gives his work its particular power. Ambivalence – or at least the sense that no one quite knew where society was headed – is a theme which, as noted in Chapter 1, runs right through the period. You don't have to dig too deep to find examples; *The Times* of 23 October 1950 carried the news that Rattigan's comedy *Who is Sylvia?* was due to open in London. At the top of the same page is an account of an exhibition of matchbox labels (an event, as the reporter helpfully points out, 'for specialists rather than for the merely curious'); further down, an article titled 'Atomic Bomb Obsolete: The Hazards of Biological Warfare' informs the reader that 'Biological science could release new diseases which would be much more powerful weapons of death than the atomic bomb' (p. 2). Any page of any newspaper from any year is liable to contain conflicting accounts of the spirit of the age; but there is something peculiarly indicative about the juxtaposition of these two stories – one playing to a sense of cosily eccentric, and rather private, Englishness, the other uneasily hinting at the possibility of genocidal annihilation. Together, these stories hint at the peculiar dilemma British society faced in the post-war period – a time, as Peter Hennessy has put it, of 'easement tinged with anxiety',[14] where increasing private comfort was threatened by events too vast and powerful to be controlled – or even to be comprehended.

Rattigan was well placed to chronicle this world. From the 1930s onwards, he had written plays in which characters struggled against the pressure exerted on them by a world which is changing. David and Joan in *After the Dance* are in thrall to the past, and Bobby Harpenden, in *While the Sun Shines*, gloomily and comically looks forward to a post-war world where aristocrats will have to engage in manual labour. In *Flare Path*, Peter Kyle, an actor whose movie career is fading, can't help but reflect on his place in the world:

> **Peter**   . . . It's the war, you see. I don't understand it, Pat – you
> know that – democracy – freedom – rights of man – and all that
> – I can talk quite glibly about them, but they don't mean
> anything, not to me. All I know is that my own little private world
> is going well, it's gone, really – and the rest of the world – the real
> world – has turned its back on me and left me out, and though I
> want to get in the circle, I can't . . .[15]

This speech could be repeated, with varying degrees of emphasis, by most of Rattigan's main characters. His work explored the tension between the inner, private world of his protagonists and a wider world that would not stay still. In *While the Sun Shines*, *Love in Idleness* and *Who is Sylvia?* this tension is exploited for comic effect. In *Love in Idleness*, for example, the plot is generated by Michael's attempts to re-create his old relationship with his mother; paradoxically, even though he sees himself as part of the new, revolutionary socialist movement that will transform the post-war world, Michael wants nothing so much as a return to the comfort of a smaller, more private life. In contrast, his mother's new lover, John (an industrialist working for the government), seems very much part of that new post-war world; however, even he is uncertainly aware that, if the world changes, his position is under threat. Mark, in *Who is Sylvia?*, is in thrall to the memory of a girl he met when he was seventeen. He spends most of his adult life trying to re-create the memory, in a series of relationships with girls who look like the original. As the play develops, we learn that this apparently private world is an open secret; at the play's end, his wife reveals that she has always known about the affairs. Interestingly, she does so by linking the private, secret world of his affairs with the public world of his work:

> **Caroline** You told me lots of things, dear, and you took the greatest trouble to make me believe them. If you tell lies to Foreign Ministers as clumsily as you tell them to me, I wonder whether anyone ever speaks to us at the United Nations.[16]

When the tension between the public and the private in Rattigan's work is discussed, critics have tended to view the matter through the prism of Rattigan's sexuality. This is an entirely legitimate response: as a gay man, Rattigan lived with the knowledge that, if his private life became public, the results would have been catastrophic. As noted in Chapter 1, Rattigan himself was clear about this, censoring the first drafts of *Separate Tables* to remove any suggestion that Major Pollock might be homosexual. These arguments have in general been rather more nuanced than the simple suggestion that Rattigan becomes explicable once his sexuality is taken into account. Christopher Innes, for example, has argued that the plays dramatise a split between 'the surface appearance of normality, and the very different reality underneath'.[17] Michael Billington sees the split slightly differently, as 'a desire to follow his liberal instincts while appeasing his supposedly conservative audience'.[18] Dan Rebellato, in the excellent general introduction to the edited playtexts, makes the point that to read the plays as 'really *homosexual*' (Rebellato's emphasis) is to misrepresent them; but the necessary subterfuges that homosexuals had to adopt did leave their mark on his work:

> Homosexuality, then, was explored and experienced through a series of semi-hidden, semi-open codes of behaviour; the image of the iceberg, with the greater part of its bulk submerged beneath the surface, was frequently employed. And this image is, of course, one of the metaphors often used to describe Rattigan's own playwriting.[19]

The implication of these arguments is clear; Rattigan might not be a disguised chronicler of homosexual life, but his sexuality – and the covert way in which he had to express it – gave him a privileged insight into the hidden workings of British society from the 1930s onwards. That society, in the late 1940s and early 1950s, was shaped by an understandable desire to retreat to the safe and the familiar; this proved impossible – the underlying tensions working within and around the country meant that the old vision of Britain could not be sustained. The media's renewed and prurient interest in homosexuality (a feature of the time) was part of a general desire to promote a return to the supposedly eternal values of family life.

However, censure was not automatic or universal. In a famous (and much-repeated) theatrical story, John Gielgud was arrested for 'indecent behaviour' in the autumn of 1953; his friends, and Gielgud himself, thought that his career was effectively over, or at least gravely damaged. This judgement proved to be wrong; the next time that Gielgud appeared on stage, in Liverpool a few days later, he received a standing ovation. Gielgud was probably protected by the visibility his celebrity gave him; but the case was widely reported. Between a witch-hunting press and the impact of widely reported events like Gielgud's arrest, homosexual society – as complex, and necessarily more sheltered and private than any other part of British life – was exposed, made public, to a far greater extent than had been the case in the 1930s when Rattigan's career was beginning. Rattigan's private world, in other words, collided with a shifting public world; this meant that his experience of a changing Britain was, in some crucial respects, similar to that of the rest of the British public. The effects of this in his post-war writing are clearly discernible. Time and again, characters find themselves adrift because they are unable to reconcile their private and public selves; the defences they build are never strong enough to keep the wider world at bay. In this context, the figure of Aunt Edna takes on a greater resonance. For Rattigan's characters, as for Rattigan himself, there is always an audience, ready to scrutinise and judge even the smallest, most personal actions; and, as the 1940s move into the 1950s, the impact of social change is felt – even by those, like Aunt Edna, who seem on the surface to be the enshrined representatives of a fixed relation between the public and the private.

The Winslow Boy

The Winslow Boy (which was one of Rattigan's most successful plays, running at the Lyric for 476 performances during 1946–7) ends with a conversation which one can imagine other dramatists regarding as something of a lost opportunity. For the first time since a highly dramatic mock cross-examination at the end of Act 2, Sir Robert Morton meets Ronnie Winslow, the boy whose innocence he has sacrificed his career to defend:

> **Ronnie**   I say, Sir Robert, I'm most awfully sorry. I didn't know anything was going to happen.
>
> **Sir Robert**   Where were you?
>
> **Ronnie**   At the pictures.
>
> **Sir Robert**   Pictures? What is that?
>
> **Catherine**   Cinematograph show.
>
> **Ronnie**   I'm most awfully sorry. I say – we won, didn't we?[20]

One can see in this evidence of Rattigan's undoubted mastery of his craft; we have had the denouement, the case has been dramatically resolved, the various protagonists have reacted and the business of the plot is over. In these circumstances, working quickly towards the final curtain makes sound dramatic sense. However, even given this, the ending is very muted. No thanks, no handshakes, no sense that Ronnie, the cause and centre of the play's action, is aware of the true impact of the verdict; as Rattigan puts it in the stage directions, he is now the 'incipient man about town' (p. 177), going out for the evening, taking advantage of a new technology that Sir Robert only barely recognises.

This is more than a bitter-sweet indication that, outside of the titanic struggle of the Winslow case, ordinary life goes on. The play is famously based on a real case – the George Archer-Shee case of 1910. In turning the case into the play, Rattigan sharpened the contrast between the family and the state; the Archer-Shees were politically well connected (George's half-brother, Martin, became an MP in 1910), and the Winslows are not. He also halts the fictional case early; in reality, the Archer-Shees pursued the Admiralty for costs for a number of years after George was declared innocent. Arthur Winslow, on the other hand, refuses to cheapen his son's innocence by seeking a financial settlement. In both cases these changes enable Rattigan to emphasise the ordinary purity of the Winslows, and the facelessness of the British legal and political establishment. It also, however, does something else; the Winslow family, and the Winslow house in which the action is set, are not hermetically sealed away from the rest of the world, but they are fundamentally private, in a way that the Archer-Shees were not. At the play's beginning, for example, Caroline, the daughter of the family, is a suffragette; but she is also bound for an entirely respectable middle-class marriage. Ronnie Winslow, after being expelled, understandably seeks sanctuary in his family home; his brother Dickie, up at Oxford, also seems more tied to the family house than his new life at university. The whole family seems wedded to each other, and to the safe world the house represents. By the play's end, however, the larger world has come flooding in; Arthur Winslow's health has suffered, Caroline's future marriage has been halted and Dickie's studies have been curtailed. The case has had a similar effect on Sir Robert; he has forgone the possibility of becoming Lord Chief Justice because of the case, and when he is alone for a moment on stage, he allows himself a moment of frailty:

> . . . **Sir Robert**, *left alone, droops his shoulders wearily. He subsides into a chair. When* **Catherine** *comes back with the whisky he straightens his shoulders instinctively, but does not rise* . . . (p. 175)

This is a significant moment. Ostensibly, *The Winslow Boy* celebrates the victory of the powerless over the powerful: as Catherine puts it, Ronnie's guilt or innocence is not significant in itself.

However, as her fiancé John reminds her, the case isn't the only external pressure the family and the country face:

> **John** . . . There's a European war blowing up, there's a coal strike on, there's a fair chance of civil war in Ireland, and there's a hundred and one other things on the horizon at the moment that I think you genuinely could call *important* . . . (*pointing at* **Ronnie**) and his bally postal order . . . (p. 152)

Catherine quickly restates the play's governing idea – that the power-less individual should always have a right of redress against the all-powerful state. This argument, understandably, is strongly re-enforced by the plot, by the positioning of Catherine and Arthur as dogged supporters of the family's cause, and by Sir Robert's willing-ness to put himself on the side of 'him . . . and his bally postal order'. However, this victory is painful, and at some moments of the play almost indistinguishable from a defeat; the case, begun in the hope that the private world of the family might be able to assert itself in the face of the power of the public world, ends with that private world fragmented. Ronnie and Dickie are no longer tied to the family home – Dickie has left, and as the final moments of the play demonstrate, Ronnie is now beginning to explore a world outside of the family (and as he does so, he loses interest in the case, which his father and sister have undertaken for his benefit). Catherine herself resolves to move from the private to the public world; she tells Sir Robert that they will meet again 'across the floor' (p. 178) of the House of Commons. Arthur has suffered most: although he is vindicated, what we see is not a man rejuvenated by his victory. Significantly, he decides against a ringing speech, in favour of the far more subdued and heartfelt 'Thank God we beat 'em' (p. 174). Before he can deliver this statement to the waiting press (representatives of the wider world, swarming immediately outside of the house) he has to be helped up from his chair by Catherine and Sir Robert. This moment, coming as it does just before Sir Robert's own collapse, serves to underline the fragility of the family and its supporters; the spoken text might provide further support for the idea of Arthur Winslow as triumphant ordinary man; the stage directions show us someone nearly broken.

The play's most striking moment is the end of the second Act, where Sir Robert demolishes the credibility of Ronnie's story, only to amaze the family by accepting the boy's innocence and agreeing to take the case. Rattigan himself was initially unsure about such an obvious *coup de théâtre*,[21] but on the first night, the scene was greeted with cheering and 'tumultuous applause'.[22] However, there is more to it than an effective manipulation of the audience. Sir Robert comes to the Winslows as a representative of the public world. He is described on his first entrance as 'immensely elegant', as a 'fop' with a 'supercilious expression' (p. 124); and he calls in to the Winslow home on his way to a dinner engagement in Devonshire House (the London residence of the Duke of Devonshire, this was one of the largest and grandest of the aristocratic houses in London). When he cross-examines Ronnie, he puts what might be called the public reading of the facts – of course the boy is guilty, and of course the whole case is a waste of public and political time. He lands on Ronnie with the full force of the establishment:

> **Sir Robert** . . . Don't be impertinent! Are you aware that the Admiralty sent up the forged postal order to Mr Ridgely-Pearce – the greatest handwriting expert in England? (p. 131)

Even though he decides (for reasons which are well explained later) to take the case, the result of the cross-examination is to leave Ronnie sobbing 'hysterically' (p. 135). The private world can take on the public world, and it can win; but that victory is damaging, and comes with a great deal of pain.

The Browning Version

In 1984, towards the end of his life, Harold Hobson reflected:

> For some time we had been listening wearily to the banal, clipped, naturalistic dialogue of modern drama with

impatience, and we thought our hearts cried out for writing of courage and colour, for the evocative word, and the bannered phrase . . . *The Browning Version* [1948] made us momentarily doubt (for *Look Back* was not far in the future) the necessity for this cry.[23]

On the face of it, the contrast that Hobson draws is between two very different types of drama, incarnated in two very different protagonists. Osborne's Jimmy Porter seems to be unburdened by any internal filters, his aim trained solely on the targets of his invective. His characteristic means of expression is the articulate, molten rant. In sharp contrast, the protagonist of Rattigan's *The Browning Version*, Andrew Crocker-Harris, a classics teacher in a public school, is measured, pedantic, plodding and (by his own admission) entirely, embarrassingly humourless. Taplow, one of his pupils, describes him as 'all shrivelled up inside like a nut' (p. 185). The emotional temperature of his language rarely rises above tepid, even when he talks about the most personal and humiliating matters:

> **Andrew** . . . I knew, of course, that I was not only not liked, but now positively disliked. I had realised, too, that the boys – for many long years now – had ceased to laugh at me. I don't know why they no longer found me a joke. Perhaps it was my illness. No, I don't think it was that. Something deeper than that. Not a sickness of the body, but a sickness of the soul. At all events it didn't take much discernment on my part to realise I had become an utter failure as a schoolmaster. Still, stupidly enough, I hadn't realised I was also feared. The Himmler of the lower fifth! I suppose that will be my epitaph. (pp. 207–8)

On a day when he is subject to a series of small and large defeats – the school governors deny him a pension; his farewell speech is moved to accommodate a more popular colleague; he has to show his successor around the house in which he has lived; his marriage finally crumbles; and the only positive event of the day – Taplow's gift, an edition of the *Agamemnon*, translated by Robert Browning – is soured by his wife, who dismisses it as 'a few bobs' worth of appease-ment' (p. 214) – one might expect anger, or at least frustrated sadness. What we hear, though, is a man who sounds as though he is a spectator to his own decline; the 'epitaph' he delivers might be for someone else.

Except for one thing; and that is the fact that Crocker-Harris cannot stop himself talking. Rather like Jimmy Porter, he demonstrates a compulsive need to communicate. Both he and Porter do so, moreover, in a way which blurs the boundaries between the public and the private. Part of the performative energy of *Look Back* comes from the sense that Jimmy's diatribes are disproportionate – that he treats his home and the people in it as an actor treats his audience. Crocker-Harris's speeches work at the opposite end of the scale. They are polished and controlled; they are not flung out to the world at large; they reveal themselves in intimate dialogues, with Taplow, with his wife's lover, with the man who will succeed him. What gives this dialogue, which is, as the extract above shows, intentionally stiff, its dramatic impact is the knowledge, shared both by Crocker-Harris and the audience, that this is the first moment that his private world has been made public. Immediately after the speech quoted above, Crocker-Harris recollects himself:

> **Andrew**   I cannot for the life of me imagine why I should choose to unburden myself to you – a total stranger – when I have been silent to others for so long. Perhaps because my very unworthy mantle is about to fall on your shoulders . . . (p. 208)

In this short extract, we see clearly the main difference between Porter and Crocker-Harris. Porter uses words to inflate his position, to give himself the stature that the world denies him; Crocker-Harris uses them to describe exactly the nature of his failure, and to efface himself.

When Crocker-Harris talks, therefore, he conveys two things simultaneously: a controlled, distanced, public politeness, and direct access to a crippling sense of failure and inadequacy. This tension between the public and the private also drives the most dramatically charged moment of the play. Taplow gives Crocker-Harris the book; and, rather like Sir Robert, Crocker-Harris has to ensure that the room is clear before he can give way. He sends Taplow out of the room to fetch medicine (Crocker-Harris is retiring because he has a heart condition):

> **Andrew**, *the moment [Taplow] is gone, breaks down and begins to sob uncontrollably. He makes a desperate attempt, after a moment, to control himself, but when* **Taplow** *comes back his emotion is still very apparent.* (p. 212)

Sir Robert manages to gather himself before others come back in; Crocker-Harris does not. His distress is not only witnessed by Taplow, but also by Frank Hunter – a more popular teacher, and his wife's lover – who is, as the stage directions have it, 'a little puzzled' (p. 212). Crocker-Harris's response, however, is not to rush from the room, or to accuse his wife's lover directly, or to ask the others to leave him alone. He greets Hunter with scrupulous politeness: 'Come in, Hunter, do. It's perfectly all right . . .' (p. 212). Once again, as in *The Winslow Boy*, Rattigan differentiates between what we hear and what we see; Crocker-Harris's voice conveys public politeness – but physically he cannot mask his anguish.

For the Winslows, the public world begins outside the front door. For Crocker-Harris, it seems, the public world begins where he ends. All the other characters in the play are attached to the life of the school; he has been marginalised – by the pupils, by his teachers and by his wife. As he tells Gilbert, the man who has come to replace him, he has tried to evolve a public persona:

> **Andrew**   . . . In early years, I discovered an easy substitute for popularity. I had, of course acquired – we all do – many little mannerisms and tricks of speech, and I found that the boys were beginning to laugh at me. I was very happy at that, and encouraged the boys' laughter by playing up to it. They didn't like me as a man, but they found me funny as a character . . . (p. 207)

The only way, it seems, that he can negotiate a compromise between his public and private selves is to simplify himself; the character that he creates, however, hardens into a caricature – and the caricature serves only to separate him from the public world of the school. However, although Crocker-Harris is an isolated figure, he is not alone; others have made the same compromise, with equally painful results. Millie Crocker-Harris creates a false history that elevates her social standing; it gives her a secure place in the social life of the school which compensates for her husband's failings. However, as her husband knows, this history is built on very insecure foundations:

> **Frobisher** . . . Your wife has often told me of her family connections. I understand her father has a business in – Bradford – isn't it?
>
> **Andrew** Yes. He runs a men's clothing shop in the Arcade. (p. 200)

However, as with her husband, her public persona has become a trap. It distances her from the other teachers and their wives; and it cannot conceal the desperation in her words and actions. Hunter is the latest (and probably the last) in a line of lovers; he breaks off the affair at the end of the play, disgusted by the cruelty with which she treats her husband (even though that cruelty is itself born from her entrapment). Even Hunter is uneasily aware that the same trap that sprung for Crocker-Harris also lies waiting for him:

> **Hunter** . . . Currying favour with the boys . . . My God, how easy it is to be popular. I've only been a master three years but I've already slipped into an act and a vernacular that I just can't get out of. Why can't anyone ever be natural with the little blighters? . . . (p. 189)

Of the main characters in the play, only the headmaster, Frobisher, seems at ease with his public persona; and as his treatment of Crocker-Harris shows, this has come at the expense of any sense of empathy with those around him.

In this context, Crocker-Harris's newfound ability to speak, however tentatively, is as much of an assertion of selfhood as any of Jimmy Porter's speeches. By the end of the play, he has achieved two small things to balance against the weight of failure in the rest of his life: he has publicly accounted for his failure, and he manages to recoup a little of the public standing he has lost. He breaks with his wife; he tells Hunter that he was aware of the affair – as he was aware of all his wife's affairs. Finally, he phones the headmaster, asserting his 'privilege' (p. 224) of speaking last at the annual prize-giving. The significance of this is that it is a public event at which, it seems, Crocker-Harris will provide an 'anti-climax' (p. 224). He will assert himself in an act of public defiance, which echoes and reverses his semi-public breakdown earlier in the play. Then he found himself unexpectedly on display, his private self made public. At the play's end, in front of the society that has marginalised him, he will use a public event as the sign of a quiet, private, small victory.

The Deep Blue Sea

The settings of Rattigan's plays are always indicative. In *The Winslow Boy*, the Winslows' home is a private sanctuary against the public world; in *The Browning Version*, it is a private apartment which is also part of a public space. *The Deep Blue Sea* takes place in a rented flat; like the Crocker-Harrises' rooms, it does not belong to its inhabitants, and as such does not provide the same kind of shelter as the Winslow house. Moreover, it is a part of a house that is in social transition:

> ... *It is a big room for it is in the first floor of a large and gloomy Victorian mansion, converted to flats after World War I, but it has an air of dinginess, even of squalor, heightened by the fact that it has, like its immediate badly-blitzed neighbourhood, so obviously come down in the world.*[24]

In earlier plays, the locations are stereotypically English, and they are not subject to history. A 1912 villa would have been a familiar part of the suburban landscape of 1946; and the incoming Labour government had not abolished public schools. The Victorian mansion in *The Deep Blue Sea*, though, has been thoroughly shaken up by the twentieth-century; given the events that Rattigan lists, it is hard to escape the sense that the play's setting is obliquely allegorical – signifying Britain, and especially the displaced, austere, uncertain Britain of the late 1940s. This is a house that has declined from its former glories; it has been profoundly shaken by two world wars; and it is now dingy, if not downright squalid – a place built for the rich, now having to accommodate itself to poverty.

Much has been made of the origins of *The Deep Blue Sea*: there is no doubt that it is linked to events in Rattigan's life – in particular the suicide of a former lover, Kenneth Morgan, in 1949; Geoffrey Wansell has argued that the play has a gay subtext, and that Hester was called Hector in the early drafts. However, as Andrew Wyllie has pointed out, it is not easy to read *The Deep Blue Sea* as a rewritten gay play:

> . . . at best the amount of inference required for a gay reading of *The Deep Blue Sea* is considerable: at worst such a reading may be nonsense. In fact, the rumour of a homosexual version of the play may be based on the character of Miller rather than that of Hester . . .[25]

This is a fair point; it is not necessary to substitute a homosexual relationship for the play's central heterosexual relationship, or to impute an illegal gay act to Dr Miller, whose previous history remains undefined, but who offers advice to Hester which is clearly based on painful past experience. It is not that such readings are illegitimate, but they do not describe the central dynamic of the play. Talking to Laurence Olivier, Rattigan said, 'The phenomenon of love is inexplicable in terms of logic. That is the theme of *The Deep Blue Sea*.'[26] Hester is caught up in a passionate affair with a man who does not love her in return; but whereas, in a pre-war play such as *After the Dance*, the theme would play out against the changes in one segment of British society, in *The Deep Blue Sea* Hester faces a public world which is in flux. The social barriers of the 1930s seem to be breaking down; the illogicality of Hester's love plays itself out against a world which no longer obeys what had seemed to be a set, logical, ordered pattern. The boundaries between Hester's private pain and the wider, judging social world no longer exist.

This relation is enacted in the opening moments of the play. The other inhabitants of the building smell gas; they break down the door of Hester's flat, to find her on the floor, having apparently committed suicide. They revive her, and as they do so the story of her life emerges. She is not married to the younger man she lives with; her husband is a prominent member of the legal establishment – so when they eventually find this out, convention dictates that he has to be contacted. However, the reactions of the rest of the household are not automatically disapproving:

Mrs Elton I don't know her real husband. And what I do know I promised faithfully I'd never tell a living soul . . . Poor lamb – she thought Mr Elton would turn her out. I found her that evening packing her things. I told her not to be silly. As if I'd tell Mr Elton a thing like that. It's none of his business, or mine, or anyone else's . . . (p. 10)

There are two points of interest in this speech. First, there is the idea that the representatives of the outside, public world, even though they break through the barriers that Hester has erected, do not enter with their minds made up. For the Winslows and for Crocker-Harris, the problem is in part that the outside world does not respect their need to be private; Mrs Elton, who has the power to judge Hester against the social norms of the time, respects that need. Second, though, there is Hester's response. As soon as Mrs Elton finds out about her, Hester starts to pack; she expects judgement – and she expects that judgement to be conventional, severe and immediate. In other words, she behaves as though the social rules that govern the public world are fixed, even though Mrs Elton's reaction shows that they are not. Hester's problem (and, as it turns out, the reason for the very tentative hope offered to her at the end) is that she has internalised a set of rules that no longer automatically apply. She is not the only one; the man she has fallen in love with, Freddie Page, would have been far more at home in the world of *Flare Path*. An ex-RAF pilot, he has struggled since the end of the war; as Hester puts it, 'his life stopped in 1940' (p. 47). Significantly, when she first meets him, he is isolated:

> **Hester** I came up to the golf club to collect you to go on to that party at the Hendersons'. You [Hester's husband] were still out playing. Freddie was there alone. He'd been chucked out of a game and was bad tempered . . . And Freddie and I sat on the veranda together for at least an hour. For some reason he talked very honestly and rather touchingly about himself – how worried he was about his future, how his life seemed to have no direction or purpose . . . (p. 47)

Interestingly, the moment where, suddenly and illogically, Hester falls in love with Freddie follows on from a meeting between two people who are excluded from the social games that surround them; Hester's husband is playing and his wife is alone, and Freddie has been thrown off the course.

Sir Robert and Crocker-Harris allow themselves one moment of emotional weakness during the course of their respective plays; Hester, on the other hand, veers between extreme control (after her suicide attempt, she responds to the house's other inhabitants with a scrupulous, reserved politeness) and overt emotion, which, as Luc Gilleman,[27] has pointed out, is tinged with melodrama. Put simply, Hester does not know how to behave; the rules that governed her previous existence no longer apply. In this context, her behavioural compass swings wildly – from careful attention to the social niceties to the kind of overwrought display of emotion that previous Rattigan characters try very hard to avoid. Once again, in this she is not alone; Freddie seeks sanctuary with his old RAF friend Jackie, both because they share common experiences, and because they understand the social code that went along with those experiences. Hester's husband, caught up in the social world that Hester has left, finds it hard to understand his wife. The young couple Ann and Philip, who also live in the house, separately confess moments of weakness to Hester, a relative stranger (Philip, that he was almost tempted into an affair; Ann, that she fears being alone). All seem to recognise, or at least to be uneasily aware, that the new world they inhabit is far more troublingly fluid than it used to be.

As with Hester, it has been assumed that another of the play's characters, Mr Miller, has a counterpart in Rattigan's life. For a time in the 1940s, Rattigan came under the influence of a rather bizarre psychiatrist called Dr Keith Newman, who exercised very tight control over his patients. According to Darlow and Hodson, Newman 'enjoyed exercising his influence over the young men he met';[28] they suggest that when he first began to treat Rattigan (who was experiencing writer's block) he exaggerated the problem, so that Rattigan would come to rely on him. For Wansell, 'Mr Miller is, to a very considerable extent, Terence Rattigan's first stage portrait of Kenneth Newman. Miller's dialogue certainly bears astonishing similarities to some of Newman's utterances'.[29] However, there is another way to read his character; and that is as Hester's counterpart. Like Hester, he has lost his place in the public world; like Hester, he was involved in a scandal (the precise details of which are never made clear; it has been suggested that he was imprisoned because he was caught in a homosexual act, or, given that he trained as a doctor, because he performed an abortion, which was also illegal at the time). Like Hester, Miller has come close to suicide: 'How close did you come to the gas fire, once?' she asks him (p. 60); and he doesn't answer her. However, he has come to terms with his uncertain place in the world; and he offers Hester, not a course of quasi-psychiatric treatment, but the judgement of someone who has been through the same process:

Miller   Listen to me. To see yourself as the world sees you may be very brave, but it can also be very foolish. Why should you accept the world's view of you as a weak-willed neurotic – better dead than alive? What right have they to judge? To judge you they must have the capacity to feel as you feel. And who has? One in a thousand. You alone know how you have felt . . . (p. 73)

In the constrained worlds of *The Winslow Boy* and *The Browning Version*, such an idea would be dismissed; Arthur Winslow cannot ignore the world's judgement about his son, and Crocker-Harris accepts the public image that the school creates for him. However, as befits a play set in a symbolic representation of the changing state of the nation, Hester and Miller find that it is possible to reject the world's view of them; at a time where the codes by which that world operates have become more fluid, going against social norms and expectations is difficult, but it is at least possible.

Separate Tables

In its setting, the double-bill *Separate Tables* exists at the opposite end of the spectrum from *The Winslow Boy*; we have moved from a set which is entirely private to a set which is entirely public: '*The dining room of the Beauregard Private Hotel, near Bournemouth. It is small, rather bare and quite unpretentious . . .*' (p. 79). The play is set in the kind of hotel in which Rattigan's mother lived for the last part of her life: as the stage directions at the beginning make clear, the permanent status of most of the guests can be seen in the motley collection of '*bottles of medicine and favourite pickles and other idiosyncratic personal accessories*' (p. 79) clearly visible on the tables. Even if the stage were unpeopled, these details might lead the observant audience member to expect that the hotel is populated by a particular type of client; elderly, retiring (in both senses of the world), or in indefinite transit between more permanent addresses.

This impression is confirmed when the characters start to speak. We learn that the elderly Miss Meacham is subject to troubling dreams. We learn that Mrs Railton-Bell, another of the hotel's more elderly residents, is living in reduced circumstances. We learn that some of the permanent guests have been there so long that, even for the staff, they seem to have faded into the woodwork; the retired teacher, Mr Fowler, is told by Mabel, one of the maids, that the kitchen has run out of the goulash he wants for dinner – but when a new guest appears, she is offered goulash. In response, Mr Fowler '*glances furiously at Mabel as she goes past him to the kitchen, but decides not to make a scene*' (p. 83). In a series of small exchanges and actions, Rattigan has sketched out an image of a section of British society; a section that feels itself to be in decline, to be trading on past prosperity and past status, and who find their growing irrelevance hard to accept. In a telling exchange during *Table by the Window*, the first of the two linked plays that make up *Separate Tables*, Lady Matheson, one of the permanent guests, engages the left-wing journalist John Malcolm in a political debate; this heated discussion soon turns to the rather more mundane details of day-to-day financial solvency:

Lady Matheson . . . Do you realise that I have to live on a little less than half of what the average dock worker makes a year?

John I know. You can't afford to have your wireless repaired – and you live by it. You had to move into a small back room when they raised the hotel prices last year. You can only afford one cinema a week, in the front rows . . . By any reasonable standards you're well below the poverty line, and, as the poor must always have my passionate sympathy, Lady Matheson, you have mine.
(p. 99)

However, it is not that the play asks us only to sympathise with a class who have found themselves unexpectedly coming down in the world. Even John – elected as a Labour MP in 1945, but convicted in 1946 'on a triple charge of assaulting a police officer in the course of his duty, of being drunk and disorderly and of causing grievous bodily harm to his wife' (p. 104) – is living in reduced circumstances; and his ex-wife Anne, who has come to the hotel to find him, is a former model whose subsequent marriages have also failed. The Major, whose court appearance for a minor sexual offence provides the plot for the second of the two plays (*Table Number Seven*), is similarly uncertain of his place in the world; so much so, that he has fabricated an alternative history – one that compensates for his inferior social status.

Discussion of *Separate Tables*, understandably, has usually focused on the fact that, as noted in the introduction, Rattigan had originally written that the Major's crime was importuning men for sex. The debate over his conduct (and his eventual vindication by most of the guests at the hotel) has been seen, quite rightly, as an oblique reference to the case against John Gielgud, and the public's response to it. However, to focus on this undeniably important part of the genesis of the play is perhaps to ignore the wider context that the setting provides. The Major's rehabilitation, like Hester's decision to continue with her life alone, is made possible by the fact that the world around them is changing; paradoxically, the fact that the division between the public and the private has broken down gives both characters – and John and Anne in the first play in the double-bill – the chance to start again. It is no longer a question of facing up to a hostile world; in *Separate Tables* both the potential hostility of that world, and its new, post-war fluidity, are clearly demonstrated.

In *Table by the Window*, John Malcolm, rather like Andrew Crocker-Harris, finds himself driven to talk about the failure that his life has been. However, where Crocker-Harris is restrained and muted, Malcolm seems at times to have been scripted, not by Rattigan, but by Osborne. For example, he berates his wife in terms that Jimmy Porter might very well recognise; she, like Alison, married beneath her in marrying him, and, like Jimmy, he attacks her for marrying outside her class:

> **John** . . . You wanted bigger game. Wilder game. None of your tame baronets and Australian millionaires . . . What enjoyment would there have been for you in using your weapons on such a husband? But to turn them on a genuine, live, roaring savage from the slums of Hull, to make him grovel at the vague and distant promise of delights that were his anyway by right, or goad him to such a frenzy of drink and rage by a locked door that he'd kick it in and hit you with his fist so hard that you'd knock yourself unconscious against a wall – that must really have been fun.
> (p. 108)

Arguably, though, Rattigan treats John with more objectivity than Osborne brings to Jimmy Porter; an ageing, occasionally violent alcoholic, John is shown as uneasily aware of the distance between his ideals and his behaviour. He might talk to the other residents about the 'revolution' wrought by Labour in post-war Britain; but, in conversation with Anne, he dismisses himself as a 'journalist, middle-aged soak and has-been, the terror of the older lady residents' (p. 104). His ex-wife is also more of a match for him than Alison is for Jimmy. After the diatribe quoted above, her response is measured and quietly damning:

> **Anne** You haven't changed much, have you? . . . The same old John pouring out the same old cascade of truths, half-truths and distortions, all beaten up together, to make a neat, consistent story. *Your* story . . . (p. 108)

John has lived through the collapse of his political hopes; Anne has lived through the end of her career and the failure of her marriages. As she says, she is afraid – of growing old, of being alone; when John asks her about her life in London, she replies, 'You can be more alone in London than in this place, John. Here at least you can walk from table to table' (p. 125). Their relationship is combustible; but it seems to be the only possibility, in the situation in which they find themselves – both alone, and both no longer in possession of the social certainties that had previously structured their lives. At the end of the play, they tentatively re-establish the relationship – and they do so in public, by sitting together in the hotel's restaurant.

In *Table Number Seven*, the Major, like Ronnie Winslow, is subject to public humiliation; unlike Ronnie, though, the Major is guilty – and his guilt threatens not only to expose his sexuality, but the carefully constructed public identity that he has built for himself since coming to the hotel. He is not a major in the Black Watch regiment; he was not educated at Sandhurst; during the war, he was a second lieutenant in the Royal Army Supply Corps, working in a supply depot in the Orkneys, rather than serving on the front line. To Mrs Railton-Bell, the permanent resident who appoints herself the moral judge of his behaviour, the Major is not only a pervert but a liar; she browbeats, persuades and cajoles most of the other guests into supporting her, using tactics that another guest likens to Senator

McCarthy's anti-communist witch-hunts (which were being conducted in the United States at the time). The Major, initially, accepts their verdict; and begins to do what they ask, making surreptitious arrangements to leave the hotel. He does so, as he confesses to Sybil (Mrs Railton-Bell's daughter), for the same reason as he assumed the character of the Major in the first place; because he is afraid, and because:

> **Major Pollock** I don't like myself as I am, I suppose, so I've had to invent another person. It's not so harmful, really. We've all got daydreams. Mine have gone a step further than most people's – that's all. Quite often, I've even managed to believe in the Major myself. (p. 156)

And yet, at the play's end, he stays – and not in open defiance of the public world (as Crocker-Harris does) or because of an overwhelmingly public endorsement (as in *The Winslow Boy*). In the last scene, he is quietly accepted into the social world of the hotel dining room; his place is reset, and he has his dinner; in the end, the only person who is isolated is Mrs Railton-Bell, who, as Rattigan puts it, is forced into a 'dignified exit' (p. 168). It would be wrong to say, though, that the Major receives a ringing endorsement from all the other guests. Their responses are variously governed by principle, fellow feeling, self-assertion and, in one case, the outcome of a moment of social embarrassment (Lady Matheson says good evening to him, and is then forced by nothing more than the desire to avoid awkwardness to continue the conversation). This is not a simple reflection of the audience's endorsement of John Gielgud; Major Pollock re-establishes his place in the public world – but that public world is itself complex and various. Crocker-Harris does what he does in defiance of the public world; Major Pollock finds himself accepted by that world – because it is composed of individuals whose sense of what is socially acceptable is no longer fixed. In this new, uncertain country, the Major is able, at least, to be his own, inadequate self. Rattigan calls the last scene a 'battle', and so it is; a quiet struggle, not between the private self and public judgement, but between varying concepts of the public world – between the kind of fixed judgements found in *The Winslow*

Boy and *The Browning Version*, and the newer, less certain, but perhaps less constraining atmosphere of a changing Britain.

The private revolution

In 1979, David Hare looked back on a decade or so of the kind of politically engaged, ideas-driven theatre that Rattigan had explicitly attacked in the 1950s. However, in defining the particular nature of the decade, Hare spoke in terms that Rattigan, perhaps, might have recognised: 'We are living through a great, groaning, yawling festival of change – but because this is England it is not always seen on the streets. In my view, it is seen in the extraordinary intensity of people's personal despair . . .'[30] The 1950s, one could argue, was as much of a yawling, groaning festival of change as the 1970s; and, like Hare, Rattigan responded to his time by chronicling the 'intensity of people's personal despair'. Hester and Crocker-Harris live with that despair; it underlies both the Major's self-created identity and John and Anne's flailing relationship. It sometimes breaks through even to the Winslows, try though they might to reject it. Time and again, the private worlds of Rattigan's protagonists are deformed by social pressure; and the victories they achieve are quiet, small, partial ones – even Arthur Winslow, whose eventual vindication destroys his health, and is no longer significant for his son. As the nature of the wider world changes, the relation between the private and the public also changes; Hester, John and Anne, and the Major survive because they no longer face a public threat that seems immutable and all-embracing. However, even here, they are still left to live with the knowledge of their own inadequacy – and with the ever-present threat that the despair Hare identifies as part of the emotional make-up of the 1970s might descend once more on Rattigan's 1950s characters. They might fight their way through to a precarious victory; but their lives are still governed by that odd, dangerous mixture of easement and threat that was a defining feature of the age.

JOHN OSBORNE: THE DRAMA OF EMOTIONS
By Luc Gilleman

> I will not refrain my mouth, I will speak in the anguish of my spirit, I will complain in the bitterness of my soul. (Job 7:11)

Osborne in the 1950s

John Osborne gained recognition during the mid-1950s, a time of transition during which Britain ceased to be a colonial power; its ancient class system was challenged, though not eroded, by the institution of the welfare state; and the country was moving towards the consumer society of the 1960s.[1] The uncertainties of that age, as well as its promise, explain the restlessness that marks its literary heroes. Osborne and other writers of his generation have left us with a vivid picture of vibrant young people living their lives against the grim backdrop of post-war England. Up in his dreary attic room, Jimmy Porter thumps his chest, crying out, 'Oh heavens, how I long for a little ordinary human enthusiasm. Just enthusiasm – that's all. I want to hear a warm thrilling voice cry out Hallelujah! [. . .] Hallelujah! I'm alive'.[2] This attempt at joyful affirmation echoes throughout the 1950s, as for instance in Act II, Scene One of Shelagh Delaney's *A Taste of Honey* (1958):

Geoff We're unique! – Young!

Jo Unrivalled! – Smashing!

Geoff We're bloody marvellous!

Such enthusiasm is too emphatic not to bring to mind the despair it is trying to transcend. It calls up the world of the 1950s, of rented bedsitters, shilling gas meters and boiled carrots.

By the beginning of the next decade, Osborne had written eight plays and started a movie company that helped to define the image we now have of Britain in the 1950s. Woodfall Film, co-founded with Tony Richardson and Harry Saltzman, delivered movie versions of *Look Back in Anger* (1959), *The Entertainer* (1960), and *Inadmissible Evidence* (1968). It also launched a string of grittily realistic movies about lower-class life that are now considered masterworks of British Free Cinema – as, for instance, *Saturday Night and Sunday Morning* (1960), *A Taste of Honey* (1961) and *The Loneliness of the Long Distance Runner* (1962). These plays and movies drew on the experiences of ordinary people who lived in the drearier parts of England. They required a different, less glamorous kind of actor who could convincingly play lower-class characters and authentically render regional accents.[3] Thus Osborne helped challenge what Nicol Williamson calls the theatre of 'sucked cheeks'.[4] Acquiring a posh accent and elegant manners were suddenly less important than being able to deliver the sound of raw emotion.

Today, Osborne is remembered mainly for *Look Back in Anger* (1956), the play that is said to mark the true beginning of post-war British drama. Yet he dominated the British stage for about fifteen years,[5] during which promising young talent as well as well-established actors lined up to fill roles in his work – actors such as Richard Burton, Albert Finney, Nicol Williamson, Paul Scofield, Ralph Richardson, Alec Guinness and Laurence Olivier.[6] The 1950s, however, was truly Osborne's decade, with the media promoting him as the 'angry' young playwright whose daring work was going to sweep away the tamer productions of Noël Coward and Terence Rattigan.[7] Of the eight plays he wrote between 1950 and 1961, three were written in collaboration: *The Devil Inside* (1950), with Stella Linden; *Personal Enemy* (1955) and *Epitaph for George Dillon* (1958), with Anthony Creighton. One was a musical, *The World of Paul Slickey* (1959), which bombed, and another was a television drama, *A Subject of Scandal and Concern* (1960), starring Richard Burton, which drew little attention. Only three plays written during that period continue to stand out: *Look Back in Anger*, *The Entertainer* (1957) and *Luther* (1961) – three bold attempts to create a sentimental theatre relevant for a changed Britain.

Look Back in Anger premiered on 8 May 1956, at London's Royal

Court Theatre. Since Rebellato's book *1956 and All That*, the importance of the play is now routinely questioned.[8] And indeed, *Look Back* did not sweep through the theatre as a force of nature. Neither was it a battering ram; the door was opened from within. The cultural establishment came to Osborne, promoted his play and rescued it when needed. To some extent, it was a media phenomenon, part of a planned programme of renewal. George Devine, artistic director of the newly reopened Royal Court Theatre, was in search of young writers. Anecdotes about Osborne and Devine's first meeting became the creation myth for the Court – a well-respected, pipe-smoking intellectual arriving late for his appointment and having to row across the watery divide that separated him from Osborne, an out-of-work actor and playwright who lived on a houseboat. What could better sum up the Royal Court's willingness to bridge the class divide?

Look Back in Anger: 'the texture of ordinary despair'

Devine and director Tony Richardson, both Oxford-educated, took Osborne, son of a barmaid, under their wing.[9] Ironically, the play they had discovered and were eager to produce takes class resentment as its subject. Reviewers coined the term 'kitchen-sink realism' to emphasise its naturalistic lower-class settings and its implicit rejection of the 'Loamshire play' or middle-class drawing-room drama.[10] Properly speaking, the set of *Look Back* is more bohemian than working-class, not a kitchen but an attic room devoted to intellectual and physical pursuits. It represents Jimmy Porter's space, with 'a jungle of newspapers and weeklies' to feed his brain, a marital bed to fulfil his sexual needs and a gas stove with food cupboard to still his hunger (p. 5). Whereas wife Alison and friend Cliff represent the upper and lower classes respectively, Jimmy is a new type, the déclassé. During the day, he tends a sweet stall in the market; at night, he plays jazz trumpet in local pubs. A lower-middle-class intellectual, educated at one of the newest universities, Jimmy is a product of the welfare state, set loose in a society that limps behind its own ideals and where the best jobs continue to go to the public school boys and the Oxbridge-educated.[11]

Cliff and Alison are recognisable types, yet they are presented in a way that challenges the audience's expectations. While Cliff may express himself in a working-class idiom familiar to theatre audiences – 'Don't let's brawl, boyo,' identifies him as Welsh to boot (p. 50) – he is also smart and ironic: 'The sweet-stall's all right, but I think I'd like to try something else. You're highly educated, and it suits you, but I need something a bit better' (p. 82). Neither would an audience have expected to find a young woman, daughter of a former colonel in the British Raj – in short, a woman used to being served rather than serving – doing the ironing while her lower-class husband discusses culture and politics. Jimmy, moreover, philosophises as naturally as he breathes. His insights and opinions are well-informed and witty. They are not presented as symptoms of lower-class vanity. He is not a typical show-off, as is the overreaching Jean in August Strindberg's *Miss Julie* (1888), for instance. As Kenneth Tynan puts it: 'Here was an educated working-class character, and he spoke with utter superiority.'[12]

In Jimmy, Osborne introduces the editorialising hero whose extensive monologues often consist of opinion pieces on political, social and cultural issues with which the audience was familiar. Jimmy holds forth wittily about any number of these – hypocritical Anglican bishops, the hydrogen bomb, American-style evangelism, the return to power of the Conservative Party – and, as in the following, famous extract, the lack of meaning and purpose in modern life:

Jimmy . . . I suppose people of our generation aren't able to die for good causes any longer. We had all that done for us, in the thirties and the forties, when we were still kids. (*In his familiar, semi-serious mood.*) There aren't any good, brave causes left. If the big bang does come, and we all get killed off, it won't be in aid of the old-fashioned, grand design. It'll just be for the Brave New-nothing-very-much-thank-you. About as pointless and inglorious as stepping in front of a bus. (p. 83)

None of the play's insights, including this one, was particularly original. 'We have, indeed [heard it all before],' Tynan pointed out, 'in novels and essays and works of philosophy; but not (and this is the crux of the matter) in the theatre' (p. 116). In raising these contemporary issues, *Look Back* revived the tradition of the state-of-the-nation play. The plays that followed in its wake – by Arnold Wesker, John Arden, Edward Bond and later Howard Brenton and David Hare, for instance – turned the stage once again into a forum where political and social opinions could be vented, as had been the case with the theatre of Pinero, Shaw and other Ibsen-inspired dramatists of the nineteenth century. This desire to become relevant to people's lives again gave post-war theatre a tremendous boost. Thanks to *Look Back*, from 1956 on, drama rivalled, even surpassed, fiction in its ability to unlock contemporary reality.[13]

And yet, when critics took issue with Jimmy's 'good, brave causes' speech, pointing out that the 1950s were not devoid of worthy causes, Osborne bridled: 'Immediately [the critics] heard this, all the shallow heads with their savage thirst for trimmed-off explanations got to work on it [. . .]. They believed him [. . .]'.[14] Critics, of course, could hardly be faulted for doing what any conventional play analysis demands, examining ideas for their thematic relevance. Other plays famous for dealing with topical issues – Shaw's *Major Barbara* (1905), for instance – are constructed around ideas the audience is expected to discuss. Ideas in Osborne, however, fulfil a different function than they do in Shaw, with whom Osborne shares a delight in articulateness and a joy in the felicitous phrase. Shaw takes care to present a well-formed, dialectical argument – a conscious control that Osborne disliked and rejected.[15] In Shaw, the conflict is embedded in argument, in the clash of ideas; in Osborne, the conflict resides in character and relationships – and ideas mainly convey emotions.

The critics, Osborne complained, 'were incapable of recognizing the texture of ordinary despair, the way it expresses itself in rhetoric and gestures that may perhaps look shabby, but are seldom simple. It is too simple to say that Jimmy Porter himself believed that there we no good, brave causes left [. . .]'.[16]

And indeed, the 'good, brave causes' speech is sandwiched between two apparently gratuitous misogynist remarks: 'Why, why, why, why do we let these women bleed us to death?' and 'No, there's nothing left for it, me boy, but to let yourself be butchered by the women' (p. 83). Framed by these expressions of prejudice and mock exasperation, the speech ceases to be a disinterested comment on contemporary life. Having just learned that Cliff will set up house by himself, Jimmy fears being alone with Helena and uses the 'good, brave causes' speech to conjure up an era when men left wives or girlfriends in order to fight more distant battles. The image is as romantic, and as fake, as Jimmy's nostalgia for India under colonial rule. The overstated misogyny signals that the 'good, brave causes' comment is not to be taken wholly seriously. In Osborne not even an inspired speech is able to transcend the moment; and as it does not deliver a privileged truth or insight, it cannot be used as a key to the play's overall meaning.[17]

If a moment of great eloquence is no longer necessarily a moment of truth, as it is in the well-made play, lines are to be examined for their immediate interactional effect, beat by beat, the way actors and directors do when rehearsing. Educated in the theatre, Osborne understood it from the actor's point of view:

Drama rests on the *dynamic* that is created *between* characters on the stage. It must be concrete and it must be expressed, even if it is only in silence or a gesture of despair. The theatre is not a schoolroom, nor is it, as many people seem to think, a place where 'discussion' takes place, where ideas are apparently formally examined in the manner of a solitary show-off in an intellectual magazine. (Preface)[18]

This means not immediately grasping for overarching themes but paying attention to the emotion pulsing within words, gestures and even silences. Osborne proclaimed, 'I want to make people feel, to give them lessons in feeling. They can think afterwards.'[19] What he seemed to have implied, however, was something more radical: not the ascendancy of feeling over thought but the demotion of thinking to a mode of feeling.

The extent to which the content of dialogue remains subservient to emotional affect can be easily demonstrated. Strip the dialogue from a scene and the stage directions continue to carry its emotional charge unaided:

> *Silence.* [**Jimmy***'s*] *rage mounting within.* [**Alison**], *recognizing an onslaught on the way, starts to panic. The wild note in her voice has re-assured him. His anger cools and hardens. His voice is quite calm when he speaks. He clutches wildly for something to shock* **Helena** *with.* [*He*] *kicks* [*the*] *cistern. Sits on it, beats* [*it*] *like bongo drums.* [*He is*] *capable of anything now.* **Cliff** *and* **Helena** *look at* **Alison** *tensely, but she just gazes at her plate.* **Cliff** *gets up quickly, and takes his arm.* **Jimmy** *pushes him back savagely, and* [**Cliff**] *sits down helplessly, turning his head away on to his hand.* [**Jimmy**] *brakes for a fresh spurt later. He's saving his strength for the knock-out.* (pp. 49–51)

Here, as elsewhere, stage directions come closest to expressing the scene's meaning. Over barely two pages, emotions oscillate between bare containment and exuberant display, with physical movement choreographed accordingly. Leave out the dialogue, and what remains resembles performance art, with Jimmy jumping up, using hands and feet to beat out the rhythm of his anger, then pushing Cliff who grabs his arm, after which Cliff collapses helplessly into a chair. Jimmy dances through the play, struts and gesticulates, performs a Flanagan and Allen double act with Cliff, even engaging him in a fight that ends with an overturned ironing board. Physical rhythms are at the heart of the play and find expression not just through choreographed movement but also through jazz, through improvised music hall numbers and stand-up comedy, and even through the classical strains of Vaughan Williams.

Speech too pulses with emotion, even to the extent that it blurs meaning, becoming surreal in its straining for effect:

> **Jimmy** . . . Mummy may look over-fed and a bit flabby on the outside, but don't let that well-bred guzzler fool you. Underneath all that, she's armour plated. [. . .] She's as rough as a night in a Bombay brothel, and as tough as a matelot's arse. She's probably in that bloody cistern, taking down every word we say. (p. 50)

The censored version used in the original production reads 'as tough as a matelot's arm', thus moving us from an exotic Bombay brothel to the incongruous image of a maritime muscleman. The 1996 edition of the *Collected Plays* restored this to the original 'matelot's arse'. This is perhaps one case where the censored version is more appropriate as the point of comparison is toughness ('armour plated') rather than decadence. Increasingly intent on shocking, Jimmy moves his listeners' attention from the ample person of Alison's mother, suddenly turned into a tough old dame, to a squalid orgy and a well-used seedy sailor, before allowing her to return eavesdropping from inside a trunk. As what is being said is constantly modulated by how and why it is being said, the play becomes a musical as much as a literary composition, with language being constantly and consciously performed. 'Jimmy Porter's inaccurately named "tirades",' says Osborne, 'should be approached as arias, and require the most adroit handling, delicacy of delivery, invention and timing.'[20] Silence, by contrast, should be allowed to speak loudly, even coarsely. Osborne insists that Alison, 'not her husband . . . was the most deadly bully. Her silence and her obdurate withdrawal were impregnable. The ironing-board was not the plaything of her submission, but the bludgeon and shield which were impenetrable to all Jimmy's appeals to desperate oratory.'[21] And indeed, only by performing silence, by giving it its full due, can one prevent the play from being dominated by a single voice.

A closer look at the interaction proves that Alison and Jimmy are more evenly matched than Osborne suggests, with both characters compelled to react in ways that enforce the stalemate. Jimmy rails at Alison because he interprets her reticence as disapproval or disinterest: 'I rage, and shout my head off, and everyone thinks "poor chap!" or "what an objectionable young man!" But that girl there can twist your arm off with her silence' (p. 57). And yet silence may well be Alison's only option, since Jimmy accepts none of her responses:

Alison (*softly*)   All I want is a little peace.

Jimmy   Peace! God! She wants peace! (*Hardly able to get his words out.*) My heart is so full, I feel ill – and she wants peace! (p. 57)

As Alison explains to Cliff, she cannot even express agreement or sympathy. 'I suppose it would have been so easy to say "Yes, darling, I know just what you mean. I know what you're feeling." (*Shrugs*.) It's those easy things that seem to be so impossible with us' (p. 24). Alison and Jimmy are caught in a classic double-bind. Only by pretending to be a bear and a squirrel can they relate to one another without misunderstandings.[22]

Despite being the engine of violent and desperate emotions, the double-bind never achieves thematic relevance in the play. Out of this unusual and complex relationship grows a fairly unremarkable narrative that runs along the well-known mileposts of the well-made play: an unexpected pregnancy, a desertion, a treacherous woman and the reconciliation of the lovers. Alison's pregnancy together with her inability to tell her husband serves as complication of the action: 'He'll suspect my motives at once. [. . .] Tonight it might be all right – we'd make love. [. . .] In the morning, he'd feel hoaxed, as if I were trying to kill him in the worst way of all' (p. 26). Alison withdraws to her parental home, inadvertently offering her friend Helena the opportunity to take her place in the marital bed and at the ironing board. In the end, Alison returns to Jimmy, having lost her baby. In a classic recognition scene (Aristotle's *anagnorisis*), she admits to being 'a lost cause' (p. 93), and Jimmy, instead of dancing about in her tears (as he had predicted he would), is forced to revise his heroic self-image. In a characteristic reversal (Aristotle's *peripeteia*), he now questions his belief in a 'burning virility of mind and spirit that looks for something as powerful as itself' and admits that he and Alison are 'rather mad, slightly satanic, and very timid little animals' (p. 95). Whatever complexity Osborne had conjured up in the couple's inter-action risks being drowned in the melodrama of the love story.

Osborne later conceded that *Look Back*, with its conventional three-Act structure, was in many ways a 'formal, old-fashioned play'.[23] Some of the exits and entrances are awkwardly planned: 'Go out and get me some cigarettes' (p. 29), for instance. Every scene ends rather too neatly on a melodramatic curtain – including the final one, with Jimmy and Alison intoning, 'Poor squirrels! . . . Oh, poor, poor bears!' (p. 95). There is even a classic letter scene, where Alison announces that she is leaving Jimmy. All this accords with the rules of playwriting as enshrined in the principles of the *pièce bien faite*. In later plays, Osborne would play fast and loose with the rules. But his collaborators on two earlier plays, Stella Linden and Anthony Creighton, had impressed upon him the need for discipline.[24] And *Look Back*'s closeness to the well-made play may have facilitated its acceptance. The daily fare of the commercial stage still consisted mainly of well-made plays – by Rattigan and Coward, for instance – as well as by the lesser-known Hugo Williams and Margaret Vyner. 'The Williams well-maders work in so far as they succour and flatter a bewildered, disinherited middle-class audience bawling after a decadent and dummy tradition,' was Osborne's verdict.[25] The world of shared assumptions and expectations implied by the well-made play was long gone.

But *Look Back* distanced itself from the well-made play by abandoning the major principle of good playwriting: that of economy, which dictates that nothing should be mentioned that remains extraneous to the action. The play mentions far too many characters who never make an appearance (Webster, Madeline, Nigel, Alison's mother, Hugh Tanner and his mother, etc.). There are far too many diversions (Cliff and Jimmy's double-act routines, for instance) whose only function seems to be to introduce a change of pace. Most importantly, the play's language is excessive. In a well-made play language plays a subservient role, driving action, revealing character and articulating ideas; in *Look Back*, it draws attention to itself, as characters showcase their linguistic and poetic virtuosity. Though a contemporary critic described the play's language as 'slangy, gay, messy and irreverent',[26] Osborne was little interested in reproducing the spontaneity of the spoken word: 'Many people made the mistake of claiming that the language of *Look Back in Anger* was naturalistic, whatever that means. The language of "everyday life" is almost incommunicable for the very good reason that it is restricted, inarticulate, dull and boring . . .'[27] Instead, Osborne perfected a highly recognisable dramatic language that was able to convey the 'texture of ordinary despair'.

Because of its intense emotional charge, its unresolved conflicts and contradictions, the effect of that language was overwhelming, stirring a popular debate about theatre and contemporary society. As Aleks Sierz points out, '*Look Back in Anger*'s centrality [may indeed be] a foundation myth', but it is one that enjoys 'strong support from the theatre community'.[28] David Hare called *Look Back in Anger* 'the play whose effect I would most like to have provoked'.[29] It is true that *Look Back* was not a technically innovative play. It did not influence the course of modern drama to the extent that Beckett or Brecht did, at their London premieres in 1955 and 1956. Its effect was altogether different. Osborne called it 'a nexus for a lot of social feelings. What emerged was eloquent of the country and of the times. Layers of expression found an outlet. There was an excitement, a new vitality in the arts. The theatre became a more fruitful and accurate picture of life than, say, Parliament.'[30] And that excitement proved infectious, drawing younger audiences to frequent the theatre and new talent to write for the stage.

The Entertainer: 'the heart of England'

One foreign playwright who immediately recognised the importance of *Look Back* was Arthur Miller. The play, he said, spoke with a vibrancy and passion more familiar to American than to British audiences. Osborne's instinctive rebelliousness and impatience with 'conventional class lines' reminded him of Mark Twain[31] and Osborne's style 'of Clifford Odets in his youth'.[32] Ironically, though *Look Back* expresses concern about the English identity in an American age, Osborne had introduced 'a very American kind of realism' to the British stage.[33] Traditionally, the British play, at least according to Miller, tends to be 'oblique and remote' whereas the American 'is pre-eminently active, relatively unreflective as such. It deals with nothing it cannot act out. It rarely comments on itself; like the people, it always pretends it does not know what it is doing. It must *be* something rather than be *about* something.'[34]

Miller's endorsement prompted Laurence Olivier, a national idol then as much as an eminent actor, to revise his opinion of Osborne and ask for a role in his next play. Olivier had disapproved of *Look*

Back, suspecting it of being unpatriotic. The play, he told Miller, was 'just a travesty on England, a lot of bitter rattling on about conditions'.[35] His decision to act in Osborne's next play proved mutually beneficial; it stimulated Olivier's career by expanding his repertoire and moved Osborne further into the mainstream. Since then many famous comedians and actors have tried on the role of Archie Rice (Max Wall, Michael Gambon and Jack Lemmon), but to this day it is mainly associated with Olivier.

The Entertainer, which premiered on 10 April 1957, at the Royal Court Theatre, stands out as Osborne's first conscious effort at technical innovation. An introductory note expresses the hope that music hall techniques would heighten the play's immediacy, 'solve some of the eternal problems of time and space that face the dramatist' and cut through 'the restrictions of the so-called naturalistic stage'.[36] The note makes no mention of contemporary innovators such as Bertolt Brecht. Osborne had been among the enthusiastic spectators when the Berliner Ensemble performed *Mother Courage and Her Children* at London's Palace Theatre in August 1956. In a letter to the *Sunday Times* he described Courage's carriage as a symbol of what could be done on the non-naturalistic stage. In comparison, 'that sturdy old animal the Ibsenite Punch, still slogging patiently for the British dramatist, is looking pretty deadbeat, and the sooner he can be packed off to some happy home in the country where his Auntie Edna can come down and tempt him with lumps of sugar the better', note the reference to Aunt Edna.[37] Despite his admiration for Brecht, Osborne rejected allegations of having succumbed to his influence in *The Entertainer* and *Luther*, claiming to go back to a venerable English tradition of a vital stage, centred around the actor, unencumbered by complex sets or stage machinery – a tradition that dates back at least to Shakespeare and that had been kept alive in the music hall.[38]

The Entertainer abandons the box set (as in the Porters' claustrophobic attic room) for a more fluid conception of space. The stage can be quickly divided or opened up by means of backcloths, 'flats' and 'swags' so that naturalistic scenes of domestic life can alternate with music hall 'numbers'. This allowed the audience to compare Archie's private life with his public appearances. In Archie, Osborne has created one of his more successful and painfully pathetic ageing characters. Archie has nothing to offer but his own fear and derision, selling the last scrap of his dignity in front of an indifferent and hostile crowd. Hustling his trade, he seems more obscenely exposed than the naked ladies in his show. Alone in the spotlight, his face hidden under pancake make-up, his uncertainties, resentment and fear are more on display than at home. Archie's private self is theatrically armoured, while his public persona is naked and vulnerable. His strategy at home is the same as on the stage: he invites the derision he expects he will get and prefers to dramatise his abjectness rather than to suffer it. With his camp sensibility and ability to hold an emotion at arm's length, to mock and comment on it, he resembles a character from a Noël Coward play:[39]

> **Archie** Phoebe, let's see you do your dance. (*This is thrown off in the usual casual, studied* **Archie** *manner.*) She dances jolly well, don't you, you poor old thing. I wonder if she'll make me cry tonight. We'll see. We'll see. (pp. 58–9)

In Archie, the conscious display of being takes precedence over being itself. It is hard to know what he truly thinks or feels. As Osborne explains in a stage direction: 'Whatever he says to anyone is almost always very carefully "thrown away". Apparently absent minded, it is a comedian's technique, it absolves him from seeming committed to anyone or anything' (p. 34).

Having lost the idealism of youth and yet without the certainties of old age, middle-aged Archie represents all those who have no other choice but to hang on to the shambles of a changed England. It is because of Archie that *The Entertainer* is now remembered as a state of the nation play, an elegiac enactment of Britain's post-war decline. 'Don't clap too hard – it's a very old building' (p. 59), he says, and in an introductory note Osborne makes sure we know that the music hall stands for post-war, post-colonial England: 'The music hall is dying, and, with it, a significant part of England. Some of the heart of England has gone; something that once belonged to everyone, for this was truly a folk art' (p. 7). That 'truly' betrays Osborne's sentimental approach to the music hall and to the English people. With its excess of feeling obfuscating critical thinking, *The Entertainer* is better at enacting nostalgia than at convincing us of the worthiness of its causes.

It is clear, for instance, that the 'heart of England' holds no place for the Polish or Irish immigrants Archie's father Billy is constantly complaining about (p. 113). The genuine sound of England is preserved in the pubs with their sing-alongs and in the music hall with their laughter at shared targets at a time when being politically correct meant precisely what it says: comedians poked fun at toffs and politicians but refrained from challenging their audience's patriotism and unthinking conservatism. As Billy puts it, 'We knew what the rules were, and even if we spent half our time making people laugh at 'em we never seriously suggested that anyone should break them' (p. 81). Leftist sentiment had no place in the music hall, and by extension in the play's vision of ordinary people. To the many easy targets (homosexuals, Irish, foreigners, etc.), Archie adds the welfare state because its 'drab equality' (p. 32) is un-English. Not to depend on others is a source of pride among the poor. When she's drunk, Archie's wife Phoebe likes to dwell on her days of poverty, if only to conclude, 'But I made something of myself. I did try to do something' – even if that 'something' meant catching a patronising and deceitful husband (vi.50).[40] And although we later learn that the family depends on handouts from Archie's successful brother, Billy too agrees that the welfare state has taken initiative and accomplishment away: 'No use leaving it to the Government for them to hand it out to a lot of bleeders who haven't got the gumption to do anything for themselves' (p. 21).

These emotional pronouncements remain largely unchallenged in the play. From the beginning, Archie's real enemy is the government, represented by the income-tax man who at the end of the play has him arrested after his last show. It is that same government who bungles the Suez Crisis, an ill-considered adventure that costs Mick, Archie's dutiful son, his life. 'What d'you make of all this business out in the Middle East?' says Billy. 'People seem to be able to do what they like to us' (p. 17). But it is not imperial ambition that Osborne faulted. In *Look Back*, Jimmy waxed nostalgic about the last days of the Raj (I.13). What Osborne regretted about the Suez Crisis was the mismanaging and thus the wasting of human life in an inglorious war. 'What made Suez a typically Tory venture,' Osborne opined, 'was not only its deception, its distaste for the basic assumptions of democracy, but the complete ineptitude of its execution.'[41]

The play questions neither the war nor the loss of life, but the absence of a living and inspiring ideology that could justify it. Mick, the dutiful son, becomes a war hero only to be killed ingloriously by the 'Wogs', a sacrifice that brings no comfort to his family. As Jean, the intellectual of the family, puts it, 'what's it all in aid of – is it really just for the sake of a gloved hand waving at you from a golden coach?' (p. 78). The question drew much comment, so that Sir Larry felt he had to distance himself from this and other controversial aspects of the play.[42] Not only does the play never move beyond that question, but also the question itself is not the critical comment it once seemed. Osborne did not disapprove of the monarchy but rather of the hollowness of its symbolism: 'My objection to the Royalty symbol is that it is dead; it is the gold filling in a mouthful of decay.'[43] Formulated this way, the remark is far from radical. Indeed, Osborne seems to be faulting not the monarchy but a decaying society for not being able to live up to its own ancient symbols.[44]

The play implies that patriotism, in post-war Britain, is but a collection of fossilised sentiments, no longer able to quell people's grief and rebelliousness. When Frank, Archie's other son and a conscientious objector, sings the blues for his dead brother Mick, the anger and irony are not lost on the audience: 'Those playing fields of Eton / Have really got us beaten. / But ain't no use agrievin' / 'Cos it's Britain we believe in' (p. 74). Britain, however, does not believe in the likes of Frank. It holds no promise when 'you're nobody, you've no money, and you're young' (p. 67). Frank has lost all hope for England and at the end of the play seeks his fortune overseas. Settled in his ways, Archie prefers prison to emigration, with a laconic, 'You can't get draught Bass in Toronto' (p. 84). More than an offhand remark, it is indicative of Archie's nostalgia for an Englishness as ephemeral as a set of attitudes yet as tangible as a pint of beer.

The play looks back wistfully from an alienating present to a past when Englishness guaranteed a sense of belonging and common purpose. 'I feel sorry for you people,' says old Billy. 'You don't know what it's really like. You haven't lived, most of you. You've never known what it was like, you're all miserable really. You don't know what life can be like' (p. 23). Billy is nostalgic for a time that never truly existed – a time when 'we were all English. What's more, we spoke English' (p. 81), and when that mythical Englishness could freely exert its cohesive powers: 'every man wore a hat in those days, didn't matter if he was a lord or a butcher – every man used to take his hat off when he passed the Cenotaph' (p. 79). This conjures up the image of a rather absurd clockwork England with hat-doffing citizens circling a monument. In the end, it remains unclear whether anything was lost – that is, anything more tangible than a dream.

Archie and Jean go their separate ways, each in pursuit of a different dream of England. In his own words, Archie is just out for himself, for 'good old number one'. And to survive he is willing to do anything, whatever the cost to his family. He would have sacrificed his wife Phoebe if Jean and Billy did not mess up his plan to abandon her for a rich young girl. When that plan falls through, he sacrifices Billy, his old father, using his reputation as a once successful comedian to sell his own show. He betrays them as easily as he sullies the idea of patriotism, which in his show assumes the shape of a nude Britannia to draw an audience. Whereas Archie in his dogged determination to survive represents an England of solitary and disillusioned individuals, Jean stands for an England imbued by a new collective spirit and sense of loyalty. She does not follow Frank abroad but stays behind to undo her father's damage by helping her stepmother Phoebe. Jean renounces the advantages of a scholarship and a rich boyfriend out of an ill-defined sense of solidarity with common folks:

> **Jean** . . . Have you ever got on a railway train here, got on a train from Birmingham to West Hartlepool? Or gone from Manchester to Warrington or Widnes. And you get out, you go down the street, and on one side maybe is a chemical works, and on the other side maybe is the railway goods yard. Some kids are playing in the street, and you walk up to some woman standing

on her doorstep. It isn't a doorstep really because you can walk straight from the street into her front room. What can you say to her? What real piece of information, what message can you give to her? Do you say: 'Madam, d'you know that Jesus died on the Cross for you?' (pp. 84–5)

This is an England devoid of grand illusions, inhabited by people immune to anything that lacks practical value, including to the notion of redemption through sacrifice. While the speech expresses her love for ordinary people, it also forebodes the futility of her own sacrifice for Phoebe, a woman who never passes up an opportunity to remind her that she is not her real daughter.

The play succeeds, however, at directing the audience's empathy not towards Jean, who acts out of principle, but toward Archie, who goes to prison out of a single-minded determination to fight his battle with the taxman to the end. When Jean turns on the scheming Archie, accusing him of selfishness, the family makes it clear she lacks under-standing. Phoebe responds with a simple 'He's always been good to me' (p. 78) and Frank advises her to 'leave them alone [. . .] You're not going to change anybody' (p. 80). And with these words, the audience too is asked not to sit in judgement. Osborne's sympathies reside with Archie, the man who claims rather too emphatically that he is 'dead behind these eyes' and does not 'feel a thing' (p. 72), who insults himself before others can, and who every night stands before an indif-ferent audience and has the courage to fail. This is the man who is allowed the last line in the play before he is led away to prison. From the wasteland of post-war Britain, he addresses the audience with a music-hall variant of Baudelaire's 'hypocrite lecteur': 'Let me know where you're working tomorrow night – and I'll come and see YOU' (p. 89). Osborne had it engraved on his tombstone. Judge such a man at your own peril.

Luther: 'the just shall live by faith'

Osborne, on the other hand, never thought twice about judging others. He did so vociferously when the Berlin Crisis of 1961 strained relations between the superpowers to breaking point. Britain, which in the late 1950s had been testing thermonuclear bombs and was now part of the US–UK Mutual Defence Agreement, joined in with belligerent rhetoric. The world seemed on the verge of an all-out nuclear war when, on 18 August 1961, Osborne sent an angry 'Letter to My Fellow Countrymen' to the *Tribune*. In hysterical terms it professes the writer's murderous intentions:

> There is murder in my brain, and I carry a knife in my heart for every one of you. Macmillan, and you, Gaitskell, you particularly. I wish we could hang you all out, with your dirty washing, on your damned Oder-Neisse Line, and those seven out of ten Americans, too. I would willingly watch you all die for the West, if only I could keep my own minuscule portion of it, you could all go ahead and die for Berlin, for Democracy, to keep out the red hordes or whatever you like.[45]

Signed 'In sincere and utter hatred', the letter provoked heated reactions in the press as well as ridicule, because Osborne had sent it from his luxurious hideout in the south of France.

Most striking about the 'Damn You, England' letter is its tone of personal grievance. It speaks with paranoid hysteria as if international relations were aimed solely at annoying Osborne. In Osborne's dramatic work political concerns appear similarly as extensions of private neuroses.[46] Jimmy Porter finds his private fears confirmed in newspaper articles about the bomb and the hypocrisy of religious and political leaders. For Archie Rice, the taxman, symbol of welfare collectivisation, personifies the threat to 'good old number one'. And in Osborne's next successful play, the bureaucracy of Rome and the rules and regulations of Catholic devotion represent the paternal authority Luther rejects. But whereas Jimmy and Archie fulminate in their private spheres, Martin Luther is the only Osborne character who achieves effective social, political and religious reform.

Luther was first staged at the Theatre Royal in Nottingham on 26 June 1961, garnered critical acclaim at the International Theatre Festival in Paris, premiered in London at the Royal Court Theatre and enjoyed a successful run on Broadway, where it received a Tony Award in 1964. In England, much attention was bestowed on the remarkable young actor from Lancashire who played Luther, Albert Finney, who had just starred as Arthur Seaton, in Karel Reisz's *Saturday Night and Sunday Morning* (1960). But reviewers were particularly struck by the distance Osborne had travelled since *Look Back*. As Michael Foot put it:

> That a playwright should step with such assurance from his crowded bed-sitting rooms and sleazy music halls on to the stage of world history; that he should have the insight to see Luther as much as a poet as a prophet; and that he should be able to interweave in the ancient drama his own modern strand of relentless astringency – these are further proofs of greatness, if any were still needed.[47]

Like Michael Foot, many recognised *Luther* as the crowning achievement of Osborne's work in the 1950s. It left even Osborne with an unusual sense of accomplishment: 'We were home,' he concluded, 'if not altogether dry.'[48]

And yet *Luther* is in some ways Osborne's least original play. It deals with a common theme, that of an individual rebelling against the established order, present, for instance, in Ibsen's *An Enemy of the People* (1893), Shaw's *Saint Joan* (1923), Brecht's *Life of Galileo* (1945), Miller's *The Crucible* (1953) and Bolt's *A Man for All Seasons* (1960). Several plays of the 1950s and early 1960s dealt with the relationship between Thomas Becket, Archbishop of Canterbury, and Henry II in the twelfth century, or with that between Sir Thomas More and King Henry VIII in the sixteenth – to which Luther's struggles with the authorities bear some resemblance. An important revival of Eliot's *Murder in the Cathedral* (1935) had taken place at the Old Vic in 1953. There were productions of Jean Anouilh's *Becket* and Christopher Fry's *Curtmantle* at the Royal Shakespeare Company in

London in 1961 and 1962 respectively. *A Man for All Seasons*, about Thomas More and Henry VIII, premiered in London on 1 July 1960. *Luther* shares with that play a number of Brechtian devices such as the expressionist set, the use of a narrator who addresses the audience and an episodic plot. So when *Luther* arrived at the Royal Court Theatre on 27 July 1961, it could count on a critical climate attuned to its theme and to historical drama in general.

For the story of Luther's rise to power, Osborne was bound by history, which he sets out quickly in a succession of bold tableaux covering a period of twenty-four years. The play sticks to well-known historical mileposts in Luther's life, such as the nailing of the ninety-five theses to the door of Wittenberg's Castle Church, his appearance at the Diet of Worms (ending with the apocryphal 'Here I stand; God help me; I can do no more'), his suppression of the Peasants' Movement and his retreat to domesticity. Few but sticklers for historical detail could take issue with Osborne's representation of history.[49] In general, Osborne follows the standard account of the Reformation, the transition between the medieval and the modern world, between a world ruled by institutions and one ruled by the individual – or, in a more modern conception, by the individual's fragmented consciousness.

Osborne's depiction of Luther's fragmented consciousness was upsetting to many; original it was not, being derived mainly from Erik H. Erikson's *Young Man Luther: A Study in Psychoanalysis and History* (1958). Erikson uses the story of Luther's life to demonstrate major stages in a young man's identity formation. Like Erikson, Osborne offers a psychological reading of Luther's lifelong physical discomforts, tracing his stomach upsets and chronic constipation to a psychological crisis in his relationship with his father and with authority in general. At the heart of that crisis lies a paralysing self-awareness, an inability to 'let go' that translates symptomatically at both ends of the alimentary canal into constipation and impeded access to speech. Like the stammering Holyoake in Osborne's television drama *A Subject of Scandal and Concern* (1960), Martin strives to speak freely and unself-consciously and yet, at critical moments, he becomes aware of the 'single words' and gets stuck: 'I heard them as if it were the first time, and suddenly [. . .] they struck at my life'.[50] This hyperawareness of what is supposed to be natural causes him to dry up – just as he does in 'the jakes', when he is reminded of the stubborn demands of the body. Only when he stops striving and allows himself to be carried by faith alone do the words flow unhindered – while often at that moment his bowels open up. Osborne's play makes much of the relation between Martin's body and the body politic of his time, quoting the historical Luther's famous phrase, 'If I break wind in Wittenberg, they might smell it in Rome' (p. 60). Protestantism, it would seem from that account, came into being not in the study or the chapel but in the bathroom – confirmed by Luther's preference for scatological figures of speech: 'I'm like a ripe stool in the world's straining anus, and at any moment we're about to let each other go' (p. 55).

Some critics were annoyed or discomfited by the play's bathroom talk.[51] However, these and other striking lines in the play are not Osborne's but the historical Luther's who expressed himself in an earthy, sometimes pungent, German. Because most obscenities in the play were culled from the great man's *Tischreden*, they were left uncensored by the Lord Chamberlain's Office. As for the rest, because of the play's wide historical span, Osborne was forced to use language economically, allowing it to hammer out themes more bluntly than was his want. The audience does not have to figure out that Martin rebels against the authority vested in his father. He articulates that thought quite clearly: 'All you want is me to justify *you*! Well, I can't, and, what's more, I won't. I can't even justify myself . . . I've done all for you I'll ever do, and that's live and wait to die' (p. 42). When Martin rejects responsibility for the brutal slaughter of peasants who followed his example in rebelling against authority, he spells out the psychological basis for his fear of anarchy: 'When I see chaos, then I see the devil's organ and then I'm afraid' (p. 89). This is untypically direct for Osborne, though it is how language is conventionally used-to reveal character, drive plot or articulate ideas.

Because of this directness, *Luther* allows us an uncommonly clear view of Osborne's assumptions about the relationship between psychology and politics. Thoughts and arguments are developed more fully in *Luther* than in other Osborne plays because public scenes are dominated by the oratorical mode of the sermon. A whole scene, for instance, is taken up by Tetzel's sermon, a cleverly constructed sales pitch for indulgences. It starts with a series of simple rhetorical questions ('Are you wondering who I am, or what I am?'), rising in a crescendo of self-aggrandisement in the end:

> **Tetzel** . . . And if you only have the coat on your back to call your own, then strip it off, strip it off now so that you too can obtain grace. For remember: as soon as your money rattles in the box and the cash bell rings, the soul flies out of purgatory and sings! So, come on then. Get your money out! What is it then, have your wits flown away with your faith? Listen then, soon, I shall take down the cross, shut the gates of heaven, and put out the brightness of this sun of grace that shines on you here today. (pp. 50–1)

The coins that upon this speech roll into the strongbox confirm Tetzel's successful imposition of his self-image upon his audience. By the end of his speech, he has grown from a common huckster into a man with the power to command God's grace.

Two scenes later, Martin's sermon forms a counterpoint to Tetzel's. Its effectiveness depends on the same ability to lend general validity to a private vision, but whereas Tetzel builds himself up, Martin breaks himself down in front of his audience. Before Luther reaches the conclusion that 'the just' shall not earn their salvation through good works but 'shall live by faith alone' (p. 63), he tells his audience how this insight occurred to him during a most private moment:

> **Martin** . . . For you must be made to know that there's no security, there's no security at all, either in indulgences, holy busywork or anywhere in this world. It came to me while I was in my tower, what they call the monk's sweathouse, the jakes, the john or whatever you're pleased to call it. I was struggling with the text I've given you: 'For therein is the righteousness of God revealed, from faith to faith; as it is written, the just shall live by

faith.' And seated there, my head down, on that privy just as when I was a little boy, I couldn't reach down to my breath for the sickness in my bowels, as I seemed to sense beneath me a large rat, a heavy, wet, plague rat, slashing at my privates with its death's teeth. [. . .] And I sat in my heap of pain until the words emerged and opened out. 'The just shall live by faith.' My pain vanished, my bowels flushed and I could get up. (pp. 62–3).

It is through sermons like this that Martin overcomes his paralysing awareness of the 'single word' and his struggle with doubt. As he says to his mentor, the Vicar-General Staupitz, 'Father, I'm never sure of the words till I hear them out loud.' To which Staupitz replies, 'Well, that's probably the meaning of the Word. The Word is *me*, and I am the Word.' When he launches them from the pulpit, Martin hears his words becoming Spirit and thus Truth. By the end of his sermon, absolute insecurity has inverted into absolute certainty and private shame into positive assertion.

Martin's sermon scene has to be read in conjunction not just with Tetzel's but also with an earlier one, in which we find Martin as a much younger man fighting his doubts during a public confession. Overwhelmed by the thought of his sinfulness, he had called out 'I am a worm and no man [. . .]. Crush out the worminess in me, stamp on me' (p. 19). Martin's language then broke down as he succumbed to an epileptic fit. At that time, he was still imposing upon himself 'an impossible standard of perfection' (p. 54). The sermon recounts the moment when he decides to give up on perfection and throw himself upon God's grace. The correctness of that decision he finds confirmed not through logical reasoning but through an overwhelming physical and mental experience, the sudden ability to evacuate his bowels as well as to articulate his inner world. The implications of such a psychological and physical imperative are vast. Martin has no programme of social or religious reform in mind when he reaches a conclusion whose effects will be far-reaching. The sermon is born from a personal need of 'a man struggling for certainty, struggling insanely like a man in a fit, an animal trapped to the bone with doubt' (p. 73). The play thus implies that out of the most private experience, responding to the most private need grows the Lutheran conviction that the way to God is not through good works but through faith.

Predicated on overwhelming feelings rather than careful thought, Martin's decisions tend towards the absolute. In matters of religion, Martin remains the 'excessive doctor' (p. 65) who rejects the principle of exchange: 'Shells for shells, empty things for empty men' (p. 62). The sale of indulgences implies a mercantile vision of virtue, as if it can be measured and doled out. For Martin, virtue is an inalienable quality that cannot be quantified. 'You can't strike bargains with God' also means that no surplus of virtue, accumulated by the saints, can be credited to your individual account through the purchase of indulgences. But the result, the play implies, is an excess of loneliness and an abdication of social responsibility. Martin rejects the idea of a community of the virtuous who look after those who struggle with sin. In its place, he posits a belief in individuality: 'only *you* could live *your* life, and only you can die your death. It can't be taken over for you' (p. 58).

This emphasis on the singularity of everyone's experience also means that when the floodgates of the mind open up, and the words are set free among the people, Martin remains innocent of the consequences (p. 69). When he tells the pope, 'I cannot understand all this hostility, and I am alarmed by it' (p. 75), he is only partly disingenuous, upholding even for himself the cherished fiction of innocence, of in moments of inspiration having regained 'the lost body of a child' (p. 80). This vision of a gap opening up between the speaker and his words is confirmed by the Knight recalling the sermon that led to the Peasants' Movement and the bloody massacre that followed in its wake. Martin, he says, was repulsive in his physicality: 'I could smell every inch of him even from where I was' (p. 86). Yet the words transcended the flawed physical vessel that gave birth to them and set everyone's imagination on fire. Again and again, though, Martin fails to live up to his own words – or to what others hear in them. In that respect, the play follows the historical record. Faced with the social anarchy unleashed by his words, Luther responded with a 1523 pamphlet 'Against the Murdering, Thieving, Hordes of Peasants' and sided with the powerful, leading to the massacre of the peasants and lesser knights the play faithfully records. In the play, Martin is finally left behind by the developments his words triggered. An obvious parallel with Brecht's *Life of Galileo* suggests itself: Galileo's scientific vision of a decentred universe also led to political unrest. The common people had heard its promise of equality – a social effect Galileo, with his innocent faith in the superiority of the truth, had not foreseen. The ending of both plays is remarkably similar. Ensconced in domesticity, Martin, like Galileo, ends up as a diminished figure who looks forward only to his next meal.

In the anguish of his spirit

Almost a Gentleman (1991), the second volume of Osborne's autobiography, ends with a line which forms the epigraph for this essay.[52] The line is revealing because, more than of anger, Osborne is the playwright of anguish and helplessness. His characters are not lovable yet insist on being heard, even if excess of feeling chases away those who are trying to love them. David Hare calls Osborne

> our poet laureate of flopsweat, of lost opportunity, of missed connections and of hidden dread, of what he himself calls 'the comfortless tragedy of isolated hearts'. John's plays are what you feel when you wake prickling in the dark: half-truth experienced as whole truth, intuition experienced as fact. John's characters, quivering, vibrating with life, have no clue how to put the nightmare away, how to chuck it, forget it, put a sock in it, repress it or even, for God's sake, how to talk the bloody thing to death. These are people to whom the fear always returns.[53]

Jimmy Porter, Archie Rice, Martin Luther, and later, Bill Maitland and Colonel Redl, are Osborne's most memorable tortured souls, doomed to failure because they rebel against nothing more tangible than life itself and the constraints it imposes. Dramatising their abjectness, they dare the audience to turn their backs on them. Finally, of course, the audience did just that. At the waning of his career, Osborne, like his characters, cast himself in a tragic light, as a man unjustly ignored by an unfeeling crowd. Suffering the humiliation of increasing irrelevancy and critical derision, '[h]e was left with a frightening bitterness', David Hare recalls. 'He thought the struggle had not been worthwhile. "It wouldn't have mattered if I hadn't lived".'[54]

ARNOLD WESKER: THE TRILOGY
by John Bull

Introduction

In a long career, Arnold Wesker has written over forty plays for the stage, but he will always be chiefly associated with the 'new wave' of British Theatre running from the mid-1950s to the early 1960s. John Osborne, with *Look Back in Anger* (1956), followed by *The Entertainer* (1957) and *Luther* (1961), is usually credited with setting the Royal Court Theatre in London on its way to developing a conscious strategy for the encouragement of new writing. However, although Wesker never quite enjoyed Osborne's early success, his first plays were in many ways more in keeping with the colourful descriptions that were coined to describe the new wave, as a kitchen-sink drama produced by angry young men. His was always a left-wing stance, and in 1960 his involvement with the Campaign for Nuclear Disarmament (CND) resulted in a month's imprisonment for taking part in a civil disobedience protest. In contrast, Osborne fairly quickly grew impatient with the politics of the radical intelligentsia, including CND and the annual Aldermaston March, and this was reflected in his work, which became increasingly concerned with private *angst*; Wesker's radicalism was more deep-rooted (he had even briefly been a member of the Young Communist League and, more importantly, the Zionist Youth Movement), and this was also reflected in his work, which sought directly to address public political issues.

It was in this period that he had staged five plays that alone would guarantee his place in the roll-call of modern theatre. The first, *The*

Kitchen, was written in 1957 while he was attending the London School of Film Technique, something that is evident in the filmic construction of the play. It draws upon his own experiences as successively a kitchen porter, a pastry cook and a chef, and depicts a single day in the kitchen of a somewhat second-rate London restaurant. It was not properly staged (at the Court) until 1961,[1] having already been released in a film version, made (appropriately) by a unit of the Association of Cinema Technicians. Ironically, all losses sustained on the four-week run were guaranteed by Twentieth Century-Fox, in return for the English Stage Company's agreement to release Rex Harrison from a contract so that he could appear in *Cleopatra*.[2] The fifth of these plays, *Chips with Everything* (1962) – a title borrowed from a disparaging remark made by Gaston, the grill chef, in *The Kitchen*[3] – also leans heavily on his past memories, in this instance of the initial weeks of training for his stint of national service in the RAF. With a long commercial transfer from the Royal Court to the Vaudeville Theatre in London's West End, *Chips* remains the most financially successful of all of his plays.

In between came the three plays, collectively known as the 'Wesker Trilogy', *Chicken Soup with Barley* (1958), *Roots* (1959) and *I'm Talking About Jerusalem* (1960). Where *The Kitchen* and *Chips* had mined his own youthful experiences, in *Chicken Soup* and *Jerusalem* Wesker offered a sweeping historical construct in which echoes of his upbringing and the immediate history of his family are fictively reconstituted in the context of pre- and post-Second World War history.

The second play, *Roots*, is linked, in that the central character, Beatie Bryant, is engaged to the Ronnie Kahn who appears in the other two plays. Beatie is loosely based on Wesker's wife Dusty who, like the character, had been a waitress in Norfolk at the time the playwright first met her.[4] This middle play presents a complete contrast to the plays that surround it, but it does share with them an insistence on remaining within and offering an analysis of a proletarian milieu, albeit in this instance a rural rather than an urban one. This, in itself, represented a major departure from established mainstream theatre, as Gerard Fry emphasised in the *Manchester Guardian*: 'the regional play pure and simple is a scarce thing in the English theatre and . . . dialect, except in low comedy or one-act plays designed for drama festivals is rarer still'.[5] It was a point made more generally by the director William Gaskill in 1961: 'You have to remember that up to 1956 working-class parts were always comic, that actors never used a regional accent in a straight part, and that plays did only depict one section of society.'[6]

Given the above, it is obvious that the trilogy can be located as a part of a larger changing societal model. However, it is possible to be more specific on this occasion. Wesker's plays were not just a product of their age: their staging was enabled through the coming together of a series of separate events. In 1954, the English Stage Company (ESC) was formed and took up residence in the Royal Court Theatre in 1956 under the artistic directorship of George Devine. The main impetus behind the formation of the company was a consensus that the British theatre was in urgent need of new blood. In 1956 Osborne's *Look Back in Anger* eventually triumphed, and seeing it had given Wesker the impetus to write *Chicken Soup*, thinking himself part of a group of like-minded people associated with the Royal Court.[7] In 1957, John Dexter was appointed as an associate director of the ESC and, that same year, the prime minister Harold Macmillan gave his famous speech in Bedford, in which he declared 'most of our people have never had it so good'. The following year, the *Observer* newspaper announced a competition for new plays, to which Wesker submitted *The Kitchen*; and the first new regional theatre to be built since the war, the Coventry Belgrade, was opened. Its first production, *Never Had It So Good* by John Wiles, a play about Coventry, recalled Macmillan's words sardonically, and gave promise of a radical agenda, something that was confirmed as early as December 1959 by a reader's report for the Arts Council of Great Britain (ACGB) on a script submitted for support: 'The dialogue is good, on a slum level, and one or two of the characters are alive, if not kicking. I can't imagine any company except Theatre Workshop [Joan Littlewood's project at the Theatre Royal, Stratford East] or perhaps Coventry attempting it.'[8]

The ACGB had awarded a £300 bursary to Wesker in September 1958, after the run of *Chicken Soup*, 'under its scheme for assisting promising new playwrights',[9] and it had been offering guarantees against loss for new plays first produced in the regions since 1954.[10] In the latter part of the decade the most frequent recipient of the maximum guarantee of £300 was the Coventry Belgrade, and it was to this theatre that John Dexter was sent to direct first Wesker's *Chicken Soup* (1958) and then *Roots* (1959), prior to their transfer to the Royal Court. It was an arrangement that suited all parties: by making this deal, the Court was able to benefit from Arts Council money that they could not themselves obtain to launch a production that could then transfer;[11] the Belgrade immediately began to establish a reputation for promoting radical new drama; and with *Roots* both John Dexter and Arnold Wesker not only enjoyed their first big theatrical success, but established the basis for a series of later collaborations.[12] *Roots* subsequently transferred to the Duke of York's and the playwright shared the *Evening Standard* award for 'Most Promising Playwright of the Year' with another Court newcomer, John Arden, whose *Serjeant Musgrave's Dance* had featured in the same season.

From a distance of more than fifty years it is difficult to convey the importance of the three plays when they were first performed as a trilogy at the Royal Court Theatre in 1960.[13] Individually, *Chicken Soup* had enjoyed an enthusiastic audience response and a fair degree of critical acclaim, leading to its inclusion in the very first volume of what was to become a major series, Penguin's *New English Dramatists*; and *Roots* proved an immediate hit, its popularity well indicated by the fact that when it was revived as part of the trilogy it occupied the Court stage for a month, far longer than the other two plays. *Jerusalem* had been judged more harshly, but whatever their original reception, it is only when the three plays are placed together that it is possible to measure the significance of Wesker's achievement.

Wesker did not have a preconceived idea of the three plays forming a unity, and *Jerusalem* was very much an afterthought, but undoubtedly the whole is greater than the sum of its parts. This is not just down to the sense that we are given of the developing interrelationship of successive generations of complex, linked family dynasties: it is the contextualisation of all this within a larger historical framework that is so important. Events in the three plays all pivot around the years 1939–45, the one period in which none of the action occurs in any of the plays. The Second World War, the hopes and worries that lead up to it, and the hopes and disillusionments that follow it, are Wesker's central preoccupation. The earliest scene (in *Chicken Soup*) is set in 1936, when Wesker was just four years old, and the most recent (in *Jerusalem*) in 1959, in a then contemporaneous England. That is a biographical link, in particular to the strongly, though not exclusively, Jewish perspective on that history; but it also affords a more general radical response to these events. Wesker said: 'the war had been a formative part of our lives, followed by the hope of 1945, and the general decline from then on. So that we were the generation at the end of that decline, desperately wanting to find something, being tired of the pessimism and the mediocrity.'[14] In a comparable way, that generation of left-wing playwrights that dates from 1968 looked back to 1945 and the end of the war in a number of their plays: David Edgar's *Maydays* (1983), David Hare's *Plenty* (1978), and Hare's and Howard Brenton's *Brassneck* (1973), for example, all open in 1945.[15] Again, this period encompassed the span of their own lifetimes but, again, there is more to it than that. Hare's 1978 television play *Licking Hitler* concludes with a character looking back through her life to the wartime years:

> **Anna** . . . Whereas we knew exactly what we were fighting against, none of us had the whisper of an idea as to what we were fighting for. Over the years I have been watching the steady impoverishment of the people's ideals, their loss of faith, the lying, the daily inveterate lying, the thirty-year-old deep corrosive national habit of lying . . .[16]

To which Arnold Wesker might reasonably nod, and say, 'Yes, but I told you that twenty years ago'.

Chicken Soup with Barley

Although the action of *Chicken Soup with Barley* sweeps through twenty years, the entire first Act occupies the events of a single day, 4 October 1936, and is organised around the momentous events of that Sunday. Oswald Mosley had planned a march through the East End of London with his British Union of Fascists (the Blackshirts) in a provocatively anti-semitic act that mobilised the local Jewish population. The play opens in the basement home of one of these Jewish families, the Kahns, Sarah and Harry, and their offspring, Ada (who is fourteen) and Ronnie (who is four). With their fellow communist colleagues they run through plans to prevent the march going through, and then take to the streets with – if we are to believe the play – virtually the whole of the East End population alongside them. In the second scene, everyone returns victorious to the house, having fought with the police but ensured that the march was stopped. It ends with a furious row between Sarah and Harry, as she has discovered that not only has he stolen money from her handbag but he has hidden at his mother's house all afternoon.

The second Act takes place in 1946 and 1947, and the Kahns have moved into a council flat in Hackney: ('The war has come and gone . . . The working class is a little more respectable now, they have not long since voted in a Labour Government').[17] Ada awaits her husband Dave's release from the army and they plan to escape to the country. Ronnie, like Sarah still true to the cause, is working in a bookshop with ambitions to be a socialist poet, and Harry, feckless in both life and politics, is continually out of work, before succumbing to his first stroke. The third Act is set in the same room in 1955 and 1956. Harry is now totally incapable of looking after himself, and Sarah is desperate. Ronnie arrives back from his job as a cook in Paris to confront his mother with his loss of belief in communism as a result of the recent Russian invasion of Hungary and Soviet Russian atrocities at home; and the play ends with Sarah arguing emotionally that it is still necessary to carry on the struggle: 'Ronnie, if you don't care you'll die' (p. 76).

If ever a play merited carrying D. H. Lawrence's famous health warning 'Never trust the teller, trust the tale' it is *Chicken Soup*. It is not just that it clearly has strong quasi-biographical elements in it (as has been pointed out frequently, Ronnie Kahn is exactly the same age as Wesker was when the play opens, and his formal name, Ronald, is an anagram of Arnold; in addition, the playwright is quite clear that Ronnie's parents are modelled on his own mother and father), but it also draws upon the collective memories of his own and other Jewish families living in the East End of London. That it does so selectively may be indicated by one small observation: the first Act of the play, quite correctly, makes much of the communists' role in the battle of Cable Street, but what it does not point out is that the Communist Party of Great Britain instructed its members not to take part in the protest and organised a meeting elsewhere in an unsuccessful attempt to divert activity. However, it is when parallels between the play and the playwright's family are sought that the problems really occur. This is unproblematic for anyone seeking to construct a biography of Wesker, and may also be worth considering in the light of one of the themes of the play, the relationship between art/culture and politics, but in the main it is an excursion up a cul-de-sac. Given that the play is unashamedly politically committed, it is important to realise at the outset that the arguments and debates that the play contains are not those of a piece of simplistic agitprop: there are tensions, there are inconsistencies and, yes, there are omissions. What is vital is that we respond to the play as we experience it, and that we do not seek to create a performance through constructing a perspective on the playwright.

Just how extreme – and, to be fair, how interesting in its own right – this can be is illustrated by Glenda Leeming in the first full-length study of Wesker's work. Having considered the exact nature of the relationship between Sarah and the playwright's mother, she quotes a statement from the playwright ('She's a much more complex person emotionally; she had some very strong values'), and concludes thus: 'The identity of Sarah and Wesker's mother confuses this statement: most of it refers to the former, the [phrase] "had some very strong values" to the latter.'[18] However, what this does do is to highlight both the central role of Sarah in the play – she has the very first and the very last words in it – and the import that must be placed on her inconsistencies. For this is a play, not about abstract political ideas but about the way in which political ideals and personal lives collide. It is sufficient, however, that we consider these collisions largely as they occur on stage.

In the first Act Sarah is given to us in the stage directions, and thus to an audience via the director/actor's reading of those directions, as a very different person from her husband: whereas 'Her movements indicate great energy and vitality', he is 'the antithesis of Sarah, amiable but weak' (p. 13). From the outset, his weakness is associated with his interest in books and the cinema by Sarah. Indeed, the very first thing he does on entering is to pick up a book and suggest to his wife, 'You should read Upton Sinclair's book about the meat-canning industry – it's an eye-opener' (p. 13). In contrast, Sarah's political commitment owes nothing to learning: a family friend says of her, 'Do you think she ever read a book on political economy in her life? Bless her! Someone told her socialism was happiness so she joined the party' (p. 62).[19] This distinction has to do with more than characterisation, let alone Wesker's interest in restaging his own parents. It affords us a reading of the play that stresses the distinction between an instinctive, emotional socialist stance and one based on intellectual reason. Sarah is ruled by her heart, and Harry by his head and, frankly, his heart is simply not in it. It is one of many oppositional positions in the play. For instance, Harry's sister, Cissie, another strong woman, occupies a political position very different from that of Sarah, even though they are both in the party. She is a trade union organiser, cool and precise in her planning, and when she leaves for the demonstration Sarah can hold back no longer: 'I hate her! . . . What's the good of being a socialist if you're not warm . . . Everything cold and calculated. People like that can't teach love and brotherhood' (p. 29).

All this underlines the fact that Sarah herself embodies a crucial set of oppositions. She is the only character who retains a firm loyalty to the Communist Party, seeing it not as the monolithic and cruel structure that Ronnie discerns by 1956 but as essentially a family, a family in which she can unite her own domestic role as wife and mother with the larger political struggle outside. She is associated in the play with 'food and tea' (p. 30), and is continually offering and providing both: indeed, the very title of the play comes from Sarah's recall of the soup that a neighbour made 'when Ada had diphtheria and I was pregnant [with Ronnie] . . . Ada still has that taste in her mouth – chicken soup with barley. She says it is a friendly taste – ask her. That saved her' (p. 74). When asked what she can do in the protest, her future son-in-law, Dave Simmonds, unthinkingly hands out a traditionally female role to her: 'If you fancy yourself as a nurse then go to Aldgate, we've got a first-aid post there' (p. 20). However, she exits the house declaring that she is going to Gardiner's Corner, one of the three male-run posts chosen to block the Blackshirts' advance. She does so, having thrust a communist flag into Harry's hands, more in hope than anticipation, but – most significantly – she does so grasping as a weapon that domestic implement that best embodies the woman's role as provider, a rolling pin (p. 24). Leeming may be right in detecting 'an element of farce' (p. 39), but the text leaves us in no doubt that we should go with Sarah's enthusiastic embrace of the struggle at this point. In scene two, having returned from the streets, Sarah first provides tea and then goes in search of her husband, who enters with a question ready-formed, 'Did she have a rolling pin in her hand?' (p. 30), recon-structing – at least in his eyes – his wife away from political activist to the role of traditional shrew on a seaside postcard.

Her choice of weapon thus opens up a number of potentially conflicting perspectives on her. Its significance is underlined by her neighbour Monty's preparation: he 'moves off quickly, taking a poker from the fireplace on his way out and concealing it in his clothes' (p. 24). He will return with the poker and, having restored it to its tradi-tional purpose, declare, 'I'll get some more coal for the fire' (p. 27). He has already opened the scene by putting water on the stove ready for Sarah to make tea and to tend – in the role of nurse that Dave had suggested for her – to an injured comrade. By the beginning of the third Act, in 1955, Monty has opted for the fireside use of the poker, and when he visits the Kahns with his wife, we learn that he has become a provider for the housewife with 'a nice little greengrocer's business in Manchester', and has not only left the party but makes sure that nobody in his new city ever finds out that he was in it (p. 61). His reasons for leaving – the disunity among supposed comrades fighting in International Brigades in the Spanish Civil War and the Soviet massacre of Jews – are expressed perfectly rationally and are, indeed, perfectly rational. It is not the case that we are led to condemn him for his desertion: unless, that is, we see the act through Sarah's perspective. It is the dichotomy that is important. The point could be pursued by considering how Harry uses the flag that Sarah had given him as the basis for a story of supposed heroism that actually reveals his cowardice and his lack of other than theoretical commitment.

Sarah opens Act Three trying hard to grapple with the complexities of an official government form. The hopes for the 1945 Labour government have long since faded, and the council-provided flat that had seemed in 1946 to offer the promise of a better life is now just one of a block of cells in which, as the visiting Cissie declares, in the last scene of the play, 'You live a whole lifetime here and not know your next-door neighbour' (p. 68). In a simple but sharply realised opening to the scene, while Sarah awaits Ronnie's return, various characters from the enthusiastic bustle of the play's opening – including Cissie, now also disillusioned with political struggle – are gathered in the Kahns' flat to play a game of cards. However, far from proving a unifying activity, it descends into a drawn-out argument, with constant disagreements about strategy and about the identity of the trump suit. It displays itself as a metaphor for the breakdown of the camaraderie and solidarity of the 1930s, and prepares us for Ronnie's reappearance once the guests have left and the helpless Harry turns down the offer of yet another cup of tea and heads for his bed.

Chicken Soup ends with the most extreme demonstration of the oppositions that the play has to offer. It is the most extreme in that it involves the mother and her son who until recently had been the only one to keep the faith with Sarah; but also because it most fully allows for the articulation of the significance of these oppositions. Ronnie throws the crushing of the Hungarian 'revolution' and the Soviet massacres at his mother, but then directly links the public realm of his invective to the other related arena of Sarah's world, the domestic. He concludes with what is now the ultimate insult and then 'wants to take back his words' but cannot: 'The family you always wanted has disintegrated, and the great ideal you always cherished has exploded in front of your eyes. But you won't face it . . . You're a pathological case, Mother – do you know that? You're still a *communist!*' (pp. 72–3). The full potential significance of the Russian invasion for Sarah is not revealed until we learn, in *I'm Talking About Jerusalem*, that she was born in Hungary.

Sarah's rejoinder is magnificent – providing a strong ending to the piece – but inadequate. In an emotional speech she affirms her continued belief in the need to continue the struggle but cannot separate it from her allegiance to the party:

> **Sarah** . . . All right! So I'm still a communist . . . When you were a baby and there was unemployment and everybody was thinking so – all the world was a communist. But it's different now. Now the people have forgotten. I sometimes think they're not worth fighting for because they forget so easily. You give them a few shillings in the bank and they can buy a television so they think it's all over . . . A world where people don't think any more? Is that what you want me to be satisfied with – a television set? Look at him! My son! He wants to die. (p. 73)

The play is, then, dramatically resolved in the sense that it provides a narrative resolution and accounts for the lives of all the characters to that point. But politically it is not, and cannot be, resolved for, to reiterate a point made at the outset, it is not a piece of simplistic propaganda, and it leaves its problems fluttering like a series of ragged red flags. Without wishing to overstress the point, Sarah's position is nearer that of a tragic heroine than is usually expressed. Certainly, if a tentative parallel can be made with the work of Bertolt Brecht, as a parental figure grieving the loss of her children, which if not physical is none the less real, her situation is closer to that of the chief protagonist in *Mother Courage* than in *The Mother*, at the end of those two plays. However, it is at this juncture that the significance of *Chicken Soup* being but one play in a trilogy can be felt. It is a play complete and entire unto itself, but the debate continues; and in the next play we will be introduced to a very different female protagonist, and to a very different social context.

Roots

The action of *Chicken Soup* spans thirty-odd years; that of *Roots* just less than two weeks. On a break from her work as a waitress in

London, Beatie Bryant goes back to Norfolk, first to stay briefly with her sister Jenny and then with her parents. The most important thing in her life is Ronnie Kahn, whom she had followed to London, and to whom she is now engaged. He is expected at the end of her stay, and Ronnie's words and thoughts dominate virtually everything that Beatie has to say to her family, as he clearly takes it upon himself to educate her in things cultural and political. The highlight of the visit is to be the arrival of Ronnie and his introduction to the family on the final Saturday. An afternoon tea is organised but as most of the immediate family gather at the Bryants' home, the postman arrives with a letter from Ronnie in which he calls off the engagement because 'it wouldn't really work, would it?' (p. 142). Beatie is at first distraught and embarrassed, but ends the play suddenly articulate and, for the first time, telling it like it is with her own voice. The plot summary is very brief because very little actually happens. Wesker: 'It was not a play of action; drama did not reside in the Aristotelian rule of cause and effect, but in expectation.'[20] What is important, apart from this movement towards the double-headed denouement – disappointment followed by triumph – is the meticulous depiction of the ordinary everyday lives of Beatie's family. The playwright recalls the first night at the Coventry Belgrade:

> The opening was breathtakingly slow. Patsy Byrne – solid, experienced, intelligent, trusting utterly in the play and John's direction – called to her child offstage, waited, went into her, moved slowly back into the room, returned to her frying-pan and cooked. Charlie Kay took his time coming in from work, placing his bike in the front room, arching his back with pain. Patsy looked at him for a long time, watching, before asking: 'Waas matter wi' you then?' Slowly, they built up the exchange that was to become the running joke in the play, about Mother Bryant saying the pain in his back was due to indigestion.[21]

Although set in rural Norfolk, the play offers no pastoral idyll. The stage directions for Jenny's house in the opening scene give a good feeling of the overall ambience of the play: 'A rather ramshackle house

. . . no water laid on, nor electricity, nor gas. Everything rambles and the furniture is cheap and old. If it is untidy it is because there is a child in the house and there are few amenities, so that the mother is too overworked to take much care' (p. 85). Wesker's wife took Jocelyn Herbert, the designer, to Norfolk to ensure the authenticity of this set and that of the parents' tied cottage where the second and third Acts are located.[22] When the play was first published, the playwright added an introductory note admitting that 'the picture I have drawn of them is a harsh one, yet still my tone is not of disgust . . . I am annoyed with them and myself'. The only character to express any joy in living in the countryside is the old Stan Mann, who dies, having made brief appearances in both households before he does. Jenny's husband, Jimmy Beale, is not alone in having physical ailments: Beatie's father suffers from a recurrent gut ache, a blemish that will allow the recent pay rise for farm workers to be partially compensated for by the estate manager busting him down to the status of casual labourer, and half the pay packet he and his wife were used to.

Apart from the director's creation of this desolate rural community, whether *Roots* really sinks or swims is down to the actor playing Beatie, and it was the events leading up to the casting of this key character that made the original production possible. George Devine and Tony Richardson of the ESC wanted changes to the script, including the appearance of Ronnie in the third Act, and when Wesker refused to accede they rejected the play. However, another council member had already read the play and liked it, as she made clear in a committee meeting: 'Dame Peggy Ashcroft asked if *Roots* . . . had been considered for production and expressed her admiration for this play which she thought contained an admirable part for Joan Plowright. Mr Devine said that he would reconsider it.'[23] Joan Plowright read the script, which she loved; John Dexter was desperate to direct it, and the Belgrade to stage it.[24] It was the part that really launched Plowright's career, and ensured that Wesker's play would be established as a part of the modern theatrical canon. *The Times*: 'the play belongs to Miss Joan Plowright, who brings bounding vitality to the one living branch growing from these dead roots'.[25]

Throughout the play Beatie brings sophisticated urban eyes and ears – albeit ones borrowed from Ronnie – to bear on her old world, and what she sees she largely does not like, from the untidiness of the houses to the dismissal of all political discourse and any notion of culture that is not simple and easy to digest. In the final scene she is goaded into defending Ronnie by giving them a moral puzzle set her by him. It is a strange but crucial interjection. A girl lives on one side of a river and two men live on the other; she loves one but her love is not reciprocated; the other loves her but his love is not reciprocated. A ferryman agrees to take her across but only on condition that she take off all her clothes, which she eventually does. The man she loves tells her that he will take her with him and she sleeps with him, only to find that he has disappeared in the morning. She turns for help to the man who loves her but, having heard what she has done, he rejects her and she is 'left alone with no clothes and no friends and no hope of staying alive'. Ronnie's question was 'Who is the person most responsible for her plight?' His answer: 'the man who say he love her but don't do nothin' to help her is most responsible because he were the last one she could turn to' (pp. 140–1).

Now, obviously, this is about to take on a very specific significance, as Ronnie, the man she loves and sleeps with, will shortly dump her by post, and is thus very much the unseen villain of the piece; but it has other resonances. Interestingly, the dilemma that he had presented does not only have him condemn himself in advance of the event, but it points to the essentially *moral* way in which Ronnie considers human behaviour: hence the impasse between him and his mother at the end of *Chicken Soup*. They both relate the sphere of the political to the moral, but reach conflicting conclusions.

The puzzle is, of course, about personal relationships and not about politics as such: and it has a very particular relevance to the state of Beatie's mind. After the receipt of Ronnie's letter, and as she is forced to admit that she never really understood what her lover was on about, she is metaphorically stripped by a family intent on her humiliation. Earlier on – after a great deal of kerfuffle involving the filling, lighting and heating of the copper – Beatie had taken a bath in the Bryants' kitchen. Her mother is horrified that someone might call and see her naked, and the daughter suggests she put up a temporary curtain, which eventually she does.

Mr Bryant 'Sides, who want to see her in her dickey suit.

Beatie I know men as 'ould pay to see me in my dickey suit. [*Posing her plump outline.*] Don't you think I got a nice dickey suit? [**Mr Bryant** *makes a dive and pinches her bottom.*] Ow! Stoppit Bryants, stoppit! [*He persists.*] Daddy, stop it now! (pp. 122–3)

Beatie brings a consciously sexual dimension into the preparations for the bath, which is rendered all the more problematic in that she is acting out in front of her parents and, in particular, her father. Mrs Bryant's immediate response is, 'Tell him he can go as soon as he like'. Her daughter, like the girl in the conundrum, is about to remove all her clothes. It is an act that can be linked to the way in which she shocks her sister Jenny in the first scene by telling her how she and Ronnie would resolve their arguments:

Beatie We'd row. Sometimes he hurt me but then, slowly, he'd build the bridges up *for* me – and then we'd make love! [*Innocently continues her meal.*]

Jenny You'd what, did you say?

Beatie Make love. Love in the afternoon gal. Ever had it? It's the only time for it . . . love – alert and fresh, when you got most energy – love in the afternoon. (p. 90)

The fact of being unclothed takes on not only sexual connotations, however. It offers insight into the difference between Beatie and her family. Her nakedness can make her vulnerable but it also symbolises her openness to new experiences and new ideas. What the narrative of the puzzle lays stress on is the movement from innocence to experience: the crossing of the river and the removal of the clothes by the girl are like components in the Freudian analysis of a dream. Beatie has already recounted a relatable occurrence as they are filling the copper with water for her bath: 'Mother! I dreamt I died last night and heaven were at the bottom of a pond. You had to jump in and sink and you know how afeared I am of water' (p. 112). This is, in essence, the imagery of baptism. However, Beatie has already crossed the water sexually. By the end of the play she will do so politically, but not with the assistance of a lascivious ferryman, for there is more than one way of crossing a river, of progressing. In the first Act, just before the 'love in the afternoon' declaration to Jenny, Beatie had attempted to rehearse Ronnie's views on the importance of words as bridges, as ways of moving, of developing: '"Well, language is words," he'd say . . . "It's bridges, so that you can get from one place to another. And the more bridges you know about the more places you can see!"' (p. 90).

All of this is crucial to understanding what exactly it is that we are witnessing at the end of the play. When the family turn on her after Ronnie's rejection and her admission of incomprehension of his world and its values, Mrs Bryant declares, 'The apple don't fall far from the tree – that it don't' (p. 144). What is being invoked here is the nature versus nurture debate: whether Beatie is a product of her origins or whether she is shaped essentially by her later experiences, including Ronnie's interventions into her life. Shortly afterwards, goaded by her mother to tell them what she knows and that they don't, she responds: '(*despairingly*): I can't mother – the apple don't fall far from the tree do it? You're right, I'm like you. Stubborn, empty, wi' no tools for livin'. I got no roots' (p. 145). What she means here is something more than the expression of her sense of no longer being connected to her family and her 'natural' roots, although it certainly does contain that sense. But when she relates the term to her listeners, she does so with an awareness of the unbreakable connection: 'you're right, I'm like you', at the same time as she demonstrates her increasing distance from them, as evidenced by, among other things, her growing eloquence. She parries her mother's attempt to re-establish the connection ('You got a family ent you?') with an argument that replaces nature with nurture: 'I am not talking about family roots – I mean – the – I mean – Look! Ever since it begun the world's bin growin' hasn't it? Things hev happened, things have been discovered, people have been thinking and improving and inventing but what do we know about it all?' (p. 146).

The breakthrough for Beatie occurs when she is able for the first time to move her perspective from the particular to the general, and to offer an analysis that is based on class division and its rooted significance in cultural and political terms.

> **Beatie** You don't wanna take any notice of what dem old papers say about the workers bein' all-important these days – that's all squit! . . . 'Blust,' they say, 'the masses is too stupid for us to come down to them.' . . . So you know who come along? The slop singers and the pop writers and the film makers and women's magazines and the Sunday papers and the picture strip love stories . . . The whole stinkin' commercial world insults us and we don't care a damn. Well, Ronnie's right – it's our own bloody fault. We want the third-rate – we got it. (pp. 147–8)

Even as the play was first produced the neat construction of a world separated by the consumption of either highbrow or lowbrow culture was more than somewhat problematic, and has become even more so in the years that followed.[26] However, her excited realisation, 'I'm talking. Jenny, Frankie, Mother – I'm not quoting no more . . . God in heaven, *Ronnie!* It does work, it's happening to me' (p. 148), provides a rousing theatrical climax in which an audience is allowed to share the character's euphoria. The conclusion is in one respect ironic, because although Ronnie never knows of Beatie's transformation, his belief in the possibility of individual rather than mass change is fundamental to the clash between him and his mother at the end of *Chicken Soup*, as is articulated most clearly in *I'm Talking About Jerusalem*:

> **Dave** Did you ever hear what happened to Beatie Bryant? . . . The girl you wanted to change.

> **Ronnie** Change! Huh! You know what my father once said to me? 'You can't change people Ronnie,' he said, 'you can only give them some love and hope they'll take it.' Well, Beatie Bryant took it but nothing seemed to happen.

> **Dave** Three years is a long time to go with a girl.

> **Ronnie** I don't regret it. Maybe something did happen . . .

Sarah I'm always telling you you can't change the world on your own . . . (p. 210)

This afterthought makes Beatie seem even more like a client in a social experiment and, indeed, it is a transformation of considerable ambiguity. Has she really found her own voice – and become her own changed person – or has she been taught well by a man whom she has quoted earlier as saying, 'It's all going up in flames . . . but I'm going to make bloody sure I save someone from the fire' (p. 115)? In many ways this is to quibble unnecessarily, since the ending so clearly separates her from her family. Her mother leads the rest of the company to the table, where they '*proceed to eat and murmur*', resolutely closing their ears to what Beatie has to say; and the point is established even more firmly for an audience by the very final acts of the play; '*The murmur of the family sitting down to eat grows as* **Beatie**'s *last cry is heard. Whatever she will do they will continue to live as before. As* **Beatie** *stands alone, articulate at last.*' It is a conclusion as emphatic in its sense of a parting of the ways and the promise of a new life as that of Ibsen's *A Doll's House*. It is not a social revolution, but a personal triumph, and at least Beatie stands rather more chance of surviving than Norah.

I'm Talking About Jerusalem

The front cover of the first published edition of *I'm Talking About Jerusalem* declares that it is 'the final play in the "Wesker Trilogy"'[27] and, even though Wesker had not planned it originally, it occupies a logical position, serving not only to pull various narrative threads of the two preceding plays together but, perhaps equally importantly, allowing the playwright to bring the action that had started in *Chicken Soup* in the year that Wesker was four, right up to his and his audience's present. We are reintroduced to Dave Simmonds, who we had learnt in the first play had enrolled in the International Brigades against Franco's fascists in the Spanish Civil War and then fought in the Second World War. In *Chicken Soup* he had been set up as the organiser and as the revolutionary hero; but he had returned, from Spain and from Europe, a changed man, shocked by the way in which the men behaved in war. He is now married to Ada Kahn, whom we had first met in the same play as a teenage activist later disillusioned with the possibility of mass revolution. In the course of the play they produce two children. In *Roots* we have been told that the pair has left London to set up home in Norfolk, and the play opens with them moving into their primitive rural house. Dave will support them initially by working as a carpenter for a local estate owner and then by producing furniture to order in his craft workshop. The reference to Jerusalem in the title is a pointer to the quasi-Utopian nature of the enterprise and, having been sacked by his boss for petty theft, Dave discovers that there is not a real market for what he produces; and the play and the trilogy ends with the removal van returning to take the family back to London.

This play offers yet a further permutation on the movement between urban and rural locations. Whereas *Roots* presented an unrelentingly gloomy and seemingly unchangeable indigenous rural population, in *Jerusalem* the city-dwellers arrive optimistically and with a vision of a Robert Owen-type socialist enterprise. As they are moving in Sarah asks what the stage directions tell us is 'the real question': 'What's wrong with socialism that you have to run to an ivory tower?' Dave's reply stresses his experience of the alienating and dehumanising effects of industrialisation: 'Since being demobbed I've worked in a factory turning out doors and window frames and I've seen men hating themselves while they were doing it. Morning after morning they've come in with a cold hatred in their eyes, brutalized!' (p. 164). His and Ada's is an individualistic project, seeking not to overthrow capitalism but to set up an alternative way of living.

That they are irrevocably intruders into a society that neither understands nor tolerates their vision is stressed by the fact that, unlike in *Roots*, we do not meet a selection of the local population. They live in isolation, both physically and politically. The only two native figures to appear represent the old order and the new, neither of which can be reconciled with Dave and Ada's particular version of the pastoral dream: the estate owner and a young apprentice taken on by

Dave. The former is a retired colonel who behaves and talks as though he were still a part of a feudal world, addressing his employee as 'Simmonds' but, in his chivalrous manner, Ada as 'Mrs Simmons' and 'Ma'am'. It is in this spirit that Dave is dismissed from his service not because he has taken a piece of unwanted and virtually valueless lino that had been lying around in a shed for months, but because he did not ask and then lied about it: thus threatening the entire 'master–servant relationship': 'I don't understand you at all, Simmonds. What did you come to the country for? It's a different way of life here, y'know. They're a slow people, the country people – slow, but sound. I know where I am with them, and they know their place with me. But with you I could never –' (p. 186). The other local is Sammy, a part of a new and young rural population. Briefly employed by Dave, the boy soon departs for the better pay of the mechanised urban factory world that the couple have rejected.

In the first scene of Act II, just two years after the end of the war, Libby Dobson comes to stay for a while. An ex-army colleague of Dave, and one who has influenced his political thinking and with whom he was planning to go into partnership, Dobson brings with him, importantly, a story of failed past socialist enterprise and a scathing critique of the current endeavour. It is a lethal combination, of empirical experience and rational argument. Challenged as to why he is so cynical about their socialism 'at an individual level', he offers them an image of the modern world in which everyone is doing their own thing, as it would come to be described in the 1960s:

> **Dobson**   . . . Would you have the world do without cars, planes, electricity, houses, roads? Because *that's* the logical conclusion. If no man should be tied to making screws all his life, then that's what it means. No screws – no transport! No labourers – no roads! No banks or offices – no commercial market! . . . Think about it. Reorganize the world so's everybody's doing a job he enjoys, so everyone's 'expressing' himself. Go on. Universal happiness? Get it! (p. 181)

A little later he tells them that while 'you've gone back to William Morris . . . I went back to old Robert Owen'. Having inherited money from his father, he had assembled four other mechanics to open a garage with him. His plan was to include yet another man once they had made sufficient profit, and so on, until there was 'a chain of garages owned and run by the workers themselves' (p. 182). However, his fellow workers got greedy and bought him out. He will prove to be correct about the unrealisability of Dave and Ada's project, but his chief role as temporary guest is to display the difference in response to the failure. The supper that Ada has prepared never gets eaten and Dobson, already permanently soured, gets more and more bitter as he works his way through a bottle of whisky, and has to be sent to bed early like a naughty child spoiling the party.

It is immediately after this that Dave loses his job but, unlike Dobson, the couple end the scene laughingly planning their future. The play then moves on six years to 1953, with Ada returning from a visit to see her father who is now completely out of it, installed in a padded cell so that he cannot hurt himself, and will shortly die. Sammy has walked off the job, and Dave asks his wife if they should think of giving up, but they end the second Act playing an energetic game about being born with their young son, Danny. There is still the determination to continue and to grow.

Nothing prepares us for the events of the first scene of Act III, when the maiden aunts Cissie and Esther (owner of a travelling market stall) visit, bringing with them the sardonic banter of the London streets, and news of Ronnie's falling in love with a waitress. Shared preparations for the evening meal and the revelation that Ada is expecting another baby delay the inevitable moment when Dave, having arrived back after failing to convince a bank manager to lend the business some money, feels forced to defend his position. He talks of himself as a prophet, and the concept of 'Jerusalem' moves closer to the visions of William Blake than the ideals of William Morris: 'You think we're cranks – recluses? Well I'll surprise you, look – no long hair, no sandals. Just flesh and blood.' Esther's subdued response closes the scene and the latest period in Dave and Ada's struggle to maintain the credibility of the enterprise: 'You want to build

Jerusalem? Build it! Only maybe we wanted to share it with you' (p. 207).

The final scene takes place on 9 October 1959, a specific and historic day, though not as momentous as that which had opened the trilogy in 1936. As the lights come up, and before preparations for packing and moving back to London continue, the radio brings the result of the previous day's general election, with 'the return to power in the House of Commons of the Conservative Party for a third time in succession since the end of the war' (p. 208). For the first time in the play contemporary public events intrude upon the attempt at a rural retreat, and the broadcast news underlines just how far away we are from the dreams of the first scene of *Chicken Soup*. This final scene of *Jerusalem* mirrors the opening one, except that the move is now a reversal, to and not from London. It also affords the reappearance of Sarah and Ronnie, ostensibly present to help with the move but actually, to allow for a final sad snatch of concluding dialogue. In the opening scene Ronnie had been a fourteen-year-old brat, foisting Beethoven on them as they get the furniture into the house, 'standing on a box conducting both the music and the movement of people back and forth'. His sudden intrusion into the last scene stresses something that has been the case throughout the trilogy, that Ronnie's absences from the action are more significant than his appearances. This is obviously the case with *Roots*, but it is noticeable that his periods away, in Norfolk and in Paris, always result in a changed set of values – or the junking of a set of values – on his return. This is particularly problematic in *Jerusalem* as, while the individual play would demand that the last words are those of Dave and Ada, whose activities have dominated the narrative, its placement as the final piece in the jigsaw dictate that the honour should go to Ronnie in dialogue with his mother. Unlike *Chicken Soup* and *Roots*, where the first and last words of the play are given to women, in *Jerusalem* they are given to Ronnie.

This creates a kind of double conclusion to the play. Dave is allowed a long speech in which he disowns his role as prophet, but says that although the project failed, 'We came here, we worked hard, we've loved every minute of it and we're still young . . . Maybe Sarah's right, maybe you can't build on your own' (pp. 215–6). Despite Ronnie's pleas, he leaves him with no second-hand dreams ('You child you – visions don't work': p. 216) and his practical actions in sorting out the house-leaving contrast with Ronnie's despairing comparison of himself with his father. He concludes the play with a desperate and repeated outburst that unites the sense of failure with the need to hope, which is evidenced by the display of anguish: 'We – must – be – mad – to cry!' And then, as the sound of the removal van fades, like Caliban on his island, Ronnie is left alone on stage as there is 'a last slow curtain' (p. 216).

Conclusion

Given that the action in Wesker's trilogy takes place immediately before and after the Second World War, it is rather surprising that there is only one reference to the Holocaust in any of the plays.[28] It is particularly surprising in view of the fact that two of the plays are concerned virtually exclusively with a number of Jewish families from London's East End. Indeed, a key component of both those plays is the insertion of Yiddish songs and dances at moments of heightened emotion. One reviewer of the original London production of *Jerusalem* laid great stress on this point: 'It is the greatest pity that the Royal Court didn't succeed in finding Jewish actors and actresses for the first and last plays of this trilogy. The Jewishness of them is an absolutely essential element and non-Jewish players simply cannot carry them off.'[29] Curiously one of the strongest reminders of the implications of the characters' 'Jewishness' comes in the one play in which they do not appear. Beatie's brother Frankie asks about Ronnie, 'What you say he is – a strong socialist? . . . And a Jew boy?', and then comments, 'Well, that's a queer mixture then' (p. 131). The trilogy makes it very clear that is not in fact a 'queer mixture' at all, but the use of the offensive term 'Jew boy' forces an audience to suddenly see life through a very different pair of eyes. That this anti-semitic remark is made by a family member without any idea that it might be problematic, and certainly could not in any way be connected with the activities of Mosley's Blackshirts, let alone those of Hitler, is what makes it so important, and points to a further significance to the chosen location of the narrative. What we are being given is not just an insight into England either side of the war, but also a specifically Jewish perspective on that England.

There is a comparable moment at the beginning of *Jerusalem* when the removal man asks Ronnie, 'Communist, are you?' His mate comments, 'That's a dirty word, ain't it?', and it is left to the first speaker to retort, 'Not during the war it wasn't' (p. 162). Despite this historical qualification, by the time that these three plays were written, 'Communist' was a dirty word for most people in England, even – perhaps especially – for those on the Left. The trilogy is full of explanations for why this should be, from the 1930s to the 1950s and the Russian invasion of Hungary. So, Wesker's characters are constructed as double aberrations – both Jewish and Communist – from an implied norm, as 'other' figures at large in an English culture. One of the extraordinary achievements of the work is the meticulously detailed depiction of the origins, life, culture and politics of such a closely defined group of characters within a structure that is recognisably that of a series of 'state-of-the-nation' plays.

This is not the only aspect of the trilogy that is concerned with 'other' figures and that counters then contemporary assumptions, however. Shelagh Delaney's *A Taste of Honey* had already premiered at the Theatre Royal Stratford East before *Chicken Soup* had had its first run at Coventry.[30] It was unique among the plays produced in the new wave in that is concerned almost exclusively with the lives of two women, a girl and her mother; but it achieves this largely by the virtual exclusion of heterosexual male characters. The trilogy goes much further though. Wesker pushes the female characters to the forefront, in particular Sarah, Beatie and Ada, but also creates wonderful, more minor parts for female actors, the maiden aunts Cissie and Esther Kahn, for example. The important thing about these characters is that the women are no longer presented as passive creatures or, at best, as victims of a male-dominated society as was usual in most post-war theatre. Most of Wesker's women are depicted as empowered beings. That he is able to do this within the largely naturalistic structure of the plays is in itself quite remarkable. The playwright addresses these gender issues as a given and not as a thing to be argued for and propagandised over; and he does so, furthermore, in a way that does not present them as impossible paragons. They are rounded characters, and they have faults as well as virtues – a point recognised by T. C. Worsley of Sarah in *Chicken Soup* in 1958: 'Mr Wesker doesn't idealize or romanticize. He presents his heroine as a living person, nagging and tiresome and tactless as well.'[31]

However, he is also well able to convey a world in which women are not empowered, and to examine their strategies for dealing with the situation. *Roots* is almost entirely about the experiences of two generations of women, a mother and her two daughters, in a world in which the wife still has to rely on handouts from the husband's pay packet in order to go about her duties, which are entirely domestic. In fact, Beatie's 'coming-out' at the end of the play is the more remarkable in that in her job as a waitress is, in essence, a directly paid version of the same domestic activity engaged in her by her mother and sister.

For these reasons alone, Wesker's trilogy continues to have a resonance; and events both in Britain and in Europe continue to parallel the political hopes, frustrations and disappointments that confront his characters. Indeed, it is one of the great strengths of the plays that the issues raised by Wesker should be so specifically related to their particular time and place, and yet continue to be relevant for subsequent generations. It is far too long since the three plays were presented in a single season as, among other things, it would confirm that they do constitute a single work. This is evidenced by a number of passages that an audience cannot properly understand without reference to the other plays (for example, virtually everything that Ronnie has to say in the final scene of *Jerusalem*); or the full significance of remarks not being able to be fully grasped until later (as, for example, the revelation, again in *Jerusalem*, that Sarah was born in Hungary). But it is much more than this. A 'reading' of all three plays allows a cross-referencing that adds depth to the characters and to the plays' themes: experiencing one play enhances our experience of the others. For example, the depiction of Harry Kahn in *Chicken Soup* must be coloured by the fact that although he never appears in

Jerusalem, we are given a tearful account of his declining condition by Ada (p. 193), before learning, through a casual remark from Ronnie, that he has died (p. 208). This sad resolution of his life generates a completely fresh understanding of Ronnie's discovery, twenty-two years earlier, of his discovery of his father's unfinished autobiography: unfinished because he could never see anything through, but now completed by death. The little that he wrote about his life in an industrialised society, well summed up by his title, 'Of me, the dummy and my family', now makes us appreciate his failure to act as an emotional response to events that, like the machines in his workplace, are out of his control (p. 48).

These connections also point us towards another linking thread in the plays: not so much the relationship between the texts and the playwright's own life and family, as the role of the writer as commentator. For Ronnie had ambitions (just as Wesker himself does) to be a writer and, specifically, a socialist writer. Although contemporary reviewers of the plays often talked of Wesker as having a naively left-wing philosophy, and of his plays as occasionally crude propaganda, what a close analysis of them suggests is something quite different. We should not assume that Ronnie is simply a mouthpiece for the playwright, for it would be more accurate to say that the many different arguments put forward by the different characters all come together to form a dialogue with which Wesker wants his audience to become involved. That is to say, that the trilogy offers no absolute conclusions, but that – as Wesker hopes – it asks all the right questions. A simple way to highlight the importance of this deliberate lack of thematic resolution is to consider *The Kitchen*. The play concludes with the restaurant owner pleading that he provides his workers with a living: he ends 'What is there more? What is there more? What is there more?' It is a question that haunts every scene of the trilogy. When *The Kitchen* was first published (in 1960) it was the script of the original short version created by the young Wesker. The final line is a stage direction, included in response to the owner's repeated question: 'We have seen that there must be something more and so the lights must slowly fade.' In 1961, the fuller version was published, the play having been revised after the learning experience that had been the writing and production of the trilogy. And now the final stage direction has been removed. Is this evidence of uncertainty on Wesker's part as to whether his audience will have seen that there is 'something more'? No, I think it signifies the playwright's intent to let the audience work things out for themselves, for it is only theory that is simple. Life, as every moment of these three plays attest, is extremely complicated.

CHAPTER 4
DOCUMENTS

The following edited interview transcripts have been taken from the Theatre Archive Project, a collaboration between the British Library and De Montfort University, originally funded by the Arts and Humanities Research Council (AHRC). The project gathers together interviews with actors, directors, writers, theatregoers and other theatre professionals; the interviews cover the period 1945–70. Complete transcripts can be found at: http://sounds.bl.uk/Arts-literature-and-performance/Theatre-Archive-Project.

The golden age

Theatre in the 1950s: plays, productions, acting, staging

Well, the West End when I started in the early 1950s was still a fairly glamorous place and those productions of H. M. Tennent were beautifully mounted and directed and designed and cast, they were of a very, very high standard and they were done with very great taste. It became very fashionable, once the English Stage Company had started and that big watershed with John Osborne and Arnold Wesker and all those people, it became fashionable to deride H. M. Tennent and it was . . . unjustifiable I think. They did wonderful work by very good writers, they discovered new writers, people like John Whiting for instance, and they presented plays with great style and taste and very . . . strong casts so I have . . . fond recollections of the West End in the 1950s . . . (*John Moffat, actor*)

And also in those seasons there was some splendid acting . . . [In] one evening [Sir Laurence Olivier] played *Oedipus Rex* in the first half . . . and he played in [Richard] Sheridan's *The*

Critic and he played Mr Puff the playwright. He had a Greek nose in *Oedipus Rex* and a splendid turned-up nose for Mr Puff! . . . And I do remember that *The Critic*, it's a comedy about the amusing productions of the [eighteenth century] . . . There was a splendid thing when they start to rehearse the play and virtually everything goes wrong, and it's the kind of dress rehearsal. And I do remember the grand finale was Mr Puff coming on try to direct and get things right, parts of the scenery fall down and he steps over a sea piece on the ground which promptly takes him up into the wings, up into the flies. Olivier just disappeared up and came down on the curtain. He was a good acrobat as well in those days! . . . Talking of stage pictures, there was another famous production by Gielgud of a play called *The Lady's Not for Burning* by Christopher Fry . . . A lovely setting by Oliver Messel . . . He was known for his magnificent stage sets. This one took place in medieval times, I do recall during the course of the play there's a thunderstorm and we had the most beautiful lighting, the stage turned slightly grey as you would get in a thunderstorm . . . (*Neil Heayes, theatregoer*)

Of course, you know about the state of English theatre, and I had come from that [. . .] tradition of Terence Rattigan's plays, and Christopher Fry and the 'well-made play'. I mean, I had been brought up through my youth, up to going to university . . . So it was a bit of a culture shock to me to come to Bristol and then find that there were all kinds of other plays that sort of didn't fit that particular bill. And it was a period of course when we – young people in England – certainly didn't know anything about the Theatre of the Absurd as it developed into . . . [There] was a whole tradition of European theatre that had been going on since the late 1800s . . . that we were completely – well I certainly was completely ignorant of. (*David Davies, actor*)

I saw a production brought over from France by Jean-Louis Barrault [French actor/director] and Madeleine Renaud [French actress], which was very exciting – mime from Paris,

just died, what's his name . . . never mind! [Marcel Marceau].
What else from abroad? Oh yes, some Greek theatre, some
Russian theatre, I saw [*The Cherry Orchard*] performed by the
Moscow Arts Company – didn't understand a word but, of
course, it was lovely, very exciting. (*James Gill, actor and stage
manager*)

There were a lot more [French productions] then than there are
now. And there had been previously throughout the nineteenth
century too. It has sort of packed up here for reasons that
escape me. It culminated with Peter Daubeny, but I have seen
in London during those years: *Le Audion* by Jean-Louis
Barrault, La Comédie Française (twice if not three times) . . .
(*Eileen Cottis, theatregoer*)

I met what I consider to be one of the great writers, had he
lived . . . and that was John Whiting. A wonderful writer, and
he and I became great friends. Just as an offshoot, he was
having his first play done in London, by Peter Brook of all
people, at the Haymarket. He had left York and I had just left
York, and we arranged to meet opposite the Haymarket in a
pub, and when John was upset his hair was all over the place
and it was white, and he came in looking like that and I said,
'What's the matter?'

Interviewer   Was the play *The Devils*?

BH   No, no, no, *Penny for a Song*. He came in looking like that
and I said, 'What's the matter?' He said, 'Do you know what that
man's just said to me?' I said, 'No.' 'He said, "I don't understand
your play, John, but I'm going to make it look pretty!"' And that's
exactly what happened and it wasn't a great success . . . (*Bernard
Hepton, actor*)

Acting: the reps

Interviewer   Why do you think so many people go on from
weekly rep to become successful in theatre?

MF   It's luck. I think, you see, the answer is you can't have a
better training. It's wonderful because it teaches what you can do

and what you can't do. But if you stayed in it for four or five years you'd become tatty.

Interviewer Why is that?

MF 'Well, I learn this, find the easy way out, who's for tennis? I think I'll wear my white togs in this and what-not' and I think it's a question of getting too smug, probably. It isn't until you get a longer term of rehearsals that you can find out.

Interviewer What was the atmosphere like . . .?

MF Wonderful. It was wonderful because you had to stick together. It sounds like an awful cliché, but it was like a happy family – it wasn't quite, you always had one or two buggers in there – you worked together as a team, they knew exactly your way of working and you knew their way of working . . . (*Malcolm Farquar, actor*)

Acting: the Old Vic

I had no idea really what the [Old Vic] training would be like. I had only been told . . . you see, I went to Rudolf von Laban Art of Movement Studio, which had been recommended by a brilliant man called Wilhelm Marcvalt who was a refugee for Nazi Germany, where he'd worked with Max Reinhardt, and had been made county drama adviser in Lincolnshire. And I did a summer course with him where there was a representative from Laban, the Art of Movement Studio, and they thought it would do me a world of good to go there first . . . [We] were encouraged to go and see variety and music hall, to do with the comic improvisation classes. We were encouraged to go to art galleries and look at painting. It was in fact an education as well as a training for theatre. And of course we would go to the theatre. We saw everything at the Old Vic because we got to the dress rehearsals. And Laurence Olivier was doing *Venus Observed* [by Christopher Fry], and as he was on the board of the Old Vic Theatre School, because he had officially opened it, he was a friend of the three men who ran it: Michel Saint-Denis, George Devine and Glen Byam Shaw. They were running the Old Vic Theatre as well as the school, so that we were at a great advantage really in that we were being trained by people who were still running a theatre and enduring criticism themselves, which we could all read. So that these men, who to us were gods, were being told off in the newspapers for not doing very well on a production. (*Joan Plowright, actor*)

The Lord Chamberlain and theatre censorship

I was . . . one of the earliest members of the Committee of the Society for Theatre Research, in which there was Muriel St Clare Byrne and all sorts of golden oldies including Sir St Vincent Troubridge . . . He was a very big florid man, obviously an Old Etonian as they all were, because they all knew what was best for us and you had to have an ex-guards officer and an Old Etonian for that one . . . Anyway, the old St Vincent Troubridge Bart was . . . one of the censors . . . and the Court wanted to put on Beckett's [*Endgame*] and the censor wanted to change [a line to] 'The pig, he doesn't exist.' It took us to realise that the convoluted mind of the censor had taken bastard . . . as a reflection on the Virgin Mary. 'The bastard, he doesn't exist!'

. . . So anyway the Court fought this tooth and nail, because Beckett wouldn't have anything to do with it . . . So finally they arranged a little private meeting with an extraordinarily distinguished audience – if you think of it that way – like Edward Bond and Keith Johnstone and you know, all the Court . . . Anyway George wouldn't have trusted anybody to deliver the line with the requisite tact – hide it! Anyway they said, 'And you meet this Sir St Vincent Troubridge; you know him.' So I met him at the door of the Court and he was clearly slightly miffed not to be met by George himself but he allowed himself to be conducted up to George's office or something like that. So there we all sat through this reading and when the line came, the line. There is a line that says 'let us pray' and there's then a pause and then George Devine said, 'The bastard, he doesn't exist.' He really hid it . . . but he didn't get away with that line. They're not fools those men, God they know what's going [on]. (*Ann Jellicoe, playwright*)

Professor Robert Anderson sent me *Tea and Sympathy*,[1] which then we had to get passed by the Lord Chamberlain . . . [He] said, 'No, the whole basis of . . . *Tea and Sympathy* is not acceptable and you can't do it in a public theatre,' and among hundreds of other plays, I'd read a play by a young American dramatist, Tennessee Williams, called *Cat on a Hot Tin Roof*[2] which I also liked very much, and again the Lord Chamberlain said 'that's banned', and. . . Arthur Miller, who . . . sent me *A View from the Bridge*[3] which I liked very much, and again the Lord Chamberlain said 'no'. I was talking one day with a lady called Muriel Large who was running the Watergate Theatre Club which was the small theatre club under the arches at Charing Cross Station, and there were then, in London, probably twenty or thirty very small theatre clubs, like the Boltons and the New Lindsay, and they of course could do plays that didn't have to be passed by the Lord Chamberlain . . . and Muriel said to me, 'I'm finding great difficulty finding plays,' and I said, 'Gosh, I've got plays that I just can't do,' and she said, 'Well, let me have them.' I said, 'Well, I don't know that they're much good to you, because they've got large casts for a small club theatre, they're expensive because of American royalties and I really don't see that you'd be interested in them,' and after a while she said to me, 'Well why don't we transfer the Watergate Club into the Comedy Theatre.' And I said, 'You're mad! We'll all end up in prison! No one's ever run an 850-seat West End theatre as a club,' and she said, 'Well, why not? Talk to your lawyers and I'll see about it!' . . . [And] I talked to a number of people, like Hugh Beaumont ['Binkie' Beaumont] and my boss then, Harold Wingate . . . and we decided in the end to take a chance and we started the New Watergate Theatre Club in the Comedy Theatre . . .

Interviewer So different commercial managers were putting money into the New Watergate to put the plays on?

AF No, no, we ran it ourselves . . . And we were very strict in that you had to buy a membership for a pound, you couldn't buy tickets until you've been a member for twenty-four hours, you could then buy a ticket as a member and up to three guests and the police were very vigilant and saw very carefully the box office was behaving itself, otherwise we'd have been shut down overnight. I mean, at the time I didn't think we were doing anything that was a major breakthrough, I wanted to do *Tea and Sympathy, Cat on a Hot Tin Roof* and *A View from the Bridge*, that's all I was interested in. I mean, now, when I lecture at various theatre courses, you know, young students say, 'Oh, you're the chap who broke the censorship laws,' but we didn't set out to break the censorship laws, we set out to produce three plays we had great faith in . . .

Interviewer Was there any contact from the Lord Chamberlain once those plays were up and running?

AF Well, other than policing that the box office behaved itself, I don't think . . . I mean, no one was spiteful about it or anything, they just saw that we were operating legally and within the law, so they shrugged their shoulders about it, and of course the . . . The major papers, you know, the *Sunday Times, Observer*, etc., had all acknowledged that these three plays were very important ones. (*Anthony Field, theatre producer, theatre project consultant, former finance director of the Arts Council*)

[What] the Lord Chamberlain hated more than anything was improvisation and of course there was a feeling that they wanted to improvise . . . And we did a play . . . which was about working on a . . . people on a building site, and there was some improvisation around the conversation. And that was absolutely anathema to the Lord Chamberlain. They were really, really, really dreadful . . . (*Jean Gaffin, theatre worker, Theatre Workshop*)

I know my colleagues were outraged [by the Lord Chamberlain] but I couldn't share their outrage, I couldn't get really . . . deeply distressed because the Lord Chamberlain had asked me to change . . . 'Jesus Christ' to 'God Almighty'. It was irritating. On the contrary, on reflection I realised that my play *Chicken Soup with Barley*, which was about communists, sympathetically drawn, could happen. There was no censorship of that, at a time when communists were demonised. That that could happen was far more important to me than that I had to change some silly words. (*Arnold Wesker, playwright*)

Binkie Beaumont and H. M. Tennent

Binkie Beaumont and Tennent, they were the big controllers, you know: you had to be in with them, and they offered a scholarship . . . I know that RADA people, you know, used to get put on to contract and I mean, it was like, I guess, Cameron Mackintosh now, you see all the programmes would say, you know, 'presented by Tennent's' and . . . it was a given, you didn't really even think about it. They were just there – they were providing it for you . . . (*Helen Neale, actor*)

The first time I ever met [Binkie Beaumont] was actually going racing and my husband, who was very much in awe of Binkie Beaumont . . . he kept saying to me, 'You must remember he is very important, you must remember this, that and the other.' And I remember I was collected in the Rolls, driven by the chauffeur called Jack, and we went off to Newmarket racing – just Binkie and I – and he was the nicest, friendliest man you could possibly meet. And I think if you crossed him he could be quite difficult, but to me he was always hugely friendly, hugely supportive, very eager always to find out what was going on. (*Patricia Noble, script-reader for H. M. Tennent*)

There was always this rather sniffy view of Tennent that they did all the commercial stuff. The plays they put on – Aunt Edna wouldn't like it! I was very aware then that there were changes afoot in the theatre and that there was exciting writing.

We all sneered at Terence Rattigan and Noël Coward; now, I think very foolishly. . . [A] play like *The Deep Blue Sea* . . . is a play with great depth to it. It's not the sort of Aunt Edna/while-away-the-time sort of play. But I think the Tynans of this world were very dismissive . . . (*Jacqueline Glasser, theatregoer and literary agent*)

Binkie was an amazing character, as you probably have heard from other people. I don't know . . . he ran H. M. Tennent Ltd, he probably was the most successful West End impresario we've had since Charles Cochrane, and he ran Tennent Productions Ltd and H. M. Tennent Ltd, which were two companies.

Interviewer There were two separate ones . . . One was educational because of the entertainment tax?

AF Yes, because of the entertainment tax . . . And he had a monopoly of all the stars and the producers and the designers . . . And Binkie, of course, was on the National Theatre Board, and anything big that came up – like the New Watergate – he would want to have a hand in, because even if he wasn't going to be in control of it, he would know what was happening and like to be, a) seen to be involved and b) to be involved . . . [Someone] that was an impresario like Binkie would be sensitive to the fact that however much he loved doing the great old plays with John Gielgud and Edith Evans and Sybil Thorndike, he also was sensitive to the new movements as they came along, and whether he hated the plays of John Osborne and Arthur Miller, he could see where audiences were going and he would capitalise on that, even if he hadn't got his heart in it. (*Anthony Field, theatre producer, theatre project consultant, former finance director of the Arts Council*)

[Binkie Beaumont] was hugely successful, he had cornered the market in glamorous productions. They were nearly always star-studded, and they gradually of course came to be seen as elitist and not part of the real world but yes, I think he was [controlling], I think he probably was. I saw him as benign, but for people who didn't fit into it, he was definitely, yes. There is the famous Angus McBean photograph . . . of Binkie, it's a Marionette Theatre with Ralph Richardson and he is holding the strings? . . . He had control of the theatres, he had control of most of the major writers, and certainly actors and actresses would die to work for him . . . He had a monopoly really, and like all monopolies, it couldn't last. (*Patricia Noble, script-reader for H. M. Tennent*)

The Arts Council

I think the grant from the Treasury was £665,000 when I joined the Arts Council, and I always remember going to bed and thinking one day, 'Please God, I'll have a million pounds a year and all my troubles will be over!' We had a very, very informal relationship with the Treasury: I would wander over with the Secretary General once or twice a year, speak to a junior civil servant at the Treasury – I always remember her name, Molly Loughnane – and we'd say, 'We want some more money,' and she'd say, 'How much?' And we'd say '£850,000' and she'd say OK, or not OK . . .

Interviewer . . . When you first started, what were the criteria on which you were assessing [theatre] . . .?

TF Well a number of us evolved this over my early years, and if an organisation applied to us for a grant and say it was a drama company presenting Agatha Christie plays on the end of the pier at Blackpool, it would go to the drama department, and the drama department would say, you know, 'We're not interested: Agatha Christie plays, end of the pier, you know, that should pay for itself,' so it would never come to our finance department at all; but Liverpool Repertory Company, that had been in existence for very many years without subsidy and the thought that they would have Arts Council funding was horrific to them because they thought, 'We're going to have all those forms to fill in and we'd have to you know bow to their precedent and all that sort of thing, we'd rather not go down that road,' they reached a stage where they said, 'We can't exist without Arts Council Funding,' added to which their Liverpool local authority would say, 'Unless you get that Arts Council funding, we won't subsidise you,' and the Arts Council were saying, 'They should get local authority funding, we won't subsidise you,' but they went hand in hand. So if Liverpool, well as it happened Liverpool Repertory Company, came to us and said, 'We want subsidy,' and the drama department said, 'All right, they do a three-weekly rep, they do a good standard of production, they do interesting plays and we should subsidise them,' at that stage it would come to the finance department and I would look at the last three years' accounts, I'd look at the budget for next year and say, 'OK, if you want to subsidise this company, in the light of their box office, in the light of the local authority interest, in the light of their costings, they could do with say £20,000 a year, grant and say £5,000 a year guarantee against loss,' and so on. But there were two distinct decisions to be made, one was the drama department and the drama panel assessing the quality of the work, and the other was the finance department assessing what sort of subsidy would be required. (*Anthony Field, theatre producer, theatre project consultant, former finance director of the Arts Council*)

Tynan and Hobson

[While] I was still living at college, we used to read Kenneth Tynan in the *Observer* on Sunday mornings and Harold Hobson in the *Sunday Times*. We read both so it was nice to compare them, most of the time while I was in college it was reading [about] things in London that I never thought I'd see . . . (*Eileen Cottis, theatregoer*)

Harold Hobson

I'd always been deeply interested in the theatre. The Playhouse then at Oxford was one of the leading theatres in Great Britain. Flora Robson, John Gielgud, Tyrone Guthrie, Richard Goolden were all members of the company, so I went to see them quickly and the theatre being a very deep interest of mine it gradually surfaced and I began to write about the theatre . . . The London editor of the *Monitor*. . . said to me one day, 'If you write a review of [the actor] Jack Buchanan in, I think it was *Stand Up and Sing*, and it's printed in the *Monitor* we will pay you for your seat,' and that was how my professional association with the theatre began . . . My theory of the theatre was that each visit to the theatre, something happens, something happens to the critic's mind and heart and the thing becomes sort of historically dense and therefore my criticisms, I should say, are records of how I happened to feel at a [particular] evening at a particular play, that they are the foundation of a historical record more than the passing of a judgement . . .

Interviewer How could you characterise your dissatisfaction with post-war British theatre, the stuff you were seeing in London?

HH It was too frivolous, too exclusively upper-middle-class. It ignored the existence of nine-tenths of the world – more than nine-tenths.

Interviewer I just wondered, there seemed to be quite a lot of reviews, particularly of [the French playwright Jean-Paul] Sartre plays, that were based on the Lyric Hammersmith that you went to see in '47 and '48 and I just wondered whether that was a policy of the theatre, or not that you can remember?

HH Yes, I think it was a policy in the theatre, it was really an anticipation of the movement in the British theatre towards the study of political questions.

Interviewer Did that mirror a greater interest in politics on the part of the general public or did you think that was something that the theatre itself was leading?

HH I think it was the theatre itself.

Interviewer We'll move on now to *Look Back in Anger*. I've read most of the reviews of the other critics and only you and Kenneth

Tynan appeared to support the play. One interesting point in *Indirect Journey* [Hobson's autobiography, published in 1978] is that you were voraciously well-read, you read everything about the theatre, articles, other dramatic criticism. Can you remember what your reaction was to these adverse criticisms to *Look Back in Anger* and whether you felt provoked by them to write a defence of it or was it entirely your own personal reaction to the play?

HH Both, I think, but it is a particularly like a critic to come across a play which he thinks is extremely good, which is a memorable experience for him, and to find that it's happened to nobody else.

Interviewer Can you remember any other plays like that?

HH Well, principally *The Birthday Party*, which I was the only London critic to praise at its first production.

Interviewer . . . [You] actually introduced the young Kenneth Tynan at Oxford to your publishers . . . so in a sense you could have been said to have started him on his career, is that correct?

HH I recommended him to Longmans.

Interviewer And what were your relations at that point and after that? . . .

HH They were very friendly, although he moved in entirely different circles.

Interviewer How would you compare your criticism to his brand of criticism . . .?

HH I think Kenneth Tynan became obsessed by Brecht and his influence was paramount in Kenneth's career, whereas I don't think there was any particular author who dominated all the rest in my view. (*Harold Hobson*)

Kenneth Tynan

. . . [we] always read the reviews. I mean, Ken Tynan . . . and Harold Hobson, were the reviewers. You never let a Sunday go without having a good laugh at Ken Tynan. And . . . he was

cruel . . . absolutely cruel. Harold Hobson was a delight . . .
[His] comments were always very sober and considerate. But
Tynan was all fireworks and, you know, with his language and
his criticisms and what have you. But he was delightful to read.
And of course yes . . . we did get some information . . . about
the plays themselves. And I always remember this . . . reading
the reviews at the time of *Look Back in Anger* and I just had to
go and see this play – 'What is it all about?' (*David Davies,
actor*)

I read Tynan every week, we all did . . . all the people I knew
who were seriously interested in the arty scene generally, but
particularly theatre, would read Tynan, and probably Hobson
and the others but Tynan was unquestionably the leader of the
pack . . . (*Anthony Smith, playwright*)

[The] one I remember of course was Ken Tynan . . . 'cause he
was so long and lanky – he used to sit in the front row of the
stalls and you used to be able to have a look over the gods and
see him there. Well in the linen room [used as the costume
room] we were up in the top of the building there: if we came
out of the linen room, down a short staircase, there was a very
smelly gents' toilet there, but to the left there was a door into
the gods. Sometimes if we wanted to see what was going on
we'd have a look there and you could see when he [Tynan] was
there. He always wore beige-coloured suits, and he used to . . .
you could see him 'cause his legs, long legs sticking out! He was
very good to us, by and large – think he liked what we were
doing. Harold Hobson . . . used to like Avis and her acting,
and he always wrote nice things about her. (*Josephine Smith,
wardrobe mistress, Theatre Workshop*)

Yes, I remember reading Tynan, because I was miffed with
Tynan because he was very unkind to Gielgud – extremely so –
and very kind to Olivier . . . there's a thing about criticism
– and it's interesting – that the critic shouldn't think more of
himself than the people he's writing about, and I'm not sure
that Tynan didn't. There are other people who write better

criticism because they're actually looking – they're wanting to say what is actually true about the performance they've seen, you know. (*Helen Neale, actor*)

Beckett and Brecht

Beckett and Godot

RG   [There] were two scripts in particular . . . and one of them was . . . *Waiting for Godot.*

Interviewer   So who passed that on to you – how did you . . .?

RG   Mr Albery [Donald Albery, a noted West End impresario]. He'd been sent it . . . and I read it and . . . I said to him, 'I think it's very difficult to read, and I suggest that from your understudies from your various theatres' – he had three – 'I could do a reading for you, from the understudies. And I would suggest that you also invite a censor . . . But it's a very interesting play and we will do a rehearsed reading.' So I directed that rehearsed reading, and I also got hold of Oscar Lewenstein and I said, 'Look you should do this bloody play with [American comic double act] Abbot and Costello . . .' Well, anyway, we did the reading and Albery decided not to have it in his theatre . . . I don't know whether he liked it or not, but it wasn't his cup of tea and they decided to give it to Peter Hall at the Arts Theatre . . . (*Renee Goddard, actor, stage manager, script-reader 1943–54*)

Interviewer   . . . [You] said [*Godot*] was one of the most memorable experiences of your life.

DB   For the simple reason that when I got home and actually talked about it to my husband, ad inf[initum], he said to me, 'What was it about exactly?' because he'd read the crits, and they were inscrutable, and I said to him, 'Well if you asked me to sit down and write a précis about this, I couldn't do it' and yet I was moved to the very depth of my being . . . I mentioned Ken Tynan once or twice in this, and I wasn't a great admirer of Ken Tynan

. . . I've got his pithy analysis of the play; something about these characters passing the time of their lives, as we ourselves are, sitting in this theatre passing our time. It struck me as being the very core and centre of it . . . [*Dorien Brooks, theatregoer*]

I was there at that little theatre on Piccadilly Circus . . . [It] was a strange theatre, it was like a Turkish bath, it was tiled, the corridors there were tiled . . . I went with three or four other people to see it because we'd read about it. I enjoyed it very much, and I have a vivid memory of the conversation afterwards, which was immediately, 'What does Godot stand for?', 'What is Godot a symbol of?' . . . I'm pleased with myself that I remember thinking – and probably saying – 'That's not the right question, all he stands for is what we are waiting for or what Didi and Gogo are waiting for on the stage . . . I don't want to symbolise it more precisely than that, it's fate or all the other things you might come up with, because it's more interesting than that, it's just an abstract quantity, what we are waiting for.' And I remember being highly entertained by it. (*Anthony Smith, playwright*)

Interviewer What did you think of what might be termed the less realistic things, people like Beckett and Ionesco who also came in, in that period?

PL Rubbish, absolute rubbish . . . Because it was meaningless, to me it was meaningless and it was meaningless for a purpose, which was to fool the audience into thinking they were being clever and I don't think this is possible. I mean, whoever saw Ionesco really? Wasn't he sitting in a dustbin, didn't he and his wife sit in a dustbin throughout the whole play? [This comment confuses Ionesco with Beckett; the characters in dustbins are in *Endgame*.] Oh really, nonsense is the word I think I was looking for. I'm not saying one has to have realism all the time but I think one has got to have comprehensible English spoken by comprehensible people, and I don't think either of those did. (*Peter Lambert, theatre director*)

Brecht

> I saw the first production of Brecht, *Mother Courage*, which was at Barnstaple of all places, at the Devon Festival in 1955 . . . and I was impressed but not as impressed as Kenneth Tynan. I never became as obsessed by Brecht as Kenneth was or as most progressive critics were. (*Harold Hobson*)

> And then we [Theatre Workshop] were further recognised by Bertolt Brecht, allowing us to do *Mother Courage*. It was conditional upon Joan playing Mother Courage. Which she said, 'Oh yes, of course I will' – she didn't have the slightest intention of playing Mother Courage at all! But anyway, things got slightly peppery because Bertolt sent over one of his assistant directors and he reported back to Bertolt that Joan was not preparing to play the part, she was rehearsing an actress, and furthermore he'd been locked out of the theatre because he wanted to make a rubber stamp reproduction of the Berliner Ensemble's production of *Mother Courage*, which Joan of course was not going to accept. So Bertolt replied immediately and said, 'If she does not play Mother Courage, she will not be allowed to do the play,' so she had to do it in the end. And so we went to the North Devon Arts Festival, and played in the Queen's Hall, Barnstaple and [*laughs*] found ourselves somewhat short of all the technical know-how, you know, that the Berliner Ensemble have with their wonderful theatres . . . (*George Cooper, actor*)

> The Berliner Ensemble came to London and . . . we all went to see it . . . and I think it was quite simple to imagine that we'd never seen anything like that before and we'd never seen such simplicity and such beauty and such power . . . So that was very, very, very impressive but on the other hand, they were foreign, so there was an element, especially in Birmingham, where you went oh well they're just foreign and then they're German aren't they so it's nothing to do with us really . . . (*Pamela Howard, scenographer*)

The Royal Court and the new drama

The Royal Court

[The] Royal Court Theatre was very pivotal . . . because it gave parts to a different type of actor, more working-class actors . . . and more actors that didn't wear a lot of make-up, actors who were visibly a new sort of actor, I think . . . (*Ian McKillop, theatregoer*)

I think there was huge excitement around the Royal Court . . . We used to feel that anything which was on there, we'd go and see it. It felt as if it was groundbreaking. To some extent with the Theatre Royal in Stratford, but not in the same way. The way [Devine] was encouraging new writing and putting on plays that probably wouldn't have seen the light of day a few years earlier . . .

Interviewer . . . [There's] a lot of people who suggest that the advent of this kitchen-sink drama and the Angry Young Men and the work at the Royal Court starting pushing the more traditional drawing-room plays out of the West End . . .

JG I don't know, they were still being put on. It's true that *The Entertainer* went to the Palace, but that was probably because it was Olivier. But it had probably always been difficult to get serious plays on in the West End. I don't think anything had changed. (*Jacqueline Glasser, theatregoer and literary agent*)

[It] was exciting to be there at the beginning. Of course we didn't know that it was going to be making history; would be a sort of important change. But indeed it was, because you know the West End theatre had . . . *Venus Observed*, Christopher Fry, T. S. Eliot and *The Lady's Not for Burning* and *Cocktail Party* and *Saint's Day* with John Whiting, and Binkie Beaumont was installed in the West End, and it was elegant, and refined, and rather poetic theatre . . . But just rather conventional and, for us students then, perhaps a little bit boring. And it was the beginning – I mean that was the sort of . . . just waiting time.

Going to be tipped over with a huge raw energy which came in with you know, the a) *Look Back in Anger* but b) Theatre Workshop, Stratford East and Joan Littlewood . . . (*Joan Plowright, actor*)

We did go to the Belgrade Coventry and we saw Wesker's *Chicken Soup with Barley* and *Roots* and *Chips with Everything* and all of that . . . and the person who designed that was Jocelyn Herbert [the designer at the Royal Court] who sadly died one or two years ago, and we met Jocelyn and Jocelyn said she'd been to the Berliner Ensemble and she'd seen the work of Brecht . . . and we saw on the stage, for instance, in *Chicken Soup with Barley* . . . well we just saw a line of washing, a light and a chair and it wasn't a real room at all and we couldn't believe it and I fell in love with Jocelyn, I mean with her work and she remained up to her death, my influence and a mentor and a friend and she'd met Caspar Neher who was the designer who worked with Brecht and she knew all about it and she was bringing that aesthetic to London . . . (*Pamela Howard, scenographer*)

[It] was very egalitarian . . . Michael and George Devine would say, 'Good evening' and everybody was, I mean we all worked hard, and the man who was what was called stage director and the chief prompt was a man called Michael Hallifax and Michael Hallifax was a very elegant, calm man who dealt with us with enormous calm and was always helpful, never lost his temper and basically ran the backstage wonderfully and he was a godsend to them . . . (*Michael Seymour, stagehand and stage electrician*)

Look Back in Anger

Interviewer What were your impressions of *Look Back in Anger*?

PB I was totally fascinated. It was real life. (*Philip Bramley: theatregoer*)

I wouldn't say *Look Back in Anger* was one of my favourites by any means. It was obviously earth-shaking, but all this business round the ironing board and all the rest of it . . . I came out of the theatre saying, 'Well, it's a good job we've seen that; we know what's going on.' It was a landmark, I know, and is always used as such isn't it? I probably thought, 'How outrageous!' [*Dorien Brooks, theatregoer*]

Look Back in Anger was put on which I went to with Wayland Young and as Wayland said at the time, 'This is a different voice. We're hearing something new.' The whole scene changed, everybody hurried to see it, I think it was Ken Tynan wasn't it, who first wrote about it and got it enthusiastic about it?

Interviewer Did you enjoy the play?

AP Oh yes, very much. (*Anne Piper, novelist and playwright*)

Well, I should explain that I saw *Look Back in Anger* in October 1956, and it did have a particular resonance for me at the time because up until that time I'd been at school, I'd done my National Service and I'd come from both of those not knowing what my career was to be. I didn't know what I wanted to do, and so I was guided by family friends who thought I ought to go to university . . . I was cross with life because it wasn't working out really as I wanted it to. And so seeing *Look Back in Anger* it really sort of came home to me. I felt, 'Yes, I'm like Jimmy Porter, I'm fed up with the world and I can rant and rave' – but of course I didn't because I'm not that sort of character. But it really did have a great impact on me, and . . . I saw it about six times, different productions over the next two or three years . . . (*John Holt, theatregoer*)

Well *Look Back in Anger* had opened at the Royal Court just before I joined the company and I just thought it was a rather good play. It seemed quite savage for its time and I know that Binkie had turned it down, it was offered to him and he didn't want to do it but it seemed to me that it was a very good play and I think that any of the actors in that company would say the same as me. I mean we didn't feel that we were doing anything very world shattering, we were just doing a play. (*John Moffatt, actor*)

I did see the first production of *Look Back in Anger* . . . I went with Joan and some other members of the company, and Joan just said, 'What an awful play!' – I mean, Joan [Littlewood] had been doing this sort of stuff . . . I thought it was interesting, I didn't get carried away by it. You see, Joan was not interested in the West End or anything like that – she wanted a People's Theatre and that was what she was working towards. Of course she would be a bit scathing of *Look Back in Anger* – it was to be expected of her! You know, I enjoyed it; I don't really remember an awful lot about it. I kept thinking to myself, 'Well, what is he going on about?' But I can see why it was so important because suddenly he was writing about different people – he was writing about these working people, that sort of thing, and not the usual West End stuff. So it was a landmark in British theatre . . . (*Julia Jones, actor, playwright, theatregoer*)

I think that things were changing, I think *Look Back in Anger* probably changed things, and then started the wheels turning or the ball rolling, and then *A Taste of Honey* came in and suddenly . . . I mean, you know, *Look Back in Anger* is a man's play, the women are . . . by the ironing board, but in this particular thing you had two very strong women, at loggerheads and shouting . . . (*Francis Cuka, actor*)

The Entertainer

Interviewer [In] *The Entertainer* where you saw Olivier, what moved you so much about that . . .?

IM It think it was, 'I have a go, ladies and gentleman, I do have a go,' and I was very moved by the songs, the 'Why should I let it touch me? Why shouldn't I sit down and try to let it pass over me?' I wasn't so moved by the famous movie moment where he talks about the black woman, but it was that sort of, I think it was so pathetic, that soft-shoe-shuffle song-and-dance thing, and the rather black . . . it was all very, very black. It was a very big theatre, whatever this theatre was called . . . and it all took place on . . . the stage of the theatre that Archie Rice was performing in and then it would cut to the room that they were arguing in, Brenda de Banzie as Phoebe, the wife of Archie, and . . . it must have been Joan Plowright as the daughter . . . But I just remember a real impression of sort of bright lights of the performances and black, black, blackness of the dreary scenes of quarrelling . . . (*Ian MacKillop, audience member*)

[On Olivier in *The Entertainer*] . . . I tell you what really impressed me . . . was Olivier's enormous professionalism and every night he would come in early – I mean, if the production started at say 7.30, he would come in at half past six while the tabs were still up. And there was a musician – a pianist – and there was a scene in, I think it was the second Act, where the character, Archie Rice, does a little dance and sings 'Why should I care' . . . Every evening he would come in and he would rehearse just that piece . . . Anyway we went on with it for, I think it ran for six weeks but at the end of that charity – the charity performance was on a Sunday . . . and . . . I'm afraid we got overtime, the stage hands, and at the end of it Olivier made an impassioned impromptu speech and the fervent thank you's all round, I can still remember he came and he shook everybody's hand, stage hand, everybody – you know, he was so kind of carried away by his whole rhetoric that he couldn't stop, you know, he went on you know flourishing 'thank you, thank you' . . . (*Michael Seymour, stagehand and stage electrician*)

Arnold Wesker

[What] was your relationship with Osborne like?

AW Curious. I always had an affectionate, soft spot for him. Because I felt that he'd opened the way, and it was *Look Back in Anger* that I saw that made me write *Chicken Soup with Barley*. So, I always felt this for him. And we would correspond intermittently. I have a collection of his postcards. His famous postcards in which he says crazy outrageous things. He always wanted me to come and visit him in Clun, in Shropshire, where he died, I think it was Shropshire. And I never did. And I slightly regret not having done so, but there was a part of me that felt that he was sort of . . . he was much more theatrical than me. I mean, he and Pinter were really theatre people, they enjoyed theatre company and I'm not very comfortable in theatre company and therefore bitchy. He would speak bitchily about people. And I'm really not comfortable listening to people bitch about others and therefore that whole theatrical green room scene was . . . I didn't feel at ease with it. So I stayed away . . .

Interviewer   Could you tell me if you saw a conflict between theatre in London and the regional theatres? . . .

AW   No. You know, there's something about the beginning of one's career where one is kind of not aware of anything except that you've written a play, someone wants to do it and you're really very excited that it's actually going to happen, so I was aware that when I got off at the station at Coventry, I saw posters advertising my play and that was an incredible thrill and then I arrived at the theatre, there in the workshop people were hammering out sets because of something I'd written in an LCC [London County Council] flat a few years previously, so that's what struck me. No, it didn't occur to me that there was something slightly patronising about the Royal Court Theatre saying, 'No, we don't feel strongly about *Chicken Soup with Barley*, but we'll let the Belgrade Theatre do it, they're going to going to bring a play to the Royal Court Theatre as part of a celebration of repertory theatres,' and there were four theatres that were bringing their productions to the Royal Court. And what the Belgrade Coventry wanted to do, the Royal Court didn't approve of, so they said, 'Look, why don't you do this play by a new young writer?' and Brian Bailey, who ran Coventry, leapt at it and it was the beginning of the career of John Dexter, who directed it, and myself. So, I didn't think there was anything wrong with that, I thought it was the way things happened, I do know that later on, I insisted that my contracts with any London theatre had to have in it, that the repertory theatres should be given the opportunity to perform the play and open it just a day after the opening in London, so they shouldn't be treated as second-class citizens. Which is what – early on in my career I realised that's what they were feeling, that they were treated as second-class citizens because they weren't allowed to do any of the plays until it had been fully exploited in London. But I must say that having argued for that and got the agreement from the Royal Court that that clause could go in the contract, very few regional theatres had the courage to do a new play, an untried play. So they may have been complaining that they were being treated as second-class citizens but in fact they also didn't have the courage to do new plays . . .

Interviewer   Were you slightly reticent when the Royal Court approached to put on the trilogy . . .?

AW   No. Not at all, I was delighted, why should I be reticent? They didn't put it on for long, you know, it was only on for about three weeks, a week for each play, but a great fuss was made of it, I mean a great fuss beyond what they actually did commercially. *Roots* was the only one of the three that transferred subsequently to the West End. And hit the hottest summer on record so no one was going to the theatre. And it had to come off after a few weeks, but no, I was thrilled that the Court did the trilogy . . .

   . . . Osborne was very sceptical of groups. He was very English about political action. I mean, I don't think he ever went on an Aldermaston March. He gave his name to the Committee of One Hundred. But I don't know if he ever marched. I may be wrong about that. But I don't have a memory of him being on a march. John Arden . . . wasn't that political to begin with but became so. When he became closer involved with Margaretta [D'Arcy: Irish writer, later John Arden's wife]. And I don't know. It's a very confused period and I know that academics are all the time trying to make it neat and put people in brackets but it was a very disparate group if you think about it. Wally [N. F.] Simpson with *One Way Pendulum* [produced at the Royal Court], his was really Theatre of the Absurd. I don't believe Harold Pinter is Theatre of the

Absurd . . . I think he's a highly stylised Naturalist, and Ann Jellicoe was writing what was much more along with Wally Simpson, Theatre of the Absurd, but it wasn't really absurd, it was just kind of way out, it was strangely structured and a strange language. But if you think about Osborne and myself, we were very conventional . . . (*Arnold Wesker, playwright*)

Theatre Workshop

Theatre Workshop before Stratford East

They acquired an old lorry, on to that was packed the set, costumes and most of the actors. They toured south, middle and north Wales, the north of England and into Scotland. Did it for years. The physical pressure on them all was just unbelievable! Everything had to be humped into the venue, the set erected and the lighting fixed. Then a very demanding performance with madam out there taking notes, and after which everything had to be dismantled. Then they would get in that lorry and drive to their next venue, or wherever they were putting their heads down for that evening. And as I say, on the journey Joan would be giving notes on the night's performance, and rehearsing. I mean they never stopped! Never stopped! It was gruelling . . . Oh! The old members of the workshop would always say to you . . . They never talked about anything else but theatre. Their own personal . . . Of course, if you had to go to the dentist, well, you had to go to the dentist, but that was just boring and got in the way about talking about the next production. Morning, noon and night – they just talked theatre. (*Murray Melvin, actor*)

Theatre Workshop at Stratford East

Interviewer So what were you first impressions of the theatre at Stratford East?

MM Oh, well that was extraordinary. I can tell you very clearly – and that's what I noticed in those two classical productions – no footlights, and then no make-up! Now middle 1950s that was unheard of, because at that time your productions were mainly painted flats, and then your lighting was lighting those flats from the front to make it look pretty and bring out the colours. I mean, that was the norm. You got to Stratford and there were no footlights. There was often just an open stage, which in those days was still pretty dramatic: to walk in and just see an open stage. You see it all the time now, but you didn't then. You put it in that context, it was incredible! And of course no make-up, because of course the lighting was European. Based nearly all white, very little colour – [German director Erwin] Piscator, [Russian director Sergei] Eisenstein, filmic . . . (*Murray Melvin, actor*)

Joan Littlewood

Interviewer So when you first went to Theatre Workshop, could you just describe the audition process?

BC . . . I did any speech I could remember from any play, a bit of Shakespeare, there was a play in which I played a lawyer – think it was called *Libel* or something – and various things like that. I would do these. Then Joan would say, 'Can you . . . [improvise], will you do some dancing?' And of course at theatre school we had had ballet and movement, apart from Laban's classes. And then we talked about the theatre, and then she would give me things to improvise. She would suddenly tell me a story and I would take something up like that as an improvisation . . . (*Barry Clayton, actor*)

Interviewer And what was Joan Littlewood like to work with? Because I've heard lots of stories and I've seen lots of documentaries on her, and I just wondered what your experience of her was?

FC It's hard to . . . well, I liked her, but she could be a pain. And she could make you suffer. I don't know whether Murray has told you this, but the first time we did *A Taste of Honey*, she . . . well, we come on, the mother and daughter come on with suitcases, and she said, 'Well we've got to get this first scene right,' and so she said, 'These suitcases haven't got anything in them! Put something in them!' and she put stage weights in them, she put God knows what in them, till they were, she really weighed them down, and then she made us go round and round the stage, with Murray being bus conductors and people who wouldn't let us on: 'Not with that suitcase you're not getting on' (*laughs*) . . . until Avis and I were at daggers drawn, and we're not speaking to her, we're about to kill Joan (*laughs*) and then she said, 'Right! Start the play!' (*In Manchester accent, quoting from the play*) 'This is the place', 'Well I don't like it!' (*Francis Cuka, actor*)

Interviewer   Would you say that that political agenda of Joan Littlewood's would influence people's interest in going to see her theatre?

PF   I never personally knew anybody who it influenced, but then I couldn't say. Just, you know, as a general impression, my impression is that the people who were interested politically would come from outside the area – that was the people who were writing for the newspapers, who were interested in that. Whereas local people just went for a night out, more, I guess. That's obviously a huge generalisation and just an impression.

Interviewer   Would you say that the devised collaborative nature showed through, or not?

PF   Sometimes it did. It wasn't so star-struck. And you had poor . . . I have to say, Avis Bunnage is ugly, or was ugly, I'm not quite sure if she has died now. But she would get star parts, and that was nice, because she was a good actress, and you don't see that often in the theatre, someone with really quite plain, getting to play the Queen, and that sort of thing. And you would – people would change parts, and so you would see them as – I saw who became Harry H. Corbett later on, he was Harry Corbett when I saw him, before he played in *Steptoe* so he was unknown then, and I saw him as – I think it was *Richard II*. And then the next week, you know, he would perhaps have quite a minor part in a play . . . (*Pat Francis, theatregoer*)

Reworking playtexts

[When] we did *The Quare Fellow*, for instance, Behan – when
we finally got him to London, [after] two attempts – came in
with this great heap of a play. Great heap, I mean it must have
had about 500 pages you know. And we sort of read it, and
obviously Joan read it first. And Joan and Gerry and . . . [others
realised] there was a wonderful play in there. But there was a
load of it, you know, garbage. Well not necessarily garbage, but
not relevant to . . . I mean, we would do a Stanislavsky analysis,
'What is the super-objective of this play? What are the best
ways the writer is telling it? Where are the . . .?' And then we
move. Because I remember the first time we ran Act One for
him, he sat in the audience, he said, (*Irish accent*) 'Bloody hell,
did I write that? It's fucking marvellous isn't it?' . . . (*Barry
Clayton, actor*)

[We] didn't really hit the jackpot until Brendan Behan came
into our life – an Irish poet, writer, reprobate, ex-member of
the IRA – who sent a script to Joan. It was called *The Quare
Fellow*. The quare fellow is a slang word, meaning the man
who's about to be hung. And the play was a rambling day – two
days – in the life of prisoners in Mountjoy Prison in Ireland,
and the run-up until the execution of this particular prisoner.
And in that day we got to meet the prisoners, some of the prisoners, and the way they behaved, and the way they didn't
behave, and their attitudes towards each other, and finally to
the hanging of the prisoner.

It was a wonderful play. We rehearsed it, not in the theatre a
lot of the time, we rehearsed it on the roof of the theatre. Joan
wanted . . . the equivalent to an exercise yard that a prison
would have had, and the stage of course was too limiting in
that respect. But she wanted to give us the freedom of being to
walk, so we went on to the roof of the theatre, where we could
see all the buses and cars and trams, all going past on the
outside, and the calls of the market people. But eventually that
all fell away as we concentrated on just literally being bored. I
mean, that's quite an exercise. We just walked round and round

in circles, totally bored, till we got bored. First of all of course we started making jokes until Joan said 'Stop it,' she said, 'You wouldn't be allowed to make a joke, you wouldn't be allowed to speak. And if you are going to speak you've got to do it so secretively that nobody else will see you.' And so we did it like a game. We spoke . . . we asked Brendan how they spoke, and they spoke out the corners of their mouth . . .

. . . And we rehearsed I think for about six or seven weeks. The play was being rewritten as we progressed. As we discovered more from rehearsals or improvisation, and we discovered more from Brendan himself who came and regaled us with all his stories of what happened, we mounted the production. We didn't know what we had on our hands . . . (*Brian Murphy, actor*)

Interviewer   Did you see *A Taste of Honey*?

JJ   Yes. First production I saw of that, it was fine. I didn't really think that it was a marvellous play, but it was very interesting. Joan made a marvellous job of it, she really made it, she made the play. Some things I am not really sure that I ought to say here, but I do remember Avis Bunnage telling me that they were on stage with . . . I think it was the second play that, what's her name, what was her name?

Interviewer   Shelagh Delaney.

JJ   Yes, that's it! Her second play, and I didn't see that – I didn't have anything to do with it at all – but Avis said that they put it on, and she was in her dressing room and Joan came into her room and said, 'Well that was a marvellous play that we wrote together Avis!' You'd better cut that out! That's a very secret thing.

Interviewer   So there was a furore about who it was who wrote the play. Is that right?

JJ   There may have been, but that is what she said to Avis. Joan quite liked to get things that were a bit raw and then she could do enormous things with them . . . (*Julia Jones, actor, playwright, theatregoer*)

Theatre Workshop and the Arts Council

Interviewer   Why do you think it was that certain companies like Theatre Workshop lost out on Arts Council funding in the earlier years?

AF   I'm not sure why. There was always a slight problem. The drama panel and we in the finance department would say, 'OK, whether it's Sheffield or Birmingham Rep or Bristol Old Vic, they are servicing an area,' and there was always a worry . . . although the English Stage Company got itself well established from the early years as a sort of purveyor of new plays, there was always a slight worry with Guildford, Leatherhead, Hornchurch, Theatre Royal Stratford, that they were so near the London conurbation they weren't necessarily servicing a region in the way that, say, Birmingham Rep was or Bristol Old Vic. And I think in a way they lost out by being on the fringe of the whole of the West End, in a way, and there was always this worry about 'Are we in fact subsidising a theatre company servicing a region or in those days of course we were also subsidising Hazel Vincent Wallace at Leatherhead, David Poulson at Bromley, but 'Should we be subsidising *Joan Littlewood* or the *Theatre Royal Stratford Company*?' And there was always this worry as to whether we were subsidising a charismatic person or a theatre . . . (*Anthony Field, theatre producer, theatre project consultant, former finance director of the Arts Council*)

Theatre Workshop and the audience.

On the first night [of *The Quare Fellow*] at Stratford East we had all the big criminals from the East End of London – the Kray brothers, notorious people – because they knew it was about being in prison, their interest was enormous. I mean, they arrived in Rolls-Royces and things like that. And what you would call their gun mo's [gun moll: generic US slang for gangster's girlfriend], with their fur coats. Most of the seats had been repaired; they had to be because we were going to have a full house. And IRA had smuggled themselves in. They at one time I think had threatened to blow the place up, but in fact they came in to watch and observe. So you can imagine what a mixed audience. Now compare that to a West End audience of that period, which was everybody in black ties and white shirts and things, suddenly we got villains and IRA members . . . And the play, oh it was amazing excitement throughout. At one point, to mark the passage of time, Joan used the National Anthem – the Irish National Anthem. And as it started to play we suddenly heard this sound like machine-gun fire. And it was all the seats tipping up; they were all coming to attention. The rest of the audience were dumbfounded, they didn't know what the hell was going on. We got frightened because we thought they were all going to face us and whip out their machine guns, and that would be the end of us. But . . . and the cheers that went on at the end was extraordinary. (*Brian Murphy, actor*)

Well this is the big problem. Joan liked to think of us as taking the theatre to the people who were robbed of their theatre – dispossessed sort of thing. I didn't really think there were all that many locals in the audience. And this would be now, what, 1953? Peter Brook actually made a comment that we were getting a Chelsea audience rather than a Stratford East 15 audience, and I think he was right, we were not getting the locals in. I'd have liked to have, you know, thought that we were attracting the locals to come and see our theatre . . . (*George Cooper, actor*)

You see the problem was, by this time, we were getting wonderful reviews from Harold Hobson and Kenneth Tynan. And Chelsea and Hampstead, if they say it was good, they would flock to the productions. And we sometimes earned £8 a week when they came. And we were having this . . . you know, it was a kind of crossover. And some said, 'Well look, we've got more money.' And Joan would say, 'Yes, but you're selling out to Binkie Beaumont [H. M. Tennent] and the Arts Council' (*laughs*). And we said, 'No, we're not, they're nobody . . . they're not offering to buy us.' (*Barry Clayton, actor*)

AFTERWORD

Dominic Sandbrook's multi-volume history of Britain from 1956 onwards dates the beginning of the 1960s (or, at least, the period which in cultural memory is given the title of the Sixties) from 1964: as this suggests, the defining features of the new decade took some time to emerge. From Macmillan's triumphant election in 1959 to the end of thirteen years of Tory rule in 1964, Britain underwent a partial transformation. The end of the 1950s was a time of economic expansion and growing political division; culturally, too, society was shifting, with a clear generational divide opening up between those now in their teens and twenties, and the rest of the nation. As with the changes in the previous decade, the effects of these changes were not felt uniformly, and nor were they as absolute as cultural mythology might make them appear. The British establishment was on shakier ground in the early 1960s, but it did not collapse; and Britain did not become an entirely different country because of the combined cultural impact of James Bond, John Lennon and Mick Jagger.

However, although these changes can (and have been) overstated, their effects were undeniable; and by the mid-1960s, many of the social certainties that had animated the work of the 1950s generation of playwrights no longer existed. Even before the social and political upheavals of the later 1960s (upheavals which had a considerable impact on the theatre), It would have been unimaginable for a play on contemporary Britain, written in the later 1960s, to have begun with the central character railing against the entrenched conservatism of an English Sunday; after Pinter's heightened, threatening naturalism, Orton's gleeful destruction of English social and sexual mores, and the multiple controversies that accompanied successive premieres of Edward Bond's work, such a beginning would have seemed staid – and badly out of time. I noted earlier that the playwrights who began their careers in the mid-1950s tended not to have long, successful careers; partly, as already pointed out, this was because the theatre did not at that time have a network that could support writers whose work veered too far from the commercially acceptable – but partly it was because of the sheer pace of the change between the Britain of 1956 and the Britain of (say) 1970. The country moved rapidly from being an imperial power in straitened circumstances to being a post-imperial country in political emergency, with a failing economy, open conflict between management and unions, and its own unacknowledged civil war, between Catholics and Protestants in Northern Ireland, leaving a trail of casualties both in Ulster and in the rest of the country. Further changes – the economic crisis of the later 1970s, the rise of Thatcherite Conservatism, with its (arguably naive) faith in the power of the free market in the 1980s and the corresponding rise of New Labour in the 1990s (as the Labour Party turned its back on the ideals of social collectivism enshrined in the creation of the welfare state in the 1940s) – served to put the society of the 1950s at an even greater distance. It was not that *Look Back in Anger* and the other plays of the time became museum pieces, but it was certainly true that they were written when the world, and Britain's place in that world, looked very different than it did even ten years later.

Of the four writers whose work has been discussed in the previous chapters, three found their careers increasingly difficult to sustain as British society changed around them. The oldest of the four, T. S. Eliot, finished his theatre career with *The Elder Statesman* in 1958; he spent his last years quietly, an established cultural institution, happily married to his second wife Valerie. Rattigan, Osborne and Wesker did not have as easy a time of it. Rattigan had already been, as he saw it, sidelined by the Royal Court generation; for much of the 1960s and 1970s he abandoned the stage altogether. Wesker's career in the British theatre stalled in the mid-1960s, after the failed experiment in cultural provision that was Centre 42. Osborne's rise was the most spectacular; and, because he had by far the highest cultural profile, his fall was the most public. Politically and culturally, he seemed to move from the Left to the Right, ending up an English patriot whose pronouncements displayed at times a breathtaking homophobia and misogyny (there was more ambiguity in his position on a number of matters, but that was lost in the media image that he helped create – that of a curmudgeonly, reactionary scourge of all things modern and liberal). In their various ways, Rattigan, Osborne and Wesker had created theatre which dealt with the difficult process of change in a society whose attitudes seemed stubbornly entrenched; in the post-1960s world, where sudden, rapid change seemed to be the only constant, all three found themselves adrift.

Terence Rattigan (1956–77): I have tried to keep pace

Binkie Beaumont, aware that, as a producer, he had to keep an eye on new developments in the theatre, invited Rattigan and the actress Margaret Leighton to the first night of *Look Back in Anger*. At the interval, having had his fill of the new text, Beaumont left, but Rattigan was persuaded by the critic Cuthbert Worsley to stay to the end. As he left the theatre, Rattigan was asked for his opinion of the evening by a *Daily Express* reporter; he replied that Osborne was saying, in effect, 'Look, Ma, I'm not Terence Rattigan'.[1] This wasn't just an ill-considered remark; it confirmed, for those eager to support the new drama, what Aunt Edna had suggested – that Rattigan's moment had passed. There was some irony in this judgement: *Look Back in Anger*, as has been noted, was structurally a very conventional three-act play, and Jimmy Porter and John Malcolm (from *Separate Tables*) were remarkably similar characters. However, in the context of the time, these similarities were largely ignored; Rattigan stood for the commercial stage (and, as a gay man, he was also, as the stereotype would have it, part of the 'homosexual mafia', led by Beaumont, which controlled access to the West End and the bigger regional theatres). Attacking him was therefore more than a simple expression of theatrical taste; it was an ideological decision.

Rattigan himself proved rather more positive about the new drama in the years to come; he admired Pinter and wrote supportively to the young Joe Orton (although he also noted sadly that getting support from Terence Rattigan might be the kiss of death for an aspiring writer). And even though he spoke out in interviews against the type of socially engaged drama that Osborne and Wesker personified, he did write to Wesker, calling *Chicken Soup with Barley* 'a fine and moving play' (in the same letter, Rattigan also said that he admired Osborne). The letter finishes: 'It doesn't matter what Ken Tynan says. It doesn't matter what the *Daily Worker* says. It does matter what Aunt Edna and I say and we both agree that you have the markings of a very fine dramatist – not faint praise, Ibsen-class.'[2] At the same time (and also apparent, sometimes painfully so, in the letters and interviews he gave in the later 1950s and the 1960s) Rattigan knew that the theatre had moved on. In the letter to Wesker, he talks of himself as a 'reactionary social democrat'; Wesker's play, he writes, had brought tears to his raddled old cheeks'. In an interview with the *Daily Express* in 1963, he went considerably further:

> I'd love to be taken a little more seriously by the critics. It is still assumed by some critics that I am still writing to lift the hearts of those Aunt Ednas of mine. I have tried to keep pace. Yet continually I am reading articles about the need to demolish the old theatre – and blow up Coward and Rattigan. I tell you, I don't dig that at all. I can't write a bit like Osborne and Wesker. I can't because you see I've grown up . . .[3]

If Rattigan had continued to produce successful plays, perhaps Aunt Edna's baleful influence would have been mitigated somewhat. Unfortunately, the plays that followed were not his best: *Variations on a Theme* (which took its plot from Dumas's *La Dame aux Camelias*), which premiered in 1958, earned another scathing review from Tynan (which took the form of an indignant monologue from Rattigan's muse, furious that he had tried to write a play without her). Other reviews, though less damning, were rather dismissive; the anonymous reviewer for *The Times* commented wearily: 'The present piece is more akin in spirit to that past misadventure in comedy than it is to the ever charming *La Dame aux Camelias*, however closely the parallels with the tragedy may be drawn.'[4] *Ross* (1960) was better written and better reviewed, and enjoyed a decent run: but its relative success was overshadowed by a theatrical disaster – a musical based on

Rattigan's first pre-war hit, *French without Tears* (*Joie de Vivre*, 1960). The production, mounted by H. M. Tennent, cost £20,000 (a considerable investment for the time); Rattigan had invested some of his own money in the show, which lasted for four performances in the West End. The audience's response was so bad that Rattigan told the cast not to take any curtain calls. The reviews were predictably harsh (Tynan's review goaded Rattigan into an angry exchange of letters with the critic). Of all the critical responses, however, Harold Hobson's was perhaps the most painful; he hated the production, not just because it was poor, but because it left him

> ... brooding over the extraordinary talent of Mr Rattigan. Here is a man who has a greater sense of the theatre than any of his contemporaries except Jean Anouilh, a man who, lacking only the fertilising flood of words, can be witty or touching, or, as in *Ross*, delicately and penetratingly perceptive in dangerous quarters of the human spirit. In the thirties several dramatists of promise appeared, Ronald Mackenzie, J. B. Priestley, W. H. Auden, and Mr Rattigan himself. What has become of them?[5]

What indeed? Partly, there had been a sharp shift in theatrical fashion; but partly, too, the world that Rattigan had written about had changed radically. It was not simply that a new generation had come to artistic, political and cultural maturity; the nature of British identity was changing – and the change was one which seemed to undermine the main thrust of Rattigan's work. He came to be associated with an unhelpful stereotype of English reserve; as a dramatist who created characters whose upper lips remained stiff (even though their lower lips might tremble from time to time). Even the necessary privacy with which Rattigan practised his sexuality was increasingly unnecessary; even before the Sexual Offences Act legalised homosexuality in 1967 (between consenting adults in private), the moral panic that characterised responses to the subject in the late 1940s and early 1950s had subsided somewhat. The Wolfenden Report (which was published in 1957 by a commission set up to investigate homosexuality and prostitution – an interesting, and revealing, yoking together of sexual practices) had stated that there was no reason why the criminal justice system should involve itself in private acts; the report might not have led to immediate legislation (the subject was still too controversial at the turn of the new decade), but it was indicative of a climate in which the subject could at least be discussed. References to gayness were usually veiled in the 1950s; in the 1960s, homosexuality could feature in a film, which starred a reliable box-office draw (Basil Dearden's *Victim* was released in 1961; its central character, a closeted solicitor who exposes criminals who have been blackmailing homosexual men, was played by Dirk Bogarde). The subject was comprehensively, and successfully, broached on stage. Joe Orton's *Entertaining Mr Sloane* and *Loot* were commercial successes; and John Osborne's *A Patriot for Me* (1965) was produced successfully by the Royal Court in 1965, even though the theatre had to run it as a club performance to escape the strictures of the Lord Chamberlain's office, which was itself two years away from abolition. Rattigan's theatre had dealt with the impact of the public world on the hidden, private self; now, it seemed, the innermost recesses of the self could be made public – and Rattigan's work seemed part of a vanished time.

Stung by what he increasingly felt was an almost automatic rejection of his work (whatever its quality), Rattigan more or less abandoned the stage during the 1960s. He did not have to rely financially on stage productions; the income from screenwriting was more than enough to finance his lifestyle. He wrote some plays for television, but stage shows were few and far between. The plays he did write were not without interest. *Ross* (which dealt with a curious incident in the life of the First World War hero Lawrence of Arabia, who joined the RAF under an assumed name after the war ended) dramatised a man in flight from self-knowledge; the play indicated (without stating overtly) that the knowledge that Lawrence was fleeing was that of his own homosexuality. The struggle between generations was presented in *Man and Boy*, where, for the first time, the father's duplicity comes close to harming his son. *Bequest to the Nation* (1970), based on a TV play, caught the tension between the private lives of Lord Nelson and Lady Hamilton (whose affair was an open secret, and an open joke), and the confines placed on them by their public lives. The play closes on a moment of painful irony; after Nelson's death, the boozy, coarse but vital Lady Hamilton is frozen into a fixed public role – bequeathed to the nation by her dead lover. *In Praise of Love* (1973), a subtle and tender play, dealt again with secrecy: this time, the secret is the impending death of one of the characters. Sebastian, whose wife Lydia is dying, comes close to articulating what might be a mission statement for Rattigan's theatre:

> **Sebastian** Do you know what 'le vice Anglais' – the English vice – really is? Not flagellation, not pederasty – whatever the French believe it to be. It's our refusal to admit to our emotions . . .[6]

Rattigan's last play, *Cause Célèbre*, based on a murder case from the 1930s, returned to the theme of *The Deep Blue Sea* – the collision between passionate love and the social norms that surround it. This time, though, the play was far more raw than Rattigan had dared to be in the 1950s; and its attack on the ingrained puritanism of a section of British society was much more overt.

After a fallow period in the 1960s, there was a minor revival of interest in Rattigan's work in the 1970s. Some of his previous successes were revived; and *Cause Célèbre* ran for 282 performances – not long by the standards of previous hits, but his best run since *Ross*. However, the revival came too late. Rattigan's health had been failing throughout the 1960s; and he had spent much of the decade as a tax exile, away from Britain – and, it seems, nursing a sense of bitterness at the sudden transformation in his fortunes. In the 1970s, the increasingly frail playwright no longer had the energy or the inclination to engage with the contemporary theatre; the relative success of *Cause Célèbre* came too late – Rattigan, seriously ill from the mid-1970s, died soon after the play opened. Interviewed by Sheridan Morley after the play opened, Rattigan mournfully reflected on the sudden, sharp decline in his fortunes from the mid-1950s onwards: "'I discovered that any play I wrote would get smashed. I just didn't have a chance with anything." Then he paused, and added, "perhaps I should have stayed and fought it out . . .'"[7] Although Rattigan might momentarily have entertained the thought that, had he been more combative his plays would have fared better, it is hard to see how this could have been the case. The world that had formed his writing had changed; and the historical forces ranged against his work were too great.

John Osborne (1961–94): watch it come down

> This is a letter of hate. It is for you, my fellow countrymen. I mean those men of my country who have defiled it. The men with manic fingers leading the sightless, febrile betrayed body of my country to death. You are its murderers. And there's little left in my brain but the thoughts of murder for you.[8]

The tone is unmistakable; a public response to a public issue (the imminence of nuclear catastrophe), expressed in terms which are bilious, extreme and personal. If, during the 1960s, critics and cultural commentators seemed to confuse John Osborne with his 1950s creation Jimmy Porter, letters such as this provided them with ample justification. Osborne was an iconic public figure for much of the 1960s and 1970s. He was famous, as Rattigan had been earlier, for being successful; he was famous, because of the constant sense of turmoil in his love life (he married the actress Mary Ure in 1957, and they divorced in 1963; he then married the critic Penelope Gilliatt, and when that marriage broke down in 1968, married the actress Jill Bennett. He married for the last time, to Helen Dawson, in 1978, and stayed with her until his death). He was famous both for his work in the theatre and for his role in supporting and developing the British film industry, through Woodfall Films (the company he helped to set up in the late 1950s); and he was famous, because he was a reliable source of quotes and controversy, whether excoriating those with their fingers on the nuclear trigger in the early 1960s, or railing against a variety of left-wing causes in the 1970s. Osborne was good copy; and the details of his life – his move politically from the Left to the Right, the success or failure of his work, the state of his marriages – provided some of the raw material for a wider debate about the changes in British society over the period.

Osborne's letter to his countrymen (sometimes referred to as 'Damn you, England') was published in *Tribune*, a left-wing magazine, in 1961; famously, the sign-off identified Osborne's location when the letter was written – Valbonne, in France. When the letter was debated – as it was for weeks in the national press, a sure sign of Osborne's cultural importance – the fact that he was in France came in for a great deal of comment. At a time when foreign holidays were still the preserve of the rich, the fact that Osborne could afford to relax outside of England was itself a source of criticism; the angry young man, living in comfort, able to rail against his countrymen from a plush French resort. This image is not entirely fair; the label of angry young man that had attached itself to Osborne wasn't a title that he had actively sought out. The incident (which, according to Osborne, caused a retired army major to hunt him down in France, and demand at gunpoint that he apologise to Britain) does, however, capture something of his relation to the Britain of the time. It is an assault on the establishment; but it is not an assault carried out by someone who feels himself part of a group or a generation. It is the intemperate response of a single individual, who poses himself, rather melodramatically, against the prevailing ethos.

The figure Osborne cuts in this letter is not too far away from the private man; through the 1960s and 1970s (in fact, right up to his death), he thought of himself as an isolated figure, who reacted against what he regarded as established modes of thought as a matter of principle. For Osborne, this explained what seemed to others to be a substantial ideological shift, from being a self-proclaimed socialist in the late 1950s to a right-wing scourge of what he saw as fashionable liberalism in the 1970s and 1980s; according to Osborne, he had stayed roughly where he was, but the nature of the establishment had changed. This is rather disingenuous; for one thing, Osborne's socialism was not a considered political position, in the way that (say) Wesker's was. It was more of a reaction against a stiflingly oppressive and conservative establishment than an endorsement of the potential power of communal action. Similarly, although Osborne grew increasingly reactionary in the 1970s and 1980s, he found some aspects of Thatcherism (the government's triumphalism and the prime minister's wholehearted embrace of the special relationship with the US) off-putting. Throughout his life, Osborne was happier reacting against what he saw as the received wisdom of the age, than he was supporting any particular position or cause.

After *Luther*, Osborne was established as the premier dramatist of the time; the tone of voice in the plays was new enough still to appear radical, and his three main successes (*Look Back in Anger*, *The Entertainer* and *Luther*) had been interestingly varied, both in style and subject matter. He had encountered failure (*The World of Paul Slickley* (1959), a rather poor attempt at a musical, had flopped spectacularly, with Osborne pursued down the street by an enraged audience). Still, he was a settled success: his plays were talking points: Woodfall Films was at the forefront of a new wave of British realist cinema – and Osborne's adaptation of Henry Fielding's eighteenth-century novel *Tom Jones* won four Oscars (including one for Osborne's script). He even ventured into television. *A Subject of Scandal and Concern* (1961) told the story of George Holyoake, the last man to be jailed for heresy in Britain; the play's narrator, an unnamed lawyer, closes the play with a direct address – almost a provocation – to the audience:

> If you are waiting for the commercial, it is probably this: you cannot live by bread alone. You must have jam – even if it is mixed with another man's blood . . . That's all. You may retire now. And if a mini-car is your particular mini-dream, then dream it. When your turn comes you will be called. Good night.[9]

The play is not one of Osborne's major works: but there is something entirely characteristic in this ending. Osborne dares the audience to respond; he challenges them explicitly – if you are the kind of person who is lulled into a contented coma by the adverts, the play suggests, you will deserve whatever it is that you get.

Osborne, over the next decade or so, made a habit of stretching the spectator's tolerance; indeed, there seemed to be something in him that warmed to an audience's hatred. The playwright Christopher

Hampton watched Osborne's response to the disastrous opening of his 1976 play *Watch It Come Down*:

> I remember thinking about all those young writers, including myself, who wrote ostensibly shocking stuff. Yet I'd never been at a play where the audience was provoked and angered by what was happening onstage. I admired *Watch It Come Down* enormously. But there was John, leaning nonchalantly on a wall at the back of the theatre, looking incredibly composed in the midst of his own play going disastrously wrong.[10]

The central characters of Osborne's plays share something of this attitude; they find themselves most at home in the midst of confrontation, as though they cannot exist without the bracing presence of hatred as a motivating force in their lives. At the same time, though, they isolate themselves; they may be defiant, but they are also alone, in a world that is indifferent or actively hostile. In *Inadmissible Evidence* (1964), the lawyer Bill Maitland is first seen defending himself in front of a phantasmagorical court, which exists only within his disintegrating mind; his increasingly desperate, flailing attempts to justify himself, and to make contact with the other characters in the play all fail. As Simon Trussler noted in an early assessment of Osborne's career, Maitland's is a tragedy of complete self-awareness; a 'consciousness of impotence in the face of destruction';[11] and one of the things that Maitland is painfully aware of is the never-ending march of a consumer society that, in a memorable phrase, turns its participants into 'flatulent, purblind, mating weasels'.[12] Redl, in Osborne's next play, *A Patriot for Me* (1965), comes to accept his homosexuality, and through this to gain access to a different stratum of pre-First World War Austrian society; all he finds there, though, are the same class divisions and political intrigues that characterise the rest of the country. The play's set-piece scene is a drag ball; one might think that such a gathering might be a place where social codes and norms might break down, but, as Osborne makes clear, a sharply divided society is reflected even here – in the quality of the dresses, and the class divisions that play themselves out during the scene. The aristocratic Baron

Von Epp (played by George Devine) might say of the masked ball: 'This is the celebration of the individual against the rest, the us's and the them's, the free and the constricted, the gay and the dreary, the lonely and the mob . . .'[13] We can see, though, that it is not; Vienna's homosexual society mirrors the rest of the country. The only character who can possibly be described as a lonely individual posed against the mob is Redl himself, and he is betrayed and killed at the play's end.

After *Patriot*, the quality of Osborne's work began to decline steadily. His next full-length plays, *Time Present* and *The Hotel in Amsterdam* (both 1968), were character studies (the first of an actress, tending her famous, dying actor father; the second of a group of characters, involved in various ways in showbusiness, who have come to the hotel of the play's title to escape their boss, K.L.). Neither play, though, has much in the way of conflict; Pamela, the actress in *Time Present*, has something of the energy of previous Osborne protagonists, although, interestingly, her vituperative assaults tend to be aimed at the rising generation of the 1960s and 1970s. She presents herself as an unashamed High Tory, at least as much because it angers Constance, a Labour MP with whom she shares a flat; her assaults on the state of contemporary Britain also serve to hide the grief of her father's death. *The Hotel in Amsterdam*, although dramatically weak (the play is virtually plotless, and the characters not intrinsically interesting enough to bear study) is an interesting variation on the usual Osborneian dynamic: K.L., the characters' boss, the person they have come to the hotel to escape, remains offstage, but shares some of the characteristics of an Osborne protagonist (he is described as '*the biggest, most poisonous, voracious, Machiavellian dinosaur in movies*'[14] – a view that might be endorsed by those who surround the central characters in other plays like *The Entertainer* or *Inadmissible Evidence*). However, his reported suicide causes the group to fragment; the end of K.L.'s life hints at a sense of despair underlying the bluster that the other characters endure. K.L., in other words, is the archetypally lonely, angry Osborne protagonist, seen, this time, from the outside. *West of Suez* has more urgency; set in a former colony in the Caribbean, the play concerns an elderly writer, Wyatt Gillman, and his family. Left behind by the receding tide of empire, all that is left for the family on this former colony is a comfortless life of boredom and bickering. Gillman himself is an intriguing mixture of eccentricity and veiled hostility; talking to a reporter near the play's end, he says he is 'Always weary, always bored, always in some sort of vague pain and always with a bit of unsatisfying hatred burning away on the old inside like a heartburn or indigestion'.[15] Unsatisfying hatred; the phrase resonates through most of Osborne's work. The anger that drives his characters cannot be assuaged, because it is not anger against anything specific; it is anger as existential condition, as a mode of operation in a world which will never provide lasting relief.

In Osborne's work up to *West of Suez* (1971), this anger (and the loneliness and vulnerability it barely masks) is contained within the world of the stage. *A Sense of Detachment* (1972) directed its anger towards the audience. Plotless, setless and constructed as an affront to the audience, it is simultaneously an aping (perhaps satirically) of the theatrical avant-garde, an attempt to create an event that brings to the theatre some of the danger of the music hall, and a threnody on the current state of the nation, the state of the theatre, the condition of the actor and the position of the audience. Six actors, caught on stage without a story to tell, fill the time with insults, hesitant conversations, readings (poetry, and promotional material for porn, read out by the oldest female actor), songs and speeches. They are interrupted by members of the audience (whose interjections are scripted, although Osborne's text exhorts the actors to retaliate, if the actual audience heckles them). It is hard to see the play as anything other than Osborne's lament, not only for an England that has irrevocably declined (the play ends with the old folk song 'Widdicombe Fair', while the cast produce bunting that carries the message 'THE-VERY-BEST-OF-BRITISH-LUCK'),[16] and for a theatre that no longer carries the same charge as it used to do (the first Act also ends with 'Widdicombe Fair', this time with a set of parodic lyrics which reference a number of playwrights – Pinter, Wesker, Christopher Hampton, Edward Albee, Edna O'Brien – 'because she's a woman' – and 'Old Uncle Sammy Beckett and all'.[17]

The play was described by B. A. Young of the *Financial Times* as Osborne's 'farewell to the theatre ...'[18] This was a prophetic comment, although not for the reasons that Young intended; the play has a dynamism, a sense of performative risk, which is theatrically very effective – as though Osborne had finally found a form that could capture that sense of 'unsatisfied hatred' that animated so much of his writing. At the time, though, *A Sense of Detachment* was seen as, in the words of one of the actors, a simple cry of 'God rot you'[19] to the country and the theatre. Osborne's routine, reflexive liberal bating, and his assaults on theatre institutions and critics for slights real and imagined, ensured that his work was disregarded; an increasing proneness to depression meant that new work dried up. From 1972 to his death in 1994, Osborne only wrote two substantial, original plays – *Watch It Come Down* (1976) and *Déjàvu* (1992). The first of these is a curious echo of John Whiting's *Saint's Day*: a group of middle- and upper-class characters, in a house in the country, some connected with the arts or with politics, are threatened both by the inherent tensions within their relationships, and by the incipient violence of the world outside the house (which eventually leads to its destruction in a hail of artillery fire). The play was commissioned by the National Theatre, as part of a celebration of the opening of its new premises on the south bank of the Thames, and as a marker of the twentieth anniversary of *Look Back in Anger*. Its failure finally drove a wedge between Osborne and the British theatrical establishment. Osborne's final play, *Dejavu*, returned to *Look Back in Anger*'s characters thirty-five years on; Jimmy Porter, or JP as the play calls him, has travelled along the same ideological route as his creator. He is now a pillar of the rural community where he lives; his anger is now directed against an establishment rooted not in unthinking conservatism but an equally unthinking liberalism. He is as lonely, however, as was Jimmy in *Look Back*; rather than his lovers, JP drives his children away, and, rather than ending the play on a moment of painfully tentative reconciliation, Osborne ends *Dejavu* with JP alone on stage, playing a piece of flamboyant classical music on his tape recorder, and conducting the absent orchestra in an act of quixotic, futile self-assertion. In this image, JP and Jimmy Porter meet; a public display of final defiance, of the angry assertion of selfhood, which is at the same time an admission of loss, of loneliness and of final defeat.

Arnold Wesker (1960–): what could be my crime?

By the end of the 1950s, Arnold Wesker was in what might have seemed a fortunate position, His work had been staged by the most prestigious theatre in London; even more than Osborne, he was the incarnation of the new spirit in the theatre – working-class, committed, ideologically literate and young. Although none of his plays had at that point set the West End alight (an important marker at the time, given the still significant power of the commercial stage) he had established himself as the heir to the revolution that *Look Back in Anger* had promised. It didn't take long to reach one of those milestones: in 1962, *Chips with Everything*, a play about Wesker's experience of National Service, gave him a significant commercial success. Of all of his generation – John Arden, Shelagh Delaney, Bernard Kops and the rest – Wesker seemed set to have the most important career: even Harold Pinter had yet to emerge as a significant new voice. Wesker, though, was aware of the possible pitfalls of being associated with a particular movement. Interviewed by Simon Trussler in 1966, he looked back over the early years of the 1960s:

> It's the way art happens in this country. It is a fashion. Do you remember a raging letter that I wrote to the *Statesman* in about 1961? Someone had said we were beginning to get tired. And immediately there loomed up an image of all of us being simply fashionable, you know, rather quaint specimens. You could do your slumming at the Royal Court, you no longer had to go to cafes on the docks. And I knew that it was going to come to an end, if somehow it wasn't consolidated . . .[20]

His comments were echoed elsewhere; the American critic Robert Brustein, writing in the *Tulane Drama Review* in 1966, made the point that the new British theatre ran the risk of being as parochial as the forms it sought to replace. 'The complicated issues of art,' he wrote, 'tend to dissolve into simple oppositions: Socialism versus Toryism, the new versus the old, experiment versus tradition, the proletariat versus the upper classes, youth versus age – and everyone connected with the theatre is neatly catalogued.'[21] To an extent this was a forgivable simplification (and as Brustein noted, did not apply to all the writers who had emerged in the late 1950s). It was, though, a danger, because it ran the risk of simplifying a complex historical moment; and, in doing so, of hampering those very writers whose work had initially seemed so vibrant and new:

> I make these complaints as a friend of the house, and would in fact be less disturbed about these writers if I weren't so profoundly sympathetic with most of their aims. But their aims have now been largely achieved and, as so often happens with successful revolutionaries, their excesses now seem to be institutionalized, ossifying into postures that should be more supple and flexible. Chief among these is a certain indifference to poetry, imagination, form, and dialectic in the drama . . .'[22]

Wesker's development in the 1960s and beyond can be thought of as an attempt to deal with the criticisms that Brustein raised; and it could be said that part of the reason for the difficulties he ran into later in the decade stemmed from his reluctance to stay within the boundaries of the debate that Brustein outlined in 1966.

Initially, though, things seemed promising. *Chips with Everything* marked a significant advance over the naturalism of the trilogy; alongside the meticulously detailed realism of *The Kitchen* (staged for the first time in its expanded form in 1961 at the Royal Court) *Chips* suggested that Wesker was a more supple, flexible dramatist than the trilogy had indicated. The play is an intriguing mixture of realism and theatrical stylisation; its central character, Pip Thompson, is an unlikely conscript; well educated and a banker's son, he seems to his seniors a natural officer. He, however, initially rejects this judgement, preferring to stay with the other recruits. He does so because, at least in his own eyes, he wants to reject his privileged background. In a crucial speech near the beginning of the play, he describes a moment of political conversion; a walk through the East End, and a stop for tea in a working-class cafe. The cafe is ordinary; but Pip describes it as though it was both the strangest (at least to him) and the most representative place, not only in the East End, but the whole country:

> I even remember the colour of the walls, a pastel pink on the top half and turquoise blue on the bottom, peeling. Peeling in fifteen different places; actually, I counted them. But what I couldn't understand was why I should have been so surprised. It wasn't as though I had been cradled in my childhood. And then I saw the menu, stained with tea and beautifully written by a foreign hand, and on top it said . . . 'Chips with everything.' Chips with every damn thing. You breed babies and you eat chips with everything.[23]

There is a powerful ambiguity to this speech. Pip, who organises the other airmen in subversive activities during the first half of the play, could be venting his anger at the lack of choice and the politically enforced regimentation of working-class life. On the other hand, the speech could sound dismissive – as though the people he describes are not fit for anything better. The actions of the play serve to prove this second reading partially wrong; without needing the kind of organisation that Pip thinks he can provide, the airmen organise themselves to stand in solidarity with one of their own against their officers. However, Pip, whose commitment to his fellow airmen has never been wholehearted, is able to defuse this potential revolt; in doing so, he accepts his superiors' judgement – becoming an officer, betraying his fellow airmen even as he saves them from punishment.

Chips with Everything defined an ideological dilemma for Wesker; he was enough of a child of the 1950s to share Richard Hoggart's dismay at the commercialised mess of mass culture; and yet at the same time he was aware of where such a dismissal might lead – towards a rejection of working-class culture as a whole. As a way of resolving this dilemma, he partially turned his back on the theatre during the 1960s. In 1960 he persuaded the Trades Union Congress to help him establish Centre 42; this organisation had, as its remit, the task of spreading culture in working-class areas. This was not simply a matter of taking high culture to the masses; rather, it was a forerunner of the community and touring theatre of the 1970s. Wesker and the other artists involved (from the theatre, these included Shelagh Delaney, Bernard Kops and the young John McGrath) in the venture wanted to engage working-class audiences directly; they mounted a series of festivals across England in 1961 and 1962 which included art exhibitions, plays, jazz and folk events, and poetry readings. Seeking a permanent base, the Centre was given the lease to the Roundhouse in north London in 1964. However, the initiative failed, for a number of reasons; despite the trade union movement's vocal support, they did not give the venture much money – and the Arts Council were as unwilling to give sustained support as they had been for Littlewood's Theatre Workshop in the 1950s. When the Centre folded in 1970 it did so because the money to keep the venture going simply wasn't there. Also, the cultural climate was changing; in the theatre, the generation that came to artistic maturity in the later 1960s espoused a more radical form of socialism than Wesker had. What seemed to him to be a necessary process of cultural consciousness-raising appeared to others (most notably John McGrath, who by 1970 had moved on from his early involvement in the Centre to a critique of the whole idea) to be an exercise in cultural imperialism – that is, the automatic assumption that some forms of art were better than others, and should be imposed on those who did not have access to them.

This was a rather unfair assumption; Wesker had been clear that the Centre's activities would include work from working-class communities – and the whole idea behind the Centre was that it would operate much more closely with its audiences than other, more established artistic enterprises. It did, however, contain a grain of truth: replying to McGrath's criticisms, Wesker said: 'What is revolutionary art? Art whose forms are different from anything we've seen before? . . . or using bourgeois art forms to say revolutionary things? . . . I've never encountered working-class art . . . I don't subscribe to the affected notions that music hall was art, or that pop music is art . . .'[24] This reflected, amongst other things, Wesker's mistrust of a culture which, to borrow a phrase from Beatie in *Roots*, took the easy way out; partly, at least as far as music was concerned, it was a generational matter – for those passing through adolescence in the later 1960s, popular music could be both an art form and a call to revolt. Partly, too, it stemmed from a more general change in the intellectual climate of the Left; the kind of disdain with which Hoggart had treated popular culture had been replaced by more nuanced discussions of the topic, in the work of Raymond Williams, for example. Wesker's mistrust of the commodification of culture was heartfelt; but it left him, by the end of the 1960s, on the wrong side of a growing political and cultural divide.

By this time, too, he had begun to acquire a reputation as someone who was difficult; and this combined with another, growing perception – that the quality of his writing was in decline. This was rather unfair: he was at least willing to try new types of writing – the poetic *The Four Seasons* (1965); the Brechtian, episodic *Their Very Own and Golden City* (1966); the elegiac *The Friends* (1970) – but the image of Wesker the naturalist and socialist proved remarkably persistent. Also, it is fair to say, Wesker's touch was less sure when his writing strove towards poetry; the ironic stylisation of *Chips* was dramatically effective, but the symbolism through which the two characters in *The Four Seasons* expressed their love was too abstract (and rather too hackneyed) to be dramatically effective. Wesker's relations with the main stages in London also suffered; throughout his life, he has been a forthright defender of his own work, especially from what he would regard as the unnecessary interpretations foisted on his work by directors. This led to strained relationships with a number of companies and directors: famously, Wesker sued the RSC over breach of contract over the production of his 1971 play *The Journalists*, because the actors refused to perform the play. According to Wesker, this was for political reasons: he had written right-wing characters who were too sympathetically presented for a militantly left-wing cast. By the end of the 1970s, although his newer work was still, periodically, produced on the London stage (*Caritas*, in 1981, was produced at the National Theatre's Cottesloe stage), Wesker was no longer thought of as part of the theatrical mainstream. The situation worsened during the 1980s, and by the time that Wesker came to write his autobiography, he had come to think of himself as an exile from the British theatre:

It is the queerest of sensations, this literary leprosy . . . I sense within the profession a kind of nervous terror of me. What is this plague which I fail to recognise, but obviously marks me like Cain? I search around as one does for stains on a shirt, shit clogged in a shoe, a torn pocket. Does my breath smell? Are my armpits unwashed? I don't remember murdering anyone. I've fulfilled all professional commitments, turned up on time, directed and made stars of actors . . . What could be my crime?[25]

Partly, the wounds were self-inflicted: Wesker was thought of as a bad risk – difficult to work with, and unwilling to listen to other opinions. Partly, too, it was because what was arguably his most important contribution to the theatre after the trilogy – Centre 42 – never gained the recognition it deserved, as the precursor to one of the most profound changes in post-war British theatre (the growth of fringe and alternative theatre in the 1970s – supported, ironically, by changes in Arts Council funding policy). Finally, though, Wesker's early success defined and confined him; his crime, if we are to use this term, was to have written a series of plays (from *The Kitchen*, through the trilogy, to *Chips with Everything*) whose success seemed to encapsulate a particular theatrical era so precisely, that they left their author little room to manoeuvre for the rest of his theatrical life.

NOTES

Introduction to the 1950s

1. Kenneth Tynan, *Theatre Writings* (London: Nick Hern Books, 2007), p. 112.
2. Dan Rebellato, *1956 and All That: The Making of Modern British Drama* (London: Routledge, 1999); Dominic Shellard, *British Theatre Since the War* (New Haven, CT: Yale University Press, 2000).
3. Michael Billington, *State of the Nation: British Theatre Since 1945* (London: Faber and Faber, 2007); Luc Gilleman, *John Osborne: Vituperative Artist* (London: Routledge, 2004); Aleks Sierz, *John Osborne's Look Back in Anger* (New York: Continuum, 2008).
4. Sierz, ibid.
5. Zachary Leader, *The Life of Kingsley Amis* (London: Jonathan Cape, 2006), p. 356.
6. Ibid.
7. Ibid., p. 357.
8. Tynan, op. cit., p. 113.
9. Peter Hennessy, *Never Again: Britain 1945–51* (London: Vintage, 1993), pp. 35–6.
10. Ibid., pp. 73–4.
11. David Kynaston, *Austerity Britain: 1945–51* (London: Bloomsbury, 2007), p. 78.
12. Peter Hennessy, *Having It So Good: Britain in the Fifties* (London: Penguin, 2007), p. 527.
13. Ibid., p. 340.
14. Dominic Sandbrook, *Never Had It So Good: A History of Britain from Suez to the Beatles* (London: Little, Brown, 2005), p. 61.
15. Ibid., forematter.
16. Ibid.; Hennessy, *Having It So Good*.
17. Hennessy, *Having It So Good*, p. 278.
18. Ibid., p. 356.
19. Sir Michael Howard, *Captain Professor: A Life in War and Peace* (London: Continuum, 2006), p. 155.
20. Hennessy, *Having It So Good*.
21. Sandbrook, op. cit., p. 86.
22. Kenneth Allsop, *The Angry Decade: A Survey of the Cultural Revolt of the Nineteen Fifties* (London: Peter Owen, 1958), p. 8.
23. Colin Wilson, *The Outsider* (London: Gollancz, 1956), blurb.
24. Sandbrook, op. cit., pp. 153–4.
25. Ibid., p. 159.

26. Humphrey Carpenter, *The Angry Young Men: A Literary Comedy of the 1950s* (London: Allen Lane, 2002), p. 175.

27. Richard Hoggart, *The Uses of Literacy* (London: Chatto & Windus, 1957), p. 248.

28. Stephen Lacey, *British Realist Theatre: The New Wave in Its Context* (London: Routledge, 1995), p. 10.

29. J. B. Priestley, *Thoughts in the Wilderness* (London: Heinemann, 1957), p. 122.

30. Alan Sillitoe, *Saturday Night and Sunday Morning* (London: Paladin, 1958), pp. 26–7.

31. Carpenter, op. cit., p. 8.

32. Kingsley Amis, *Lucky Jim* (London: Penguin, 1992), p. 63.

33. David Kynaston, *Family Britain: 1951–57* (London: Bloomsbury, 2009), p. 511.

34. Sandbrook, op. cit., pp. 528–9.

35. Carpenter, op. cit., p. 57.

36. Ibid.

37. Stefan Collini, *Absent Minds: Intellectuals in Britain* (Oxford: Oxford University Press, 2006).

38. Quoted in Sandbrook, op. cit., p. 158.

39. Tom Maschler, *Declaration* (London: MacGibbon & Kee, 1957), pp. 8–9.

1 The British theatre 1945–60

1. John Whiting, in Charles Marowitz, Tom Milne and Owen Hale, *The Encore Reader: A Chronicle of the New Drama* (London: Methuen, 1965), pp. 105–6.

2. Ibid., p. 106.

3. Dominic Shellard, *British Theatre Since the War* (New Haven, CT: Yale University Press, 2000), p. 2.

4. J. B. Priestley, *Theatre Outlook* (London: Nicholson & Watson, 1947), p. 6.

5. See Colin Chambers, *The Story of Unity Theatre* (London: Lawrence & Wishart, 1989).

6. Dan Rebellato, *1956 and All That: The Making of Modern British Drama* (London: Routledge, 1999), p. 57.

7. Philip Roberts, *The Royal Court Theatre and the Modern Stage* (Cambridge: Cambridge University Press, 1999), p. 14.

8. George Rowell and Tony Jackson, *The Repertory Movement: A History of Regional Theatre in Britain* (Cambridge: Cambridge University Press, 1984).

9. Theatre Archive Project interview, Malcolm Farquhar, 2 February 2004.

10. Michael Billington, *Harold Pinter* (London: Faber and Faber, 2007).

11. Theatre Archive Project interview, Robert Aldous, 22 March 2010.

12. Michael Billington, *State of the Nation: British Theatre Since 1945* (London, Faber and Faber, 2007).

13. Quoted in Marowitz et al., op. cit., p. 40.

14. Ibid., pp. 40–1.
15. David Rabey, *English Drama Since 1940* (London: Longman, 2003), p. 7.
16. Steve Nicholson, *The Censorship of British Drama* (Exeter: University of Exeter Press, 2005), p. 279.
17. Irving Wardle, *The Theatres of George Devine* (London: Jonathan Cape, 1978), p. 205.
18. Terence Rattigan, *Plays: Two* (London: Methuen, 1985), p. 170.
19. Geoffrey Wansell, *Terence Rattigan* (London: Oberon Books, 2009), p. 265.
20. Ibid., p. 268.
21. Dominic Shellard, *Kenneth Tynan: A Life* (New Haven, CT: Yale University Press, 2003), p. 113.
22. Kenneth Tynan, *Theatre Writings* (London: Nick Hern Books, 2007), pp. 22–3.
23. Quoted in Dominic Shellard, *Harold Hobson: Witness and Judge* (Edinburgh: Edinburgh University Press, 1995), p. 145.
24. Tynan, op. cit., p. 197.
25. Penelope Gilliatt, quoted in Shellard, *Harold Hobson*, p. 181.
26. Ibid., p. 98.
27. Tynan, op. cit., p. 36.
28. Ibid., pp. 36–7.
29. Ibid., p. 37.
30. Roberts, op. cit., p. 9.
31. Billington, *State of the Nation*.
32. Rebellato, op. cit.
33. Bill Gaskell, *A Sense of Direction* (London: Faber, 1988).
34. T. S. Eliot, quoted in S. L. Bethell, *Shakespeare and the Popular Tradition* (London: Staple Press, 1944), unnumbered text.
35. Rabey, op. cit., p. 9.
36. Quoted in Billington, *State of the Nation*, p. 19.
37. Noël Coward, *Plays 5* (London: Methuen, 1983), p. 113.
38. Tynan, op. cit., p. 107.
39. Nick Smurthwaite, 'Revival of a Realist', *The Stage*, 5 February 2004.
40. Quoted in Billington, *State of the Nation*, p. 64.
41. Eric Salmon, *The Dark Journey: John Whiting as a Dramatist* (London: Barrie & Jenkins, 1979), p. 9.
42. Ibid., p. 129.
43. James Knowlson, *Damned to Fame: The Life of Samuel Beckett* (London: Bloomsbury, 1996), p. 412.
44. Ibid., p. 414.
45. Quoted in Peter Roberts (ed.), *The Best of Plays and Players 1953–1968* (London: Methuen, 1987), p. 59.
46. Tynan, op. cit., p. 72.
47. Quoted in Peter Roberts, op. cit., pp. 59–60.
48. Quoted in Shellard, *British Theatre Since the War*, p. 93.

49. Robert Leach, *Theatre Workshop: Joan Littlewood and the Making of Modern British Theatre* (Exeter: University of Exeter Press, 2006), p. 27.

50. George Devine, quoted in Marowitz et al., op. cit., p. 15.

51. Tynan, op. cit., p. 124.

52. *The Times*, 31 March 1956, quoted in Ruth Little and Emily McLaughlin, *The Royal Court: Inside Out* (London: Oberon Books, 2007), p. 17.

53. Philip Roberts, op. cit., Rebellato, op. cit., Shellard, *British Theatre Since the War*.

54. John Russell Taylor, *Anger and After: A Guide to the New British Drama* (London: Methuen, 1963).

55. Little and McLaughlin, op. cit., p. 43.

56. Philip Roberts, op. cit., pp. 56–7.

57. Quoted in Richard Findlater (ed.), *At the Royal Court: Twenty-Five Years of the English Stage Company* (London: Amber Lane Press, 1981), pp. 84–5.

58. Joan Littlewood, *Joan's Book* (London: Minerva, 1994), p. 538.

59. Leach, op. cit.

60. Ibid., p. 103.

61. Littlewood, op. cit., p. 189.

62. Barry Clayton, Theatre Archive Project interview, Kate Harris, 8 October 2007.

63. Shellard, *British Theatre Since the War*.

64. Tynan, op. cit., p. 193.

65. Caryl Churchill, quoted in Philip Roberts, op. cit., p. 78.

66. Tynan, op. cit., p. 217.

67. Ibid., p. 226.

68. Marowitz et al., op. cit., p. 63.

69. Ibid.

70. Maggie Gale, *West End Women: Women and the London Stage 1918–1962* (London: Routledge, 1996), p. 196.

2 Introducing the playwrights

1. T. S. Eliot, *Selected Essays* (New York: Harcourt, Brace & Co., 1932), p. 93.

2. Ibid.

3. T. S. Eliot, *For Lancelot Andrewes: Essays on Style and Order* (London: Faber and Gwyer, 1928), p. ix.

4. Geoffrey Wansell, *Terence Rattigan* (London: Oberon Books, 2009), p. 36.

5. Terence Rattigan, *After the Dance* (London: Nick Hern Books, 1995), p. 28.

6. John Osborne, *Looking Back: Never Explain, Never Apologise* (London: Faber and Faber, 1999), p. 8.

7. John Heilpern, *John Osborne: A Patriot for Us* (London: Chatto & Windus, 2006), p. 53.

8. Osborne, op. cit., pp. 93–4.
9. Ibid., p. 119.
10. Ibid., p. 206.
11. John Osborne, *Epitaph for George Dillon* (London: Faber and Faber, 1958), p. 61.
12. Arnold Wesker, *As Much as I Dare* (London: Century, 1994), p. 29.
13. Ibid., pp. 51–2.
14. Ibid., p. 254.
15. Ibid., p. 494.
16. Ibid., p. 465.

3 Playwrights and plays: T. S. Eliot

1. Letter to Djuna Barnes, 19 August 1949, Djuna Barnes Papers, Archives and Manuscripts, University of Maryland.
2. See E. Martin Browne, *The Making of T. S. Eliot's Plays* (Cambridge: Cambridge University Press, 1969).
3. Denis Donoghue, *The Third Voice: Modern British and American Verse Drama* (Princeton, NJ: Princeton University Press, 1959), p. 6.
4. Browne, op. cit., p. 281.
5. T. S. Eliot, 'Seneca in Elizabethan Tradition', in *Essays on Elizabethan Drama* (New York: Harcourt Brace, 1956), p. 7 (emphasis added).
6. Browne, op. cit.
7. T. S. Eliot, ' "Rhetoric" and Poetic Drama', in *Selected Essays* (New York: Harcourt Brace, 1960), p. 27.
8. T. S. Eliot, 'John Marston', in *Essays in Elizabethan Drama*, p. 173.
9. Browne, op. cit., p. 259.
10. T. S. Eliot, 'The Possibility of a Poetic Drama', in *The Sacred Wood* (London: Methuen, 1967), p. 70.
11. Kristin Smidt, *The Importance of Recognition: Six Chapters on T. S. Eliot* (n.p., 1973), p. 161.
12. T. S. Eliot, *Poetry and Drama* (Cambridge, MA: Harvard University Press, 1951), p. 39.
13. T. S. Eliot, *The Cocktail Party*, in *The Complete Poems and Plays, 1909–1950* (New York: Harcourt Brace, 1967), p. 326 (all subsequent quotations from this edition).
14. Alan Dent, 'Fly in the Ointment', *News China* (n.p., 6 May 1950)
15. M. Monier-Williams, *Sanskrit English Dictionary* (Oxford: Clarendon Press, 1872).
16. Henry Clarke Warren (ed., trans.), *Buddhism in Translations: Passages Selected from Buddhist Sacred Books* (Cambridge, MA: Harvard University Press, 1922), p. xxiv.
17. Christopher Innes, *Modern British Drama: The Twentieth Century* (Cambridge: Cambridge University Press, 2002), p. 461.

18. Ibid., p. 463.
19. Eliot, *Poetry and Drama*, p. 38.
20. Clive Barnes, 'Theatre: The A.P.A.'s "Cocktail Party" ', *New York Times*, 8 October 1968, p. 42.
21. Warren, op. cit., p. 376.
22. Peter Harvey, *An Introduction to Buddhism: Teachings, History, and Practices* (Cambridge: Cambridge University Press, 1990), p. 45.
23. Quoted in David Chinitz, *T. S. Eliot and the Cultural Divide* (Chicago, IL: University of Chicago Press, 2003), p. 53.
24. Harvey, op. cit., p. 52.
25. Katherine Worth, *Revolutions in Modern English Drama* (London: G. Bell, 1972), p. 55.
26. Hugh Kenner, *The Invisible Poet* (New York: McDowell, 1959), p. 330.
27. Browne, op. cit., p. 254.
28. T. S. Eliot, *The Confidential Clerk* (New York: Harcourt Brace, 1954), p. 40 (all subsequent quotations from this edition).
29. Lyndall Gordon, *T. S. Eliot: An Imperfect Life* (Now York and London: Norton, 1998), p. 478.
30. Ibid.
31. Carol Smith, *T. S. Eliot's Dramatic Theory and Practice: From Sweeney Agonistes to The Elder Statesman* (New York: Gordian Press, 1977), p. 188.
32. Joyce M. Holland, 'Human Relations in Eliot's Drama', *Renascence*, 22, 1970, pp. 151–61.
33. Smith, Carol H., 'Eliot's "Divine" Comedies: *The Cocktail Party*, *The Confidential Clerk*, and *The Elder Statesman*', in David Chinitz (ed.), *The Blackwell Companion to T. S. Eliot* (Malden, MA: Blackwell, 2009), p. 251.
34. Browne, op. cit., p. 292.
35. Ibid., p. 293.
36. Ibid.
37. Ibid., pp. 293–4.
38. R. T. Davies, 'Mr. T. S. Eliot's "The Confidential Clerk" ', *Theology*, 56(4), October 1953, p. 413.
39. Robert A. Colby, 'Orpheus in the Counting House: *The Confidential Clerk*', *PMLA*, 72(4), September 1957, p. 792.
40. Jeffrey M. Perl, 'T. S. Eliot's Small Boat of Thought', *Common Knowledge*, 13(1–2), Spring/Fall, 2007, p. 343.
41. Innes, op. cit., pp. 472, 473.
42. Quoted in Browne, op. cit., p. 259.
43. S. L. Bethell, *Shakespeare and the Popular Tradition* (London: Staple Press, 1944), p. 33.
44. Eric Salmon, *Is the Theatre Still Dying?* (Westport, CT: Greenwood Press, 1985), p. 83.

45. Richard L. Homan, 'T. S. Eliot's *Confidential Clerk*: Prelude to Pinter?', *Educational Theatre Journal*, 28(3), October 1976, p. 399.
46. Harold Pinter, *The Homecoming* (New York: Grove Press, 1965), p. 31.
47. Browne, op. cit., p. 285 (original emphasis).
48. Ibid., p. 281.
49. Ibid., p. 307.
50. Sophocles, *The Three Theban Plays*, trans. Robert Fagles (New York: Penguin, 1984), p. 381.
51. T. S. Eliot, *The Elder Statesman* (New York: Harcourt Brace, 1958), p. 130 (all subsequent quotations from this edition).
52. Leo Aylen, *Greek Tragedy and the Modern World* (London: Methuen, 1964), p. 336.
53. Anthony S. Abbott, *The Vital Lie: Reality and Illusion in Modern Drama* (Tuscaloosa: University of Alabama Press, 1989), p. 160.
54. David E. Jones, *The Plays of T. S. Eliot* (Toronto: University of Toronto Press, 1960), p. 192.
55. Jewel Spears Brooker (ed.), *T. S. Eliot: The Contemporary Reviews* (Cambridge: Cambridge University Press, 2004), p. 567.
56. Quoted in Gareth and Barbara Lloyd Evans (eds), *Plays in Review, 1956–1980: British Drama and the Critics* (London: Batsford Academic and Educational, 1985), p. 73.
57. Quoted in David A. Moody, *Thomas Stearns Eliot: Poet* (Cambridge: Cambridge University Press, 1994), p. 165.
58. Quoted in Browne, op. cit., p. 332.
59. Moody, op. cit., p. 269.
60. Brooker, op. cit., p. 570.

3 Playwrights and plays: Terence Rattigan

1. Terence Rattigan, *Collected Plays Volume 2* (London: Hamish Hamilton, 1953), pp. xi–xii.
2. Geoffrey Wansell, *Terence Rattigan* (London: Oberon Books, 2009), p. 215.
3. Rattigan, op. cit., p. xii.
4. Ibid., pp. xiv–xv.
5. Ibid., p. xvi.
6. Ibid.
7. Ibid., p. xx.
8. Wansell, op. cit., p. 253.
9. Kenneth Tynan, *Theatre Writings* (London: Nick Hern Books, 2007), p. 34.
10. Ibid.
11. Ibid.
12. Ibid., p. 35.

13. Terence Rattigan, *Plays: One* (London: Methuen, 1982), p. 232 (all subsequent quotations from this edition).
14. Peter Hennessy, *Having It So Good: Britain in the Fifties* (London: Penguin, 2007), p. 7.
15. Terence Rattigan, *Flare Path* (London: Nick Hern Books, 2011), p. 57.
16. Rattigan, *Collected Plays Volume 2*, p. 283.
17. Dominic Shellard, *British Theatre Since the War* (New Haven, CT: Yale University Press, 2003), p. 61.
18. Michael Billington, *Sate of the Nation: British Theatre Since 1945* (London: Faber and Faber, 2007), p. 38.
19. Dan Rebellato, Introduction, *Cause Célèbre* by Terence Rattigan (London: Nick Hern Books, 2011), p. xvi.
20. Rattigan, *Plays: One*, pp. 177–8.
21. Wansell, op. cit., pp. 164–5.
22. Ibid., p. 164.
23. Harold Hobson, *Theatre in Britain: A Personal View* (Oxford: Phaidon, 1984), p. 148.
24. Terence Rattigan, *Plays: Two* (London: Methuen, 1985), p. 3 (all subsequent quotations from this edition).
25. Andrew Wyllie, *Sex on Stage: Gender and Sexuality in Post-War British Drama* (Bristol, Intellect, 2009), p. 85.
26. Wansell, op. cit., p. 225.
27. Luc Gilleman, 'From Coward and Rattigan to Osborne'. *Modern Drama*, 51(1), Spring, 2008.
28. Michael Darlow and Gillian Hodson, *Terence Rattigan: The Man and His Work* (London: Quartet, 1979), p. 102.
29. Wansell, op. cit., p. 233.
30. David Hare, 'A Lecture Given at Queen's College, Cambridge', in *Licking Hitler* (London: Faber and Faber, 1978), p. 66.

3 Playwrights and plays: John Osborne

1. Wartime rationing ended only in 1954, but already in 1957 Conservative prime minister Harold Macmillan claimed that the British people had 'never had it so good'. For a detailed account of the early post-war period (1945–57), see David Kynaston, *Austerity Britain: 1945–51* (London: Bloomsbury, 2007) and *Family Britain: 1951–57* (London: Bloomsbury, 2009).
2. John Osborne, *Look Back in Anger* (London: Faber and Faber, 1956), p. 11 (all subsequent quotations from this edition).
3. This launched the careers of actors hailing from the Midlands or northern England: Rita Tushingham (from Liverpool), Tom Courtenay (from Yorkshire) and Albert

Finney (from Lancashire), for instance. 'Soon RADA elocution classes would be practising not the usual strangled, diphthonged yelps of stage "received pronunciation" but
the flat vowels of the "North-Midlands".' See Harry Ritchie, *Success Stories: Literature
and the Media in England, 1950–1959* (London and Boston, MA: Faber and Faber,
1988), p. 124.

4. *John Osborne and the Gift of Friendship*, dir. Tony Palmer, perf. John Osborne, Tony
   Richardson, Laurence Olivier and Nicol Williamson (Digital Classics DVD, 2006).

5. Nicol Williamson, in ibid.

6. After Olivier, promising young talent as well as famous actors lined up to fill roles in
   Osborne plays. Richard Burton starred in the movie of *Look Back in Anger* (1959) and
   the TV drama *A Subject of Scandal and Concern* (1960); Albert Finney rose to fame in
   the award-winning *Luther* (1961) as well as in Osborne's movie adaptation of *Tom
   Jones* (1963); Nicol Williamson gave legendary marathon performances in *Inadmissible
   Evidence* (1964); the Austrian-Swiss movie actor Maximilian Schell played Colonel
   Redl in *A Patriot for Me* (1965). And the list goes on: Paul Scofield in *The Hotel in
   Amsterdam* (1968); Ralph Richardson in *West of Suez* (1971); and Alec Guinness in
   the TV production of *The Gift of Friendship* (1972). For about twelve to fifteen years,
   starting with Laurence Olivier taking on the role of Archie Rice, Osborne's work
   dominated the British stage, attracting its star actors.

7. Ironically, today, plays by Coward and Rattigan are more often revived than those of
   Osborne, whose oeuvre is uneven, but also more troubling and demanding of its
   audience.

8. Dan Rebellato, *1956 and All That: The Making of Modern Biritish Drama* (London:
   Routledge, 1999). Rebellato claims that many of the changes attributed to *Look Back
   in Anger* in fact pre-date the play. For a reading that emphasises the contributions of
   Look Back to modern drama, see Luc Gilleman, 'From Coward and Rattigan to
   Osborne', *Modern Drama*, 50(1), Spring, 2008.

9. Biographical information for this study of Osborne's plays is based mainly on the
   authorised biography by John Heilpern, *John Osborne: A Patriot for Us* (London:
   Chatto & Windus, 2006), and on Luc Gilleman's *John Osborne: Vituperative Artist*
   (London: Routledge, 2004). Both make use of the John Osborne archives at the Harry
   Ransom Humanities Research Center in Austin, Texas.

10. Ritchie, op. cit. p. 9.

11. See Kenneth Allsop, *The Angry Decade: A Survey of the Cultural Revolt of the Nineteen
    Fifties* (London: Peter Owen, 1958) for a contemporary study of the 'blocked' society
    of the 1950s. For an informed sociological reading of 1950s literature and drama, see
    Alan Sinfield, *Literature, Politics and Culture in Postwar Britain* (London and New
    York: Continuum, 2007).

12. Tynan, in *John Osborne and the Gift of Friendship*, op. cit.

13. This is also the view of several writers, most notably of David Hare in 'I Have a Go
    Lady, I Have a Go' (lecture given at Hay-on-Wye, 2002, quoted in Heilpern, op. cit.,
    p. 45). Osborne pointed out that, before *Look Back*, 'The placement of the most

successful playwrights, Priestley, Coward or Rattigan, was well below the salt of the Novelist or Poet'. He believed he changed this by reinvigorating dramatic speech, by the 'pursuit of vibrant language and patent honesty' (ibid.).

14. Tom Maschler, *Declaration* (London: MacGibbon & Kee, 1957), p. 69.

15. Osborne claims that Shaw's prefaces speak more passionately than his plays. Having acted in several of them in provincial repertory theatre, Osborne came to dislike the contrast between Shaw's intellectualism and the cheapness of his emotions: 'Shaw . . . usually sounds like a giddy spinster or a eunuch who has slipped into something unsuitable when he strives after emotion' – John Osborne, *A Better Class of Person* (London: Faber and Faber, 1981), p. 257. He called Shaw 'the most fraudulent, inept writer of Victorian melodramas ever to gull a timid critic or fool a dull public'.

16. Quoted in Maschler, op. cit., p. 69.

17. Harold Ferrar makes a similar point when he warns against searching for 'mythic patterns' in Osborne: 'Unlike Pinter or Beckett, Osborne is not concerned with incorporating his themes into timeless-seeming mythic patterns but prefers a traditional domestic form in which ideas inhere in relationships and conflicts. He is willing to sacrifice density of poetic texture in favour of a hyperactive whirlwind rhetoric that mirrors not a cosmic tradition but the frantic second-to-second living of pain-filled lives, "the very narrow strip of hell" we inhabit' – Harold Ferrar, *John Osborne* (New York and London: Columbia University Press, 1973), p. 11.

18. This is also the epigraph to Alan Carter's *John Osborne* (Edinburgh: Oliver & Boyd, 1973).

19. John Osborne, 'They Call It Cricket', in Maschler, op. cit., p. 65.

20. John Osborne, *Damn You, England: Collected Prose* (London: Faber and Faber, 1994), p. 47.

21. Ibid., p. 44.

22. For a reading of the play in terms of the double-bind, see Luc Gilleman, 'The Logic of Anger and Despair: A Pragmatic Approach to *Look Back in Anger*', in Patricia D. Denison (ed.), *John Osborne: A Casebook* (New York and London: Garland, 1997).

23. Osborne, *Damn You, England*, p. 48.

24. Osborne, *A Better Class of Person*, pp. 194–6.

25. Osborne, *Damn You, England*, pp. 20–1.

26. A. Alvarez, 'Anti-Establishment Drama', *Parisian Review*, 26, 1959, p. 610.

27. Osborne, *Damn You, England*, p. 46.

28. Aleks Sierz, *John Osborne's Look Back in Anger* (New York: Continuum, 2008), p. 3.

29. David Hare, 'A Defence of the New', in *Obedience, Struggle and Revolt: Lectures on the Theatre* (London: Faber and Faber, 2005), p. 104.

30. Quoted in Stephen Watts, 'Playwright John Osborne Looks Back', *New York Times*, 22 September 1963, p. 3.

31. Henry Brandon, 'The State of the Theatre', interview with Arthur Miller, *Harper's* 221, 1960, p. 63.

32. Arthur Miller, *Timebends: A Life* (New York: Grove, 1987), p. 417.

33. Ibid.

34. Brandon, op. cit., p. 63.

35. Miller, op. cit, p. 416.

36. John Osborne, *The Entertainer* (London: Faber and Faber, 1961), p. 7 (all subsequent quotations from this edition).

37. Osborne, 'Ensemble Performance', in *Damn You, England*, p. 5.

38. Osborne, 'All Words', in ibid., p. 18.

39. In his private scenes, Archie, as played by Olivier, is not unlike Elyot Chase in *Private Lives* (1930). One of Olivier's first successful stage appearances had been as Victor in that play when it premiered on 18 August 1930. Coward, of course, reserved the role of Elyot Chase for himself.

40. Osborne's conception of the working class was nostalgic and sentimental, based on childhood memories of his maternal grandmother who worked at Woolworth's: 'Almost every working day of her life, she has got up at five o'clock to go out to work, to walk down what has always seemed to me to be the most hideous and coldest street in London. Sometimes when I have walked with her, all young bones and shiver, she has grinned at me, her face blue with what I thought was cold. "I never mind the cold – I like the wind in my face." She'd put her head down, hold on to her hat and *push*' (Osborne, 'They Call It Cricket', pp. 80–1). Vivid, but time-blurred, such memories are also behind his conception of Ma Tanner, the old char who sets Jimmy Porter up in his sweet stall and who slaves away to support son and husband. Osborne's opinions about the welfare state were well known. He disliked its crudely materialistic appeal, its technocratic principles and lack of ideals.

41. Osborne, 'They Call It Cricket', p. 84.

42. Osborne, 'Angry Again', in *Damn You, England*.

43. Osborne, 'They Call It Cricket', p. 76.

44. Much later, in 1993, in an article for the *Spectator*, Osborne returned to these lines, explaining, 'No one realised that this was not mockery of the institution, but of the lunatics who were using it to shore up the debilitating inertia and conformity that dominated life at the time' ('Royalty Accounts', in *Damn You, England*, p. 199). By then Osborne had become an outspoken advocate of the monarchy, the Church of England, the Book of Common Prayer and Britain's past military exploits.

45. Harold Macmillan was the Conservative prime minister; Hugh Gaitskell was leader of the Labour opposition. Osborne, 'All Words', in *Damn You, England*, p. 194.

46. Turning around a feminist slogan, for Osborne the political is personal. In 'They Call It Cricket' (p. 83), he defines his socialism as 'an experimental attitude to feeling', remembering how his grandfather referred to a socialist as 'a man who doesn't believe in raising his hat'.

47. Michael Foot, 'Osborne's *Luther*', *Tribune*, 4 August 1961.

48. John Osborne, *Almost a Gentleman* (London: Faber and Faber, 1991), p. 193.

49. Evelyn Waugh in the *Sunday Telegraph* pointed out several mistakes and particularly took issue with Osborne's suggestion that Luther retreated into domesticity, 'when, in

fact, he had 15 years before him of huge prestige'. But in this *Luther* was probably inspired by the penultimate scene of Brecht's *Life of Galileo*.

50. John Osborne, *Luther* (London: Faber and Faber, 1965), p. 40 (all subsequent quotations from this edition).

51. Alan Brien complained in the *Sunday Telegraph* that he 'counted at least 25 references to the bowels which not only seemed to betray a horrified delight of the playwright rather than of the character in the images but which also came near to arguing that the Reformation was invented to cure one man's constipation'.

52. Osborne, *Almost a Gentleman*, p. 273.

53. David Hare, 'I Have a Go', in *Obedience, Struggle and Revolt*, op. cit, p. 44.

54. David Hare, *Acting Up: A Diary* (London and New York: Faber and Faber, 1999), p. 231.

3 Playwrights and plays: Arnold Wesker

In these footnotes the prefix THM references the English Stage Company Archives, and the prefix ACGB the Archives of the Arts Council of Great Britain. Both these archives are held in the Theatre Collection of the Victoria and Albert Museum, London. I am very grateful for the assistance of the museum's staff in undertaking this and other pieces of research.

1. Although a shorter version of *The Kitchen* was given two Sunday-night productions at the Royal Court Theatre on 13 and 20 September 1959 (these were actually plays rehearsed up to dress rehearsal point, but performed in front of whatever was playing on the main stage).

2. See Minutes of Council Meeting of English Stage Company, 2 October 1961: THM/273/1/2/7

3. Arnold Wesker, *Three Plays* (Harmondsworth: Penguin, 1976), p. 23.

4. Indeed, the published text is dedicated 'To Dusty'.

5. Quoted in Glenda Leeming, *Wesker the Playwright* (London: Methuen, 1983), p. 48.

6. Robert Rubens, 'Conversations at the Royal Court: William Gaskill', *Transatlantic Review*, 8 (Winter 1961).

7. On this see Leeming, op. cit., p. 9.

8. ACGB/40/4/3.

9. See the letter from N. V. Linklater, drama director ACGB, to George Devine, 3 June 1959: ACGB/40/4/1.

10. For the full details of the attached conditions see ACGB/40/3/3.

11. The Council Minutes of the English Stage Company for 28 June 1958 make it clear that they had sent *Chicken Soup* to Coventry: THM/223/1/5/4. It was a process they continued right up to the 1961 run of *The Kitchen*, which was preceded by a week at the Belgrade. It resulted in some disputes between the Court and the Belgrade over the

rights to royalties: see the ESC minute's for 10 February 1960, for example: THM/223/1/5/6.

12. Before he died in 1990, Dexter had directed seven of Wesker's plays.

13. They premiered on 7 June, 28 June and 27 July 1960.

14. Charles Marowitz and Simon Trussler (eds), *Theatre at Work* (London: Methuen, 1967), p. 83.

15. See John Bull, *New British Political Dramatists* (London: Macmillan, 1984).

16. David Hare, *The History Plays* (London: Faber and Faber, 1984), p. 128.

17. Opening stage direction to II, i. All references to the text of the 'Trilogy' are to Arnold Wesker, *The Wesker Trilogy* (London: Penguin, 1964) unless otherwise stated.

18. Leeming, op. cit., p. 43.

19. In scene one she confuses Cable Street with Sidney Street, location of the famous siege in 1911, at which Harry retorts, 'I don't get my facts mixed up, anyway', p. 18.

20. Arnold Wesker, 'Living-room revolt', *Guardian*, 26 January 2008.

21. Ibid.

22. See Wesker on this, ibid.

23. THM/273/1/2/5: minutes of meeting of 23 January 1959.

24. On this see 'Living-room revolt', op. cit.

25. 'Play with New and Good Idea', *The Times*, 1 July 1959.

26. The habitual preoccupation of the proletarian Kahn family with listening to classical music on the radio has been remarked on by a number of critics and reviewers; although, of course, that may in itself be further evidence of class prejudice.

27. Penguin, 1960.

28. *I'm Talking About Jerusalem*, p. 214.

29. T. C. Worsley, *Financial Times*, 28 July 1960.

30. It opened on 27 May 1958.

31. T. C. Worsley, *New Statesman*, 15 July 1958.

4 Documents

1. A 1953 play by Robert Anderson, which contains a male character who is suspected of homosexuality.

2. A 1955 play by Tennessee Williams, which again features a male character who is suspected of homosexuality.

3. A 1955 play by Arthur Miller, which not only includes a male character who accuses another male character of homosexuality, but which also features a kiss between two men.

Afterword

1. Geoffrey Wansell, *Terence Rattigan* (London: Oberon Books, 2009), p. 284.
2. www.theatrevoice.com/4128/arnold-wesker-reads-terence-rattigans-letters-to-him/.
3. Wansell, op. cit., p. 351.
4. *The Times*, 9 May 1958, p. 16.
5. Michael Darlow and Gillian Hodson, *Terence Rattigan: The Man and His Work* (London: Quartet, 1979), pp. 257–8.
6. Terence Rattigan, *Plays: Two* (London: Methuen, 1985), p. 247.
7. Wansell, op. cit., pp. 415–16.
8. Quoted in John Heilpern, *John Osborne: A Patriot for Us* (London: Chatto & Windus, 2006), p. 239.
9. John Osborne, *A Subject of Scandal and Concern* (London: Faber and Faber, 1961), pp. 46–7.
10. Heilpern. op. cit., p. 386.
11. Simon Trussler, *The Plays of John Osborne: An Assessment* (London: Gollancz, 1969), p. 124.
12. John Osborne, *Inadmissible Evidence* (London: Faber and Faber, 1965), p. 24.
13. Ibid., p. 77.
14. John Osborne, *The Hotel in Amsterdam* (London: Faber and Faber, 2003), p. 20.
15. John Osborne, *West of Suez* (London: Faber and Faber, 1971), p. 70.
16. John Osborne, *A Sense of Detachment* (London: Faber and Faber, 1973), p. 59.
17. Ibid., p. 26.
18. Quoted in Heilpern, op. cit., p. 377.
19. Osborne, *A Sense of Detachment*, p. 60.
20. Simon Trussler, 'His Very Own and Golden City: An Interview with Arnold Wesker', *Tulane Drama Review*, 11(2), Winter, 1966, p. 195.
21. Robert Brustein, 'The English Stage', *Tulane Drama Review*, 10(3), Spring, 1966, p. 129.
22. Ibid., p. 130.
23. Arnold Wesker, *Chips with Everything* (London: Jonathan Cape, 1962), p. 16.
24. Catherine Itzin, *Stages in the Revolution* (London: Merthuen, 1980), pp. 107–8.
25. Arnold Wesker, *As Much as I Dare* (London: Century, 1994), p. 8.

SELECT BIBLIOGRAPHY

Recommended books on post-war British theatre

Billington, Michael, *State of the Nation: British Theatre Since 1945* (London: Faber, 2007):
A good general introduction to the development of British post-Second World War
playwriting; Billington provides one of the best analyses of the state of British playwriting before 1956.

Gilleman, Luc, *John Osborne: Vituperative Artist* (London: Routledge, 2004): A comprehensive overview and analysis of Osborne's work, with close analysis of the major
plays.

Holdsworth, Nadine, *Joan Littlewood* (London: Routledge 2006); Leach, Robert, *Theatre
Workshop: Joan Littlewood and the Making of Modern British Theatre* (Exeter: University
of Exeter Press, 2006): Two recent, comprehensive introductions to the work of
Littlewood and Theatre Workshop. Holdsworth looks in depth at Littlewood's direc-
torial practice; Leach covers all aspects of Theatre Workshop's career, including the
company's finances and its rather precarious relationship with the Arts Council.

Lacey, Stephen, *British Realist Theatre: The New Wave in Its Context* (London: Routledge
1995): A frequently cited text on post-Osborne theatre; Lacey places the work in a
comprehensively discussed historical framework, which covers the cultural, political
and economic changes that shaped the drama of the decade.

Rabey, David, *English Drama Since 1940* (London: Longman, 2003): A very good introduction to post-war British writing, which gives due weight to otherwise neglected
writers – in particular John Whiting.

Rebellato, Dan, *1956 and All That: The Making of Modern British Drama* (London:
Routledge, 1999): One of the key texts in contemporary theatre writing; a revisionist
discussion which analyses the Royal Court revolution in the light of 1950s attitudes to
gender and culture.

Roberts, Philip, *The Royal Court Theatre and the Modern Stage* (Cambridge: Cambridge
University Press, 1999): Still the best history of the Court; the chapters on the theatre's
early days are particularly instructive.

Shellard, Dominic, *British Theatre Since the War* (New Haven, CT: Yale University Press,
2000): A clearly written introduction to the period, which relates the development of
playwriting to changes in the British theatre industry, as well as to wider changes in
the politics and culture of the time.

——, *Kenneth Tynan: A Life* (New Haven, CT: Yale University Press, 2003): Shellard's
biography of Kenneth Tynan provides information not only on the development of

Tynan's career, but on the theatre culture of the time; it contains substantial quotations from the most significant reviews, and places Tynan's writing against a changing theatrical culture.

Taylor, John Russell, *Anger and After: A Guide to the New British Drama* (London: Methuen, 1963): A key text; not so much because it provides a definitive analysis of the writing of the period, but because it is one of the earliest (and one of the clearest) statements of the *Look Back in Anger* myth.

Tynan, Kenneth, *Theatre Writings* (London: Nick Hern Books, 2007): The most useful recent compendium of Tynan's reviews; the editor, Dominic Shellard (see above) includes contextualising information about the culture and history of the period – including key historical documents (the *Observer* editoral on Suez, Harold Hobson's review of *Waiting for Godot*).

Website

Theatre Archive Project: www.bl.uk/theatrearchive. This website is an invaluable resource for the period; it provides first-hand accounts of making and seeing theatre from the end of the Second World War to the 1960s. There are interviews with actors, directors, designers and audience members; in particular, the website contains accounts from members of Theatre Workshop, and with the cast of the first production of Harold Pinter's debut play, *The Room*.

Playwrights and the 1950s: general reading

Abbott, Anthony S., *The Vital Lie: Reality and Illusion in Modern Drama* (Tuscaloosa: University of Alabama Press, 1989).

Ackroyd, Peter, *T. S. Eliot* (London: Hamish Hamilton, 1984).

Allsop, Kenneth, *The Angry Decade: A Survey of the Cultural Revolt of the Nineteen Fifties* (London: Peter Owen, 1958).

Alvarez, A., 'Anti-Establishment Drama', *Parisian Review*, 26, 1959.

Amis, Kingsley, *Lucky Jim* (London: Penguin, 1992).

'Angry Again', review of *The Entertainer*, *Daily Mail*, 9 September 1957.

Arrowsmith, William, 'English Verse Drama II: *The Cocktail Party*', *Hudson Review*, 3(3), 1950, pp. 411–30.

Asman, Kevin G., 'The Failure and Promise of "Socialism as Personal Contact", in Arnold Wesker's *Roots*', in Reade W. Dorman (ed.), *Arnold Wesker: A Casebook* (New York and London: Garland Publishing, 1998), pp. 34–48.

Aylen, Leo, *Greek Tragedy and the Modern World* (London: Methuen, 1964).

Babbitt, Irving, *The Dhammapada: Translated from the Pali with an Essay on Buddha and the Occident* (1936) (New York: New Directions, 1965).

Barnes, Clive, 'Theatre: The A.P.A.'s "Cocktail Party"', *New York Times*, 8 October 1968, p. 42.

Bethell, S. L., *Shakespeare and the Popular Tradition* (London: Staple Press. 1944).

Billington, Michael, *Harold Pinter* (London: Faber and Faber, 2007).

——, *State of the Nation: British Theatre Since 1945* (London: Faber and Faber, 2007).

Brandon, Henry, 'The State of the Theatre', interview with Arthur Miller, *Harper's*, 221, 1960, pp. 63–9. Reprinted in *Conversations with Arthur Miller*, ed. Matthew C. Roudané, Jackson and London: University Press of Mississippi, 1987, pp. 56–67.

Brenton, Howard and David Hare, *Brassneck* (London: Eyre Methuen, 1973).

Brien, Alan, 'The Changing World of John Osborne', *Sunday Telegraph*, 9 July 1961.

Brooker, Jewel Spears (ed.), *T. S. Eliot: The Contemporary Reviews* (Cambridge: Cambridge University Press, 2004).

Brown, John Russell, *Modern British Dramatists* (Englewood Cliffs, NJ: Prentice Hall, 1968).

Browne, E. Martin, *The Making of T. S. Eliot's Plays* (Cambridge: Cambridge University Press, 1969).

Brustein, Robert, 'The English Stage', *Tulane Drama Review*, 10(3), Spring, 1966.

Bull, John, *New British Political Dramatists* (London: Macmillan, 1984).

Carpenter, Humphrey, *The Angry Young Men: A Literary Comedy of the 1950s* (London: Allen Lane, 2002).

Carter, Alan, *John Osborne* (Edinburgh: Oliver & Boyd, 1973).

Chamberlain, Lesley, 'Through a Cocktail Glass Darkly', *Modern Drama*, 31(4), 1988, pp. 512–19.

Chambers, Colin, *The Story of Unity Theatre* (London: Lawrence & Wishart, 1989).

Chinitz, David, *T. S. Eliot and the Cultural Divide* (Chicago, IL: University of Chicago Press, 2003).

Colby, Robert A., 'Orpheus in the Counting House: *The Confidential Clerk*', *PMLA*, 72(4), September 1957, pp. 791–802.

Collini, Stefan, *Absent Minds: Intellectuals in Britain* (Oxford: Oxford University Press, 2006).

Coward, Noël, *Plays 5* (London: Methuen, 1983).

Darlow, Michael and Gillian Hodson, *Terence Rattigan: The Man and His Work* (London: Quartet, 1979).

Davies, R. T., 'Mr T. S. Eliot's "The Confidential Clerk"', *Theology*, 56(4), October 1953, pp. 411–14.

Delaney, Shelagh, *A Taste of Honey* (London: Eyre Methuen, 1959).

Dent, Alan, 'Fly in the Ointment', *News China*, 6 May 1950, n.p.

Dexter, John, 'Working with Arnold', *Plays and Players*, April 1962.

Donoghue, Denis, *The Third Voice: Modern British and American Verse Drama* (Princeton, NJ: Princeton University Press, 1959).

Dorman, Reade W., *Arnold Wesker Revisited* (London: Macmillan, 1995).

—— (ed.), *Arnold Wesker: A Casebook* (New York and London: Garland Publishing, 1998).

Edgar, David, *Maydays* (London: Methuen, 1983).

Eliot, T. S., *For Lancelot Andrewes: Essays on Style and Order* (London: Faber and Gwyer, 1928).

——, *Selected Essays* (New York, Harcourt, Brace & Company, 1932).

——, *The Use of Poetry and the Use of Criticism* (Cambridge, MA: Harvard University Press, 1933).

——, *After Strange Gods: A Primer of Modern Heresy* (London: Faber and Faber, 1934).

——, Letter to Djuna Barnes, 19 August 1949, Djuna Barnes Papers, Archives and Manuscripts, University of Maryland.

——, *Poetry and Drama* (Cambridge, MA: Harvard University Press, 1951).

——, *The Confidential Clerk* (New York: Harcourt Brace, 1954).

——, 'Seneca in Elizabethan Tradition', in *Essays on Elizabethan Drama* (New York: Harcourt Brace, 1956), pp. 3–55.

——, 'John Marston', *Essays on Elizabethan Drama* (New York: Harcourt Brace, 1956). 162–178.

——, *The Elder Statesman* (New York: Harcourt Brace, 1958).

——, '"Rhetoric" and Poetic Drama' (1919), in *Selected Essays* (new edn) (New York: Harcourt Brace, 1960), pp. 37–42.

——, 'The Possibility of a Poetic Drama', in *The Sacred Wood* (London: Methuen, 1967), pp. 1–16.

——, *The Cocktail Party* in *The Complete Poems and Plays, 1909–1950* (New York: Harcourt Brace, 1967), pp. 295–388.

Erikson, Erik H., *Young Man Luther: A Study in Psychoanalysis and History* (London and New York: Norton, 1962).

Ferrar, Harold, *John Osborne* (New York and London: Columbia University Press, 1973).

Findlater, Richard (ed.), *At The Royal Court: Twenty-Five Years of the English Stage Company* (London: Amber Lane Press, 1981).

Foot, Michael, 'Osborne's *Luther*', *Tribune*, 4 August 1961.

Gale, Maggie, *West End Women: Women and the London Stage 1918–1962* (London: Routledge, 1996).

Gaskell, Bill, *A Sense of Direction* (London: Faber and Faber, 1988).

Gilleman, Luc, 'The Logic of Anger and Despair: A Pragmatic Approach to *Look Back in Anger*', in Patricia D. Denison (ed.), *John Osborne: A Casebook* (New York and London: Garland, 1997), pp. 71–90.

——, *John Osborne: Vituperative Artist* (London: Routledge, 2004).

——, 'From Coward and Rattigan to Osborne', *Modern Drama*, 51(1), Spring, 2008.

Gordon, Lyndall, *T. S. Eliot: An Imperfect Life* (New York and London: Norton, 1998).

Hare, David, 'A Lecture Given at Queen's College, Cambridge', in *Licking Hitler* (London: Faber and Faber, 1978).

——, *Plenty* (London: Faber and Faber, 1978).

——, *The History Plays* (London: Faber and Faber, 1984).

——, *Acting Up: A Diary* (London and New York: Faber, 1999).

——, *Obedience, Struggle and Revolt: Lectures on Theatre* (London: Faber and Faber, 2005).

Harvey, Peter, *An Introduction to Buddhism: Teachings, History, and Practices* (Cambridge: Cambridge University Press, 1990).

Heilpern, John, *John Osborne: A Patriot for Us* (London: Chatto & Windus, 2006).

Hennessy, Peter, *Never Again: Britain 1945–51* (London: Vintage, 1953).

——, *Having It So Good: Britain in the Fifties* (London: Penguin, 2007).

Hobson, Harold, *Theatre in Britain: A Personal View* (Oxford: Phaidon, 1984).

Hoggart, Richard, *The Uses of Literacy* (London: Chatto & Windus, 1957).

Holland, Joyce M., 'Human Relations in Eliot's Drama', *Renascence*, 22, 1970, pp. 151–61.

Homan, Richard L., 'T. S. Eliot's *Confidential Clerk*: Prelude to Pinter?', *Educational Theatre Journal*, 28(3), October 1976, pp. 398–404.

Howard, Sir Michael, *Captain Professor: A Life in War and Peace* (London: Continuum, 2006).

Innes, Christopher, *Modern British Drama: The Twentieth Century* (Cambridge: Cambridge University Press, 2002).

Itzin, Catherine, *Stages in the Revolution* (London: Methuen, 1980).

John Osborne and the Gift of Friendship, dir. Tony Palmer, perf. John Osborne, Tony Richardson, Laurence Olivier, Nicol Williamson, Digital Classics DVD, 2006.

Jones, David E., *The Plays of T. S. Eliot* (Toronto: University of Toronto Press, 1960).

Knowlson, James, *Damned to Fame: The Life of Samuel Beckett* (London: Bloomsbury, 1996).

Kynaston, David, *Austerity Britain: 1945–51* (London: Bloomsbury, 2007).

——, *Family Britain: 1951–57* (London: Bloomsbury, 2009).

Lacey, Stephen, *British Realist Theatre: The New Wave in Its Context* (London: Routledge, 1995).

Leach, Robert, *Theatre Workshop: Joan Littlewood and the Making of Modern British Theatre* (Exeter: University of Exeter Press, 2006).

Leader, Zachary, *The Life of Kingsley Amis* (London: Jonathan Cape, 2006).

Leeming, Glenda, *Wesker the Playwright* (London: Methuen, 1983).

——, *Wesker on File* (London: Methuen, 1985).

—— and Simon Trussler, *The Plays of Arnold Wesker* (London: Gollanz, 1971).

Littlewood, Joan, *Joan's Book* (London: Minerva, 1994).

Little, Ruth and Emily McLaughlin, *The Royal Court Theatre: Inside Out* (London: Oberon Books, 2007).

Marowitz, Charles, Tom Milne and Owen Hale, *The Encore Reader: A Chronicle of the New Drama* (London: Methuen, 1965).

Maschler, Tom, *Declaration* (London: MacGibbon & Kee, 1957).

Miller, Arthur, *Timebends: A Life* (New York: Grove, 1987).

Monier-Williams, M., *Sanskrit English Dictionary: Etymologically and philologically arranged with special reference to Greek, Latin, Gothic, German, Anglo-Saxon, and other cognate Indo-European languages* (Oxford: Clarendon Press, 1872).

Moody, A. David., *Thomas Stearns Eliot: Poet,* 2nd edn (Cambridge: Cambridge University Press, 1994).

Nicholson, Steve, *The Censorship of British Drama* (Exeter: University of Exeter Press, 2005).

Osborne, John, *Look Back in Anger* (London: Faber and Faber, 1956).

——, *Epitaph for George Dillon* (London: Faber and Faber, 1958).

——, *A Subject of Scandal and Concern* (London: Faber and Faber, 1961).

——, *Inadmissible Evidence* (London: Faber and Faber, 1965).

——, *West of Suez* (London: Faber and Faber, 1971).

——, *A Sense of Detachment* (London: Faber and Faber, 1973).

——, *Damn You, England: Collected Prose* (London: Faber and Faber, 1994).

——, *Luther,* in *John Osborne: Plays Three* (London and Boston, MA: Faber and Faber, 1998), pp. 1–80.

——, *The Hotel in Amsterdam* (London: Faber and Faber, 2003).

——, *Looking Back: Never Explain, Never Apologise* (London: Faber and Faber, 1999).

Perl, Jeffrey M., 'T. S. Eliot's Small Boat of Thought', *Common Knowledge,* 13(1–2), Spring/Fall, 2007, pp. 337–61.

Pinter, Harold. *The Homecoming* (New York: Grove Press, 1965).

Priestley, J. B, *Theatre Outlook* (London: Nicholson & Watson, 1947).

——, *Thoughts in the Wilderness* (London: Heinemann, 1957).

Rabey, David, *English Drama Since 1940* (London: Longman, 2003).

Rattigan, Terence, *Collected Plays, Vol. 1* (London: Hamish Hamilton, 1953).

——, *Collected Plays Vol. 2* (London: Hamish Hamilton, 1953).

——, *Plays: One* (London: Methuen, 1982).

——, *Plays: Two* (London: Methuen, 1985).

——, *After the Dance* (London: Nick Hern Books, 1995).

——, *Flare Path* (Nick Hern Books, 2011).

Rebellato, Dan, *1956 and All That: The Making of Modern British Drama* (London: Routledge, 1999).

——, Introduction, *Cause Célèbre* by Terence Rattigan (London: Nick Hern Books, 2011).

Ritchie, Harry, *Success Stories: Literature and the Media in England, 1950–1959* (London and Boston, MA: Faber and Faber, 1988).

Roberts, Peter (ed,), *The Best of Plays and Players 1953–1968* (London: Methuen, 1987).

Roberts, Philip, *The Royal Court Theatre and the Modern Stage* (Cambridge: Cambridge University Press, 1999).

Rowell, George and Tony Jackson, *The Repertory Movement: A History of Regional Theatre in Britain* (Cambridge: Cambridge University Press, 1984).

Salmon, Eric, *The Dark Journey: John Whiting as Dramatist* (London: Barrie & Jenkins, 1979).

——, *Is the Theatre Still Dying?* (Westport, CT: Greenwood Press, 1985).

Sandbrook, Dominic, *Never Had It So Good: A History of Britain from Suez to the Beatles* (London: Little Brown, 2005).

Selmon, Michael, 'Logician, Heal Thy Self: Poetry and Drama in Eliot's *The Cocktail Party*', *Modern Drama*, 31(4), 1988, pp. 495–511.

Shaughnessy, Robert, *Three Socialist Plays* (Buckingham: Open University Press, 1992).

Shellard, Dominic, *Harold Hobson: Witness and Judge* (Edinburgh: Edinburgh University Press, 1995).

——, *British Theatre Since the War* (New Haven, CT: Yale University Press, 2000).

——, *Kenneth Tynan: A Life* (New Haven, CT: Yale University Press, 2003).

—— (ed.), *British Theatre in the 1950s* (Sheffield: Sheffield University Press, 2000).

Sierz, Aleks, *John Osborne's Look Back in Anger* (New York: Continuum, 2008).

Sillitoe, Alan, *Saturday Night and Sunday Morning* (London: Paladin, 1958).

Sinfield, Alan, *Literature, Politics, and Culture in Postwar Britain,* 3rd edn (London and New York: Continuum, 2007).

Smidt, Kristin, *The Importance of Recognition: Six Chapters on T. S. Eliot* (n.p., 1973).

Smith, Carol H., *T. S. Eliot's Dramatic Theory and Practice: From Sweeney Agonistes to The Elder Statesman* (New York: Gordian Press, 1977).

——, 'Eliot's "Divine" Comedies: *The Cocktail Party, The Confidential Clerk*, and *The Elder Statesman*', in David Chinitz, (ed.), *The Blackwell Companion to T. S. Eliot* (Malden, MA: Blackwell, 2009), pp. 251–62.

Smurthwaite, Nick, 'Revival of a Realist', *The Stage*, 5 February 2004.

Sophocles, *The Three Theban Plays*, trans. Robert Fagles (New York: Penguin, 1984).

Taylor, John Russell, *Anger and After: A Guide to the New British Drama* (London: Methuen, 1963).

Trussler, Simon, 'His Very Own and Golden City: An Interview with Arnold Wesker', *Tulane Drama Review*, 11(2), Winter, 1966.

Tynan, Kenneth, 'T. S. Eliot', in Gareth and Barbara Lloyd Evans (eds), *Plays in Review, 1956–1980: British Drama and the Critics* (London: Batsford Academic and Educational, 1985), pp. 67–75.

——, *The Plays of John Osborne: An Assessment* (London: Gollancz, 1969).

——, *Theatre Writings* (London: Nick Hern Books, 2007).

Wansell, Geoffrey, *Terence Rattigan* (London: Oberon Books, 2009).

Wardle, Irving, *The Theatres of George Devine* (London: Jonathan Cape, 1978).

Warren, Henry Clarke, ed. and trans., *Buddhism in Translations: Passages Selected from the Buddhist Sacred Books.* Harvard Oriental Series, vol. 3 (Cambridge, MA: Harvard University Press, 1922).

Watts, Stephen, 'Playwright John Osborne Looks Back', *New York Times*, 22 September 1963, p. 3.

Waugh, Evelyn, 'Wilful Monk', review of *Luther*, by John Osborne, *Sunday Telegraph*, 27 August 1961.

Wesker, Arnold, *Chicken Soup with Barley* (Harmondsworth: Penguin, 1959).

——, *Roots* (Harmondsworth: Penguin, 1959).

——, *I'm Talking About Jerusalem* (Harmondsworth: Penguin, 1960).

——, *The Kitchen* (London: Jonathan Cape, 1960).

———, *The Wesker Trilogy* (London: Jonathan Cape, 1960; Harmondsworth: Penguin, 1964).

———, *Chips with Everything* (London: Jonathan Cape, 1962).

———, *Three Plays* (*The Kitchen*; *The Four Seasons*; *Their Very Own and Golden City*) (Harmondsworth: Penguin, 1976).

———, *As Much as I Dare* (London: Century, 1994).

———, 'Living-room revolt', *Guardian*, 26 January 2008.

Wilcher, Robert, *Understanding Arnold Wesker* (Columbia: University of South Carolina Press, 1991).

Wilson, Colin, *The Outsider* (London: Gollancz, 1956).

Wilson, Edmund, *The Bit Between My Teeth: A Literary Chronicle of 1950–1965* (New York: Farrar, Straus and Giroux, 1966).

Worth, Katherine, *Revolutions in Modern English Drama* (London: G. Bell, 1972).

Wyllie, Andrew, *Sex on Stage: Gender and Sexuality in Post-War British Drama* (Bristol: Intellect, 2009).

Theatre Archive Interviews

Theatre Archive Project interview, Robert Aldous (22 March 2010).

Theatre Archive Project interview, Malcolm Farquhar (2 February 2004).

Theatre Archive Project interview, Barry Clayton (8 October 2007).

INDEX

Note: Play titles are entered in the index under authors' names, if known. Page references in **bold type** denote main references to topics.

NOTES ON CONTRIBUTORS

Sarah Bay-Cheng is Associate Professor and Director of Graduate Studies in Theatre at the University at Buffalo, the State University of New York, where she teaches courses in drama, contemporary theatre and intermediality. Her research interests include avant-garde theatre and film, poetic drama, and intersections of technology and performance. Her book publications include *Mapping Intermediality in Performance* (Amsterdam University Press, 2010), *Poets at Play: An Anthology of Modernist Drama* (Susquehanna University Press, 2010) and *Mama Dada: Gertrude Stein's Avant-Garde Theater* (Routledge, 2005).

John Bull is Emeritus Professor of Film and Theatre at the University of Reading. He is the author of *Vanbrugh and Farquhar* (Macmillan, 1998), *Stage Right: Crisis and Recovery in British Contemporary Mainstream Theatre* (Macmillan, 1994) and *New British Political Dramatists* (Macmillan, 1984). He has contributed to *The Methuen Drama Guide to Contemporary British Playwrights* (Methuen Drama, 2011), has published numerous articles and chapters on modern British and European theatre and performance, and has also edited a collection of the early work of Howard Brenton.

Luc Gilleman was Professor of English at Smith College, Massachusetts, where he taught classes in modern drama, British literature, literature and science, and literary and cultural theory. He is the author of *John Osborne: Vituperative Artist* (Routledge, 2002). His articles on modern drama can be found in a number of publications, including *Modern Drama, Theatre Journal, Theatre Topics, New England Theatre Journal, Journal for Dramatic Theory and Criticism, The Pinter Review* and *Theatre Symposium*.